BEYOND
JUSTICE

BEYOND JUSTICE

The Auschwitz Trial

REBECCA WITTMANN

HARVARD UNIVERSITY PRESS
Cambridge, Massachusetts
London, England
2005

Library of Congress Cataloging-in-Publication Data

Wittmann, Rebecca, 1970–
Beyond justice : the Auschwitz trial / Rebecca Wittmann.
p. cm.
Includes bibliographical references and index.
ISBN 0-674-01694-7
1. Auschwitz Trial, Frankfurt am Main, Germany, 1963–1965.
I. Title.

KK73.5.A98W58   2005
341.6'9'0268—dc22   2004060567

For my parents,
Horst and Evelyn Wittmann

Contents

Illustrations

BEYOND JUSTICE

Introduction

State Attorney Kügler: "Did you investigate who was respon-
sible for the gassings?" Former SS Judge Wiebeck: "Back then
that did not interest us. Those were supreme acts beyond jus-
tice (justizfreie Hoheitsakte).*"*

—FROM HERMANN LANGBEIN, *Der Auschwitz-Prozess*

A RE WAR CRIMES beyond justice? What *is* justice in cases of
mass devastation and annihilation? The word "justice," according to the *Oxford English Dictionary*, means "equity," "the quality of
being morally just," "rectitude," "the vindication of right through the
court of law," and "the infliction of punishment." Modern justice is
generally sought through the administration of law in judicial proceedings. Is there a way to successfully try the perpetrators of genocide, to mete out just sentences, and to atone for mass atrocity?[1] Are
the courts, the victims, and society searching for legal justice, or for
justice to history and memory?

The successes and failures of these proceedings—as purely legal
exercises, as history lessons, as preventive measures, as meaningful
catharses—are the subject of extensive debate. Scholars in many
fields have recently turned their attention to the way the international community prosecutes war crimes and genocide.[2] The Nuremberg trials of Nazi criminals in the late 1940s became the pervasive legal backdrop for the many different sorts of proceedings that

1

were to follow throughout the twentieth century, from the Eichmann trial in Israel to the criminal tribunals to address ethnic cleansing in Bosnia and genocide in Rwanda, to the Truth and Reconciliation Commission in South Africa. International trials of genocidal crimes, always conducted before a large and intensely involved public audience, attempt both to seek a just verdict and to teach moral historical lessons, whether the trial organizers admit to the latter goal or not; scholars such as Lawrence Douglas and Mark Osiel have recently made compelling arguments that these trials can in fact "galvanize collective interest in the past."[3]

But what happens when a nation tries to deal with its own genocidal past, using its own criminal code, in its own state courts? Without the international criminal charges that are now central to our understanding of war crimes trials, without the concepts of war crimes, genocide, or crimes against humanity, without the supervision of the international community, is it possible to deal successfully with crimes of unprecedented magnitude?

The Auschwitz concentration camp has become the most important representation of Nazism and the Holocaust. This was not yet so in Germany in the decades immediately following the war. During the mid-1960s, the authorities in the public prosecutor's office of the state of Hesse, West Germany, organized a trial of a group of people alleged to have been responsible for some of the evil perpetrated at Auschwitz. The trial was intended to be an event of great significance. In the mind of its principal organizer, Attorney General Fritz Bauer, the trial was to put the entire "Auschwitz complex" before the court, both the "small men" who had carried out the "Final Solution" and those who had created the measures, policies, and laws that had given the Holocaust an air of legality. According to Bauer, "Germany was not made up only of the Nazi Hitler and the Nazi Himmler. There were hundreds of thousands, millions of others, who carried out the 'Final Solution' not only because they had orders, but because it was their worldview as well, which they willingly admitted."[4] This concept, Auschwitz on trial, was at the core of German public confrontation with the Nazi past in the 1960s.

Why should we care about this trial? Why does it warrant a detailed investigation, and why now? To answer these questions, it is important to set the trial in context. The trial of twenty Auschwitz "perpetrators"—representing a cross section of criminals who participated in the atrocities at the camp between 1940 and 1945—took place in Frankfurt am Main starting in December 1963 and lasted more than 180 days. It was not the first criminal procedure against Nazi criminals in Germany, but it was by far the largest, most public, and most important ever to take place in West Germany using West German judges and West German law. The motley group of defendants included two camp adjutants (second in command to the commander of the camp), five members of the Political Department, two dentists, a doctor, the camp pharmacist, four barrack commanders, four medical orderlies, a camp security commander, a "disinfector," and a "capo" (a prisoner appointed by the Schutzstaffel, or SS, who worked as a barracks or labor squad leader).

The trial opened with a seven-hundred-page indictment which included the testimony of 254 witnesses, both survivors and former SS officers from Auschwitz, plus a three-hundred-page history of the camp written by the historians Hans Buchheim, Martin Broszat, and Helmut Krausnick of the Institute for Contemporary History in Munich. This historical account provided many Germans with their first knowledge of the workings of genocide at Auschwitz. Shortly after the trial it was published as a two-volume work titled *The Anatomy of the SS State*, representing the first major inquiry not only into the camp itself but also into the structure of its bureaucracy. National and international press coverage was extensive. In West Germany each court day was covered by all the major newspapers, including the *Frankfurter Allgemeine Zeitung*, the *Frankfurter Rundschau*, the *Frankfurter Neue Presse*, and *Die Welt*, despite the prohibition of the use of cameras in the courtroom. The trial ended with a nine-hundred-page judgment in August 1965, in which all but three defendants were convicted either of murder (*Mord*) or of aiding and abetting murder (*Beihilfe zu Mord*). Sentences ranged from life in prison, for six of the defendants, to between three and ten years, to acquittal.

In view of this, it is surprising that no monograph on the trial exists in either German or English.[5] The lack of research on the trial itself is in part the result of the federal German protective time limit, which prevented the release of documents or transcripts pertaining to a trial for thirty years from the last day of the trial. In addition, a paragraph in the federal criminal procedure (*Strafprozessordnung*—StPO) forbade the transcribing of the trial.[6] Instead, the trial was audiotaped, with each witness's cooperation, only for the "purpose of the protection of the memory of the court."[7] It is only now that the Fritz Bauer Institute for the Documentation and Research of the Holocaust in Frankfurt am Main has undertaken the enormous task of transcribing the five hundred hours of tape. This is possible because of what appears to have been a lapse on the part of the presiding judge, Senator Hans Hofmeyer, whose duty it was to destroy the tapes after the court had used them for sentencing purposes. Hermann Langbein said in a newspaper article soon after the trial: "A large chunk of responsibility for ensuring that the Auschwitz Trial stands the test of time belongs to the documentations made during and after the trial. Are these documentations truly capable of the difficult task of conveying the proceedings in detail and the urgency of the language, of doing justice to the tortured and the tempted?"[8] The tapes were deposited in the basement of the public prosecutor's office in Frankfurt, where they remained until the Radio Broadcasting Company of Hesse began re-recording them onto more durable digital audiotapes in 1993. Until then, it seems, they were left to disintegrate. As a result there is much confusion and ignorance about the Auschwitz Trial. Although meticulously documented and publicly recounted in the 1960s, the trial is often mistaken for part of the International Military Tribunal at Nuremberg or not recognized at all.

The Auschwitz Trial is slowly emerging, however, as the symbol of West Germany's ongoing confrontation with its past. The Jewish Museum in Berlin displays documents and audiotapes and shows a film of the trial; the Fritz Bauer Institute staged an exhibition in the spring of 2004 commemorating the fortieth anniversary of the trial, during which the transcriptions of the trial tapes were finally made available to the public.[9] Newspapers like the *Frankfurter Allgemeine Zeitung*, the *Frankfurter Rundschau*, and *Die Zeit* once again carried extensive articles about this extensive trial. And significantly, recent literature on war crimes trials, particularly the work of Ian Buruma and Mark Osiel, points to the Auschwitz Trial as the true turning point in postwar West German understanding of Nazi crimes, as it "evoked and articulated pervasive sentiments of indignation and reprobation," and "captured the imagination of millions of young Germans as virtually nothing about the country's past had done before."[10]

How and why is the Auschwitz Trial only now emerging in historical discourse about the Holocaust? What does this belated response tell us about its impact on German public consciousness of Nazi crimes? Most important, in light of the deficiency of material and knowledge surrounding the trial not only in Germany but especially internationally, what conclusions can be drawn about the trial's success in achieving the prosecution's initial goal, the trying of the Auschwitz complex? The answers to these questions lie in the magnitude of the trial itself and its place within the record of convictions in West German Nazi trials in general. However one chooses to interpret the events of each trial and to assess the success each had in doing justice, the statistics regarding the actual trials of Nazis are dismal. Of approximately 100,000 people investigated in Germany and suspected of committing mass murder and participating in the machinery of the "Final Solution," only about 6,500 were actually brought to trial, and the large majority of these before 1949.[11] In this context, the Auschwitz Trial represents a historical watershed not only because of the size of the proceedings but because of the nature and timing of the trial itself. One of the most extraordinary aspects of this trial was the sheer amount of information it made available to the West German public for the first time since the end of the war. No longer could people claim that they had no access to facts about what the Nazis had done in the East. No longer could they claim that they were the greatest victims of the war, a claim that had enjoyed great popularity in the immediate postwar period and allowed Germans to focus on the brutality of the Allies and especially the Soviets in their campaign to drive German settlers out of the East and to imprison and torture German soldiers.[12] Germans now had to confront the detailed and extensive evidence produced by historians and the hundreds of witnesses who demonstrated the involvement of ordinary Germans in unspeakable crimes in Poland. They could read about the rise of Nazism, the support that millions of Germans had given the movement in the 1930s, the creation of the SS state, the recruitment and enthusiastic registering of hundreds of thousands of people in the SS, and most important, the implementation of the program to destroy Europe's Jews. Here on trial were the guards and functionaries at the lowest rung of the Nazi hierarchy, men who were often unfit for military duty but wanted to serve Nazi aims and had made it their job to murder innocent men, women, and children on a daily basis. This was sensational, attention-grabbing news that most Germans could not ignore.

And yet, I argue, the information that the public received was distorted. The sincere effort of the public prosecution to indict Auschwitz, to teach lessons about the culpability of all involved in the murder of innocents, was hindered by the law as it was defined. Prosecutors had to adhere to rigid interpretations of the murder statute and subjective definitions of perpetrators and accomplices that in the end condemned only those who had gone beyond the acts of murder ordered by Himmler and Hitler. In effect, those who carried out the state-ordered genocide were convicted—if they were convicted at all—only as accomplices to murder. They remained ordinary citizens who were basically decent and reluctant to perform their tasks, while the others, the sadists and "excess perpetrators" (*Exceßtäter*), were monsters or devils who bore no resemblance to the majority of society. The killing of millions in the gas chambers— the main form of murder at Auschwitz, after all—became a lesser crime, calling for a lighter sentence, than the murder of one person carried out without orders from superiors. This was the information that the public got about Auschwitz, and I argue that it ultimately hampered rather than helped the growing efforts at *Vergangenheits-bewältigung*, or overcoming the past. While the Auschwitz Trial certainly did demonstrate to Germans that the crimes perpetrated at Auschwitz were, as Ian Buruma later put it, the "key event of World War II," the history lesson that was convincing because it was taught by German courts was not the condemnation of systematic atrocity that the prosecution had intended.[13] Instead, the German public learned to censure and denounce the sadistic excess perpetrators of Auschwitz but to exonerate the order-followers whose crimes of complicity were never the true focus of the trial, the law, or the extensive press coverage.

Why was the law so constricting? Why did prosecutors, intent on showing the criminality of the Nazi regime, end up trying to prove that defendants had acted *against* Nazi orders? A legal theoretical debate that had already begun by 1945 informed much of the law used in West German trials and led to the decision by the newly formed West German justice system to try Nazi criminals according to the national penal code. To some extent, the West German state implemented that judicial method in response to the perceived problems with the Allied policies. Chapter 1 therefore examines the criminal code itself, giving an overview of the postwar West German criminal justice system and focusing on three major elements.

First, I look at the prohibition of 1949 on retroactive legislation *(Rückwirkungsverbot)*, which made invalid all ex post facto laws (those charging individuals with crimes that were allegedly not illegal when committed).[14] This prohibited recourse to Occupation Control Council No. 10 and the charge of crimes against humanity. Instead, the court called on the long-standing criminal code of 1871, which included a murder charge (paragraph 211) and a distinction between perpetrator and accomplice (paragraphs 47–49). Second, I assess the actual murder charge and its stipulation that the prosecution must prove the subjective motivation and individual initiative of each perpetrator in order to convict him of murder. The law is of course not impersonal: people stood behind the decision to use a subjective rather than objective definition of murder, whereby the perpetrator was the person who willed or intended the crime, rather than the person who pulled the trigger. I briefly discuss the legal debate during the 1960s that led to this hugely important decision. A grasp of these legal issues is imperative if one is to gain a full understanding of the trial proceedings themselves—the atmosphere in the courtroom, the strategies adopted by the prosecution and defense, and the role of the judge in arbitrating the trial. Finally, I investigate the debate on the statute of limitations (*Verjährungsdebatte*), which also had a significant impact on the trial. This debate began in the late 1950s in the Bundestag and dealt with the twenty-year statute of limitations on murder and the fifteen-year limitation on manslaughter. The courts could only charge the defendants according to the decisions reached as a result of this debate.

The main focus of *Beyond Justice* is the Auschwitz investigation itself. The pretrial period provides the most extensive body of documentation produced by this trial, with more than thirty thousand pages of evidence, some four hundred witness interrogations, and the investigation of as many as eight hundred suspected perpetrators at Auschwitz (including not only SS guards from the camp but prisoner capos suspected of murder and brutality as well). These pages also chronicle the decisions made by the courts and the prosecution in their efforts to have a manageable yet comprehensive trial that would adequately judge criminals of varying levels of responsibility and show the corrupt nature of the Auschwitz complex. The prosecution often made what seem to be baffling decisions to close investigations or postpone them for later trials; yet such excising of suspects and sometimes even defendants proved strategically necessary.

Judges and prosecutors interrogated witnesses thoroughly (most witnesses were deposed twice) because these interrogations provided the main proof for the case against the defendants; the trial relied much more heavily on witness testimony than on documentation. The prosecution therefore had to carefully choose the "best" witnesses for the trial. I investigate the influential factors in these decisions.

The historical narrative continues through Chapter 3, in which I examine the indictment. This fascinating document centers on the three-hundred-page history of the Auschwitz concentration camp. Because the German criminal code required the state to prove each defendant's individual guilt, the prosecutors needed to include this historical account to emphasize the magnitude and uniqueness of their crimes. The charges and evidence provided in the indictment are further indications of the prosecution's attempt to put the Holocaust at the center of the trial. It is in the indictment that the paradoxical nature of the trial—and the thrust of my argument about its deficiencies—begins to show itself most clearly. The prosecution exposed the crimes of Nazism in a very comprehensive way through the historical background of the SS and Auschwitz; but prosecutors also had to rely on Nazi regulations (which they include in the indictment) to demonstrate each defendant's individual initiative. While indicting Auschwitz, they were thus also obliged to give its camp regulations an air of validity. This contradiction reached its height with the introduction of former SS judges into the proceedings.

The audiotapes are extremely effective in conveying the atmosphere of the trial's everyday proceedings, which I explore in Chapter 4. The tapes were difficult to obtain: the Ministry of Justice initially told me that I could not listen to the originals because they were too badly damaged; when I wrote back demonstrating my awareness that copies of the tapes existed and asking to hear those, the officials relented. These tapes provided an opportunity that historians seldom obtain. I could actually listen to the voices of the witnesses, the defendants, and the court officers rather than merely read their words on paper. The lack of a written transcription created a few disadvantages: I was unable to turn quickly to any particular person's testimony, and it was nearly impossible to get through five hundred hours of tape. In addition, the prosecution, defense lawyers, and judges spoke out of turn and did not identify themselves. This habit made their voices difficult to distinguish from one another. But there were advantages as well. I was able to gain a strong sense of the atmosphere in the courtroom, of the tensions that filled the room, of the judge's sensitive treatment of different survivors and his reactions to outbursts by the spectators or the defendants. And I could experience the courtroom in all of its absurdity; during the particularly gruesome testimony of one witness, for example, I was jolted out of the image of camp life by the sound of children playing. The windows of the courtroom must have been open, and children at a nearby school were playing during recess. Everyday life thus crept into the trial's sometimes otherworldly horrors and created a sense of immediacy that shaped my examination of this trial.

In my investigation of the audiotapes, I selected a cross section of witnesses on the basis of research I had done with the pretrial files. Because the Fritz Bauer Institute carefully documented the chronology of the tapes and the witnesses who appeared on them, I could choose which tapes I wanted to hear. I focus in Chapter 4 on the role of the judges, the prosecution, and the defense: their strategies, tactics, and conflicts.

By far the largest part of the trial was made up of witness testimony. I concentrate on two kinds of witnesses in Chapter 4: the survivors of the camp and former SS members. The survivors made an essential contribution to the prosecution by recounting the horrors at Auschwitz and reconstructing the actions of the accused at the camp. The audiotapes in this case provide a more nuanced understanding of witness testimony than a transcript could. Not only is it possible to perceive the changing tone of the judge's interrogations, but one can also appreciate the effect on the court of listening to the simultaneous translation of statements made in Polish (the majority skillfully rendered by one woman, Wera Kapkajew), Ukrainian, and Czech.

The court required witnesses to tell in painstaking detail about their experiences almost twenty years earlier. This procedure removed any element of depersonalization or incomprehensibility through the sheer number of the victims and the weight of evidence and presented to the court and the world the names, faces, personalities, and activities of those who had been victims of the defendants on trial. At the same time, the witnesses sometimes reinforced the "innocence" of those who did not act brutally or on personal initiative, describing those who murdered reluctantly as, relatively speaking, "decent men" *(anständige Männer)* and inadvertently diminishing the criminal nature of the camp system itself.

The vivid memories of the witnesses created a remarkable picture of the camp's functioning. Many of the survivors had occupied relatively important positions at the camp: Hermann Langbein, for example, was the "secretary" to the head doctor (Dr. Wirths) from 1942 to 1945. Others who testified were secretaries (mostly women) in the Political Department, "corpse bearers" *(Leichenträger)*, and even a member of the "Special Unit" (Sonderkommando) of the crematorium, which was in charge of taking bodies from the gas chambers to the crematorium. This unit was generally "replaced" every six weeks (that is to say, its members were murdered) to ensure secrecy.[15] These witnesses provided invaluable insight into the workings of the camp and eerily brought the everyday life and death of Auschwitz into the proceedings of the court. I present the testimony of a cross section of these witnesses, comparing it with their pretrial depositions and assessing their significance not only at the trial but also in the retelling of history.

In studying the second type of witness, the former SS officers, I investigate the theme of carrying out orders, the "corruption" of certain defendants, and the standards which were used to evaluate their behavior. I concentrate particularly on the testimony of certain former SS judges—especially the enigmatic Konrad Morgen—sent by the *Reichsführer* SS Heinrich Himmler and the police court in Munich to Auschwitz to investigate alleged corrupt practices.[16] Their statements about the brutality of such defendants as Wilhelm Boger (who created his own instruments of torture and stole gold and other valuables from the "Canada" bunker) and Klaus Dylewski (who carried out an execution "without a valid death sentence") shifted attention away from Nazi policies of brutality to individual acts of cruelty, and consequently implied—again paradoxically—that Nazi orders were "acceptable" and "legal."[17] This phenomenon created the impression that those who herded thousands into the gas chambers were less guilty than those who shot prisoners without a legal death sentence handed down by Nazi officials. Although the prosecution summoned witnesses who provided proof of the individual initiative of certain defendants, the presence of the witnesses also undermined the attempts of the prosecution to show, by using the 1871 criminal code, that the acts committed at Auschwitz were indeed crimes at the time they were carried out. As a result, only the most grotesque and shocking of crimes were severely punished, while mass murder conducted through the machinery of genocide, the gas chambers and the crematoriums, receded into the background.

The daily events of the trial, the atrocities that were described there, and the increasing emphasis on acts of unspeakable cruelty were all transmitted to the public through the press, whose coverage created a "pornography of horror" that I explore in Chapter 4. The graphic representation of the "sadists" and "monsters" on the stand contributed to a general public detachment from the defendants. Reporters described the cruel actions of a few in grotesque detail and largely ignored the rest of the men on trial or presented them as reluctant participants caught up in the killing machinery. In this representation the press was reflecting the general tone of the legal proceedings; the court's focus on monstrosities proved fortuitous for newspapers dependent on sensational headlines for sales. Press coverage provides us with a window onto what the public absorbed of the trial and further demonstrates that the main message from the Auschwitz Trial was that in this "hell on earth" there had been a only few wanton, depraved criminals, while most of the guards were not culpable for any crime greater than reluctantly following orders.[18]

Chapter 5 examines the closing statements and the judgment imposed on the defendants. The closing statements encapsulate the arguments of both prosecution and defense. The judgment gives not only the individual verdict for each defendant but also lengthy explanations for the acquittals, convictions, and punishments. The court's ruling demonstrates how difficult it was to reconcile the crimes, the context in which they were committed, and the legal limitations imposed on the court. The written judgment reads like an exposé of Judge Hofmeyer's psychological battle with himself, whose duty it was to enforce ordinary law to punish extraordinary crimes. Did Fritz Bauer and his attorneys succeed in putting the machinery of genocide on trial? Were atonement and just punishment achieved, as the prosecution had hoped? I explore these questions and evaluate the judgment in light of the prosecution's goals.

The complexities of German postwar justice, press reporting, and public response are at the heart of this book. We now know the importance of understanding the role of the "small men" who participated in the atrocities of the Holocaust. Recent scholarly inquiry and research have focused on the "ordinary man" and on perpetrator mentality, sometimes to the exclusion of discussion about ideological training and systemic antidemocratic corruption.[19] The men on trial in Frankfurt represent the order-followers and not the architects of genocide. My examination of the followers' guilt is in no way an attempt to exculpate the "desktop" murderers. I am interested, however, in discovering how the law as it was defined presented, punished, and made examples of the Auschwitz defendants, and how the full force of the legal system came down only on those who were exceptions to the rule.

The Auschwitz Trial contributed to a historical understanding of the Nazi period and the Holocaust that had been lacking in Germany until the 1960s.[20] It is generally agreed that before the awakening of that decade—an awakening that began in earnest in 1967 and which the Auschwitz Trial advanced—only a handful of works written in Germany dealt with the Holocaust. While the 1950s and 1960s did bring increasing scholarship and research into the subject, particularly by historians such as Eugen Kogon, Karl Dietrich Bracher, Wolfgang Scheffler, the scholars at the institute in Munich, and survivors like Hermann Langbein and Lucie Adelsberger, this period was generally marked by a culture of silence. Norbert Frei, a specialist on the history of trials in postwar Germany, says that after the founding of the Federal Republic "the initially respectable attempts at requital by the West German justice system came to a quick standstill. Instead, there was an overwhelming call for a *Schluß-strich*," that is, for considering the case closed. The few works that did appear in Germany were often written by survivors wishing to make their stories known, but they were not widely read; Hannah Arendt's *Eichmann in Jerusalem*, which appeared in German translation in 1964, offered the general public the first encounter with the nature of Nazi evil, and it shocked the readers—not only in Germany but around the world—with its portrayal of the "banal" Adolf Eichmann.[21]

With this examination of the Auschwitz Trial I want to show the contradictory results of the proceedings. Although the trial created a new public awareness of what Auschwitz was, it also offered a distorted representation of that history—particularly the responsibility of Nazi henchmen. The prosecutors had a very specific goal: to teach a lesson about the Nazi past. But the result of the trial was a paradoxical one at best. The West German criminal code was inadequate because of limitations inherent in the murder law, and because of the way legal theorists and judges chose to interpret that law. The court therefore could not render a fair verdict, and although the trial provided Germans with invaluable documentation of Nazi crimes, it did not offer the justice for which the prosecution had so ardently worked.

◆ CHAPTER 1 ◆

Pretrial History

BETWEEN 1950 AND 1962 the West Germans investigated 30,000 former Nazis, indicted 12,846, tried 5,426, and acquitted 4,027. Statistics vary somewhat from source to source, but all show a relatively high figure for acquittals and a low number of heavy sentences. Of those sentenced, only 155 were convicted of murder.[1] The West German justice system opened investigations only after historians, sociologists, and psychologists began to examine the legacy of the Allied prosecutions at Nuremberg. Domestic scholars were not dealing with the subject at all in the 1950s, and it was only grudgingly taken up again in West Germany after foreign observers—such as the historian Gerhard Reitlinger and the American prosecutor Telford Taylor—used the abundant documentary evidence produced at Nuremberg to draw German public and judicial attention back to the Nazi past. Even then, public prosecutor's offices pursued these crimes, as Fritz Bauer put it, "wearily and without passion," limiting their investigations to charges made by survivors who saw their persecutors walking free in the streets, or to crimes that had been committed in their regional jurisdiction—for example, during Kristallnacht.[2]

Why was there such reluctance to pursue Nazi crimes, even the most heinous? Fritz Bauer, the attorney general of Hesse in charge of the Auschwitz case and an outspoken legal analyst, was preoccupied with this question as early as the 1960s. He argued that there were at least three explanations. First, most investigations were "coincidental and improvised"; second, the Nuremberg trials had initially created a sense of finality around Nazi investigations; and third and most important, the limitations of the West German criminal procedural code produced inertia in the courts.[3] In the 1970s and 1980s, scholars continued to probe the problems with German trials; pioneering works include those by Adalbert Rückerl, former head of the Zentrale Stelle der Landesjustizverwaltungen (ZS, the Central Office of the Land Judicial Authorities for the Investigation of National-Socialist Crimes), whose books laid the groundwork for further studies of Nazi trials. Henry Friedlander has also written numerous articles examining the German judiciary and Nazi crimes, and Ingo Müller, in his study of Nazi and postwar judges, has argued that there was a great deal of continuity in the judiciary, such that many Nazi judges retained their posts in the postwar period and were therefore inclined to be very lenient with Nazi defendants. In recent years dissertations have proliferated attempting to explain the poor record of convictions in both East and West Germany. Annette Weinke, for example, in an expansive study of postwar trials, argues that the lack of cooperation between East and West hampered their investigations of Nazi perpetrators. Kerstin Freudiger also examines a large number of Nazi trials and concludes that the judiciary made every effort to interpret the law in such a way as to exonerate defendants or at least work in their favor to produce fewer convictions and shorter sentences. Michael Greve similarly argues that the judiciary was extremely lenient in its treatment of Nazi perpetrators. Greve, like Müller, contends that the significant presence of former Nazi judges in the postwar judiciary made it impossible for real justice to be served; despite the fact that international pressure produced an increased number of trials in the 1960s, convictions were increasingly for aiding and abetting rather than for perpetration of murder.[4] Historians and legal scholars have been grappling with the problems of Nazi trials in Germany, and with a few exceptions, they conclude that Nazi crimes were not sufficiently punished or dealt with by the German judiciary. I concur with this general sentiment, but I do not agree with the wholesale condemnation of the German justice system; my examination of the motives and efforts of the Frankfurt prosecution will demonstrate why.

From Nuremberg to Auschwitz

Why did West German jurists decide to use the West German criminal code? Why did the courts not adopt the international criminal charges as, for example, the Israelis had during the Eichmann trial, which occurred just two years before the Auschwitz Trial? In hindsight, it becomes clear that the German penal code was often unsuitable for the prosecution of Nazi crimes, whereas the international criminal charges at least dealt with the elimination of national groups based on racial ideology (crimes against humanity). The roots of the problems surrounding Nazi trials in West Germany lay in the transition from International Military Tribunal of Nuremberg to German national criminal law. The German code had a strict ban on retroactivity and therefore comprised no prohibition on genocide, which became illegal only in 1954, in a new statute. I contend that the decision to try Nazis in Germany using the standard penal code was the result of both external and internal pressures. Before delving into the German case, I will briefly explore Allied policies of investigation, prosecution, and denazification in occupied Germany, with emphasis on the most important and famous trial of Nazi criminals—the Nuremberg Trial of 1945–1946 before the Allied International War Crimes Tribunal—to explain the West German judiciary's decision to reject international laws and try Nazi criminals according to their own national penal code.

Allied Policies, 1945–1949

The Allied decision to try the major Nazi war criminals was in part a reaction to the failure of the war crimes provisions of the Versailles treaty at the peace conference in Paris in 1919. In Paris, the issue of German war crimes was addressed and consigned to the Commission on Responsibilities of the Authors of the War and Enforcement of Penalties. The Treaty of Versailles included four paragraphs dedicated to war crimes, condemning the Germans for waging an aggressive war and for "a supreme offence against international morality and the sanctity of treaties."[5] The provisions of the treaty included recognition, on the part of the Germans, of the Allies' right to try them. Unfortunately, these trials degenerated into a debacle; whereas the initial goal was to try Wilhelm II and other top German military officials for war crimes, the end result was a chaotic proceeding in Leipzig in 1921 in which no major figures stood trial. The Americans (under Wilson's strong influence) distanced themselves from the proceedings and chose instead to focus on the creation of the League of Nations. Historian Gary Bass argues that the trials in fact inflamed the German right, excited further tension between Germany and France, and helped to destabilize the Weimar Republic.[6] These trials have virtually faded from public memory because of their failure and because the principal outcome of the Treaty of Versailles was the draconian policies of immense punitive reparation payments and the demilitarization to which Germany was subjected. In addition, according to Telford Taylor, a member of the American team prosecuting at Nuremberg and chief prosecutor at the subsequent trials, Germany seemed to be a much more dangerous threat during World War II. Writes Taylor, "the perceived evil of Nazism was far deeper and more pervasive than was that of Imperial Germany."[7]

In response to this, the International Military Tribunal (IMT) at Nuremberg was a carefully thought-out attempt to undo the mistakes of the past and to prevent the rise of another Hitler. As early as 1943, the Allies had thoroughly debated how they would deal with

Nazi war crimes after the war was over; Stalin's suggestion to execute a few thousand top Nazi officials was rejected in favor of the trial model. In April 1945, at the founding conference of the United Nations in San Francisco, the delegates discussed the idea of an international tribunal and the Americans sought international support for the project. Just a few days after Hitler's suicide, the Americans proposed "due process for defendants." Although the Allies had not yet singled out the defendants or defined the charges against them, the procedure for prosecuting Nazi war criminals began to take the form of what was intended to be a fair trial at which each of the accused would be given the opportunity to defend himself.[8] After some debate, the Soviets, British and French agreed to the American proposition that an International Military Tribunal was the best way to deal with Nazi crimes.

Allied representatives assembled in London in June 1945 to create an agreement on the trial process that became known as the Nuremberg charter. They agreed on the most important governing condition of the trial—namely, that only Nazi crimes would come under the jurisdiction of the court. The Soviets, for example, did not want to be charged with the massacre of thousands of Polish officers at Katyn in 1940; in fact they included this crime as a charge in the indictment against the Germans. The Americans had also killed civilians and wanted to avoid a tu quoque argument from by the defense. The charter then, stipulated clearly that war crimes meant crimes committed in connection with Germany's waging of aggressive war. Only Germany would be held responsible. Both "conspiracy to commit crimes against peace" and "crimes against peace" (referring to aggressive war) became paragraphs in the IMT charter that had as much weight as "war crimes" and "crimes against humanity."[9]

Conflict arose over what type of proceedings should take place. The Soviets quite openly envisioned purely punitive measures, designed primarily to punish the Nazi criminals already presumed guilty. The Americans pushed their agenda to create an indictment and to conduct a fair trial in which the defendants were presumed innocent and had the right to defense attorneys and due process.

The Americans also wanted the trial to take place in Nuremberg, not only because the city was in American-occupied territory but because it had been the site of many Nazi rallies. On August 8, 1945, after a summer of debate in London, The charter of the International Military Tribunal came into existence. The charter of the IMT laid the groundwork for the trial at Nuremberg of the leading Nazis, by determining the structure of the trial, the roles of the countries involved (and their prosecutors), and the rules intended to ensure a fair trial for the defendants. Most important, paragraph 6 of the charter defined the crimes that would be prosecuted:

(a) *Crimes against Peace*: namely, planning, preparation, initiation or waging of a war of aggression, or a war in violation of international treaties, agreements or assurances, or participation in a common plan or conspiracy for the accomplishment of any of the foregoing;

(b) *War Crimes*: namely, violations of the laws or customs of war. Such violations shall include, but not be limited to, murder, ill-treatment or deportation to slave labor or for any other purpose of civilian population of or in occupied territory, murder or ill-treatment of prisoners of war or persons on the seas, killing of hostages, plunder of public or private property, wanton destruction of cities, towns, or villages, or devastation not justified by military necessity;

(c) *Crimes against Humanity*: namely, murder, extermination, enslavement, deportation, and other inhumane acts committed against any civilian population, before or during the war, or persecutions on political, racial or religious grounds in execution of or in connection with any crime within the jurisdiction of the Tribunal, whether or not in violation of domestic law of the country where perpetrated.[10]

The wording of the charge of crimes against humanity had immense significance in the proceedings of the trial. First, it is important to note that the Allies' accusation encompassed Nazi crimes against any civilian population, before or during the war. The scope of definition meant that the Germans could be charged with persecuting their own population, even before the beginning of the war. This interpretation was rarely applied, however, and only in the context of the key phrase already mentioned: the jurisdiction of the tribunal. In fact prewar crimes were largely ruled out.[11]

Once the charter had been agreed to, the Allies decided on the defendants and drafted the indictment. The Americans were determined to try not only the highest-ranking German perpetrators but also the "leading representatives of groups or organizations to be deemed criminal."[12] On October 6, 1945, the Allies indicted twenty-four defendants (two of whom—Robert Ley, head of the *Arbeiterfront*, who committed suicide, and Gustav Krupp von Bohlen und Halbach—were later excluded) on four counts: 1) The Common Plan or Conspiracy (formerly the last statement applying to all three clauses of the charter), 2) Crimes against Peace, 3) War Crimes, and 4) Crimes against Humanity.[13] As for the destruction of European Jewry, Count 4 of the indictment had a new section that extrapolated from the statement in the charter: "Persecution on Political, Racial, and Religious Grounds in Execution of and in Connection with the Common Plan Mentioned in Count One [aggressive war]." It stated: "These persecutions were directed against Jews. They were also directed against persons whose political belief or spiritual aspirations were deemed to be in conflict with the aims of the Nazis. Jews were systematically persecuted since 1933; they were deprived of their liberty, thrown into concentration camps where they were murdered and ill-treated."[14] In the end, fifteen of the defendants were convicted on this charge. Both Julius Streicher and Baldur von Schirach were convicted solely of crimes against humanity. This provides an illustrative example of the limitations of contemporary understanding of the mass murder of the Jews; Streicher was presented as the ideologue behind the Final Solution, and the pivotal role of other defendants, such as Hermann Göring, was overlooked in the effort to focus on their guilt in crimes against peace.

The Nuremberg trial met with three widely expressed criticisms in Germany. First, the trial was seen as a form of "victor's justice." Many Germans found this unacceptable for fundamental procedural reasons, and because they felt that the Allies could not be impartial.[15] Second, Germany's constitution since unification in 1871 had contained a strict ban on retroactivity, as we shall see later. In light of this stipulation, critics observed, Nuremberg imposed an ex post facto adjudication—in assuming the existence of crimes that were not defined as such at the time the acts were supposedly committed. Finally, the tu quoque argument, discussed earlier, carried weight for the Germans who had been victims of Allied bomb attacks. According to legal expert Adalbert Rückerl, the devastation that the air raids inflicted on the mass of the German population left the people outraged at the Allies, uninterested in trials of the Nazis, and determined only "to find food and accommodation for themselves and their families."[16]

The Trial of the Major German War Criminals ended in October 1946. The judges acquitted three defendants, sentenced twelve to death, and gave sentences of differing lengths to the rest. The trial was followed by other Allied trials, but none, interestingly, conducted by all the Allies together. Instead, as had been decided in December 1945 by the Control Council Law No. 10, each occupying power proceeded against Nazi criminals as it saw fit.[17] These subsequent trials were conducted separately by the Allied powers, but the largest and most famous were the American trials. Twelve in all were conducted at Nuremberg, lasting until mid-1949. The Americans divided the defendants into criminal groups according to occupation. They held a doctors' trial (mentioned earlier), a lawyers' trial (in which the defendants included leading judges—this trial was to be the subject of the film "Judgment at Nuremberg"), the IG Farben trial (at which the chemical company that manufactured the poison gas Zyklon B and employed slave labor was tried), and the *Einsatzgruppen* trial of Otto Ohlendorf and twenty-three heads of the special "operations groups," which had swept through Eastern Europe and murdered some one million Jews before the death camps were established.[18] The Americans also launched proceedings against guards at various concentration camps (most famously in the Da-chau trial, for example) and in all had a fairly successful conviction record: of 1,941 people indicted by the American courts, 1,517 were sentenced. In all, between 1945 and 1949, the Americans interned 100,000 former Nazi officials. In all three Western zones, the Allies interned almost 200,000 former Nazi higher-ups.[19]

The years between 1945 and 1950 marked a slow transition from Allied control of the German justice system to the emergence of a fairly independent German judiciary. Although it may appear that the justice system was reorganized solely by the Allies, the exclusive use of the German code in Nazi trials was in fact orchestrated by German jurists who exerted pressure on the Allies to prevent national or district courts from using Control Council Law No. 10. Why? This question can be answered in part by assessing the legal system imposed by the Allies prior to the establishment of the Federal Republic. At the start of the Allied occupation, German courts ceased to function, and it took approximately five years for these institutions gradually to come back to life. We shall see later in this chapter that after the establishment of the Federal Republic, the German penal code was based on the original code of 1871. The Allies, who took it upon themselves to determine the legal foundations of postwar Germany, decided that any laws instituted by the Nazis that were obviously criminal (for example, those endorsing racial discrimination) would be revoked.

The Allied Control Council Laws were designed to reconstruct the German state. Law No. 4 on "the Reorganization of the German Judicial System" prohibited German courts from trying any crimes committed against the Allies. Control Council Law No. 10, which referred to the four international criminal charges, also stipulated that the German courts could try only crimes "committed by persons of German citizenship or nationality against other persons of German citizenship or nationality, or stateless persons." As a result, it fell to the Allies to prosecute all crimes committed by the Germans against Allied nationals and all war crimes, including crimes against the Jews.[20]

In addition, the Germans were not eager to apply the international charges of the IMT charter. The historian Henry Friedlander argues that the charges themselves could have been advantageous to the Germans for a few reasons: it made "no distinction between perpetrator and accomplice, rejected defense of superior orders, and provided for penalties higher than the German penal code." Not only did the German penal code supply lenient sentences for manslaughter and for aiding and abetting murder, but it was so difficult to prove perpetration of murder that the maximum punishment could rarely be applied. In addition, the German penal code threw out the defense of superior orders, or *Befehlsnotstand*, but it could be used to distinguish between a perpetrator and an accomplice. Still, German jurists argued bitterly over the basic character of Control Council Law No. 10. Although the four counts of the IMT could be useful in convicting defendants of genocide, and although they contained no distinction between perpetrator and accomplice, they seemed, as ex post facto legislation, to assail the very core of the German constitution and its ban on retroactivity. Friedlander states that "finally, in 1951, the Allies yielded to massive German pressure and prohibited the use of Law No. 10 in German courts. Thereafter, conviction of Nazi criminals could be obtained only on the basis of the German penal code."[21]

As a consequence, then, ex-Nazis would be dealt with as common criminals. Rückerl asserts that this outcome is exactly what the German public wanted after the experience of Nuremberg. Germans were tired or war, and of war crimes as a category. They were preoccupied with food, shelter, and reconstruction. In many ways, the German public saw the Allied judicial proceedings as political revenge rather than criminal justice. They prevented the courts from trying serious crimes; the IMT charter smacked of retroactivity and victors' justice; and the denazification trials were fraught with controversy, as questionnaires were forged, lower-ranking Nazis often received heavier punishments than their superiors, and persons charged were "reeducated" for six months, then whitewashed with a *Persilschein* (literally, laundry detergent coupon) and released.

Rückerl says that the reason "they regarded the murder of millions of Jews, political opponents and insane persons as a political act rather than a primarily criminal one may be found in the reporting of the trials mounted by the IMT in Nuremberg and its enormous impact on public opinion. The trials were characterized by an intermingling of military, political and purely criminal events in a manner which rendered it virtually impossible for an unprejudiced observer to obtain the facts needed to unravel the tangle of evidence."[22]

The only viable adaptation to this situation for the German Ministry of Justice was to create purely criminal proceedings that shunned the Allied Control Council system. This was also a way for the newly independent, democratic West German government to demonstrate that it was capable on its own of coping with Nazi crimes. By using the long-standing code—and pointing to the fact that the murder statute had never gone out of effect—the Federal Republic could show that Nazism's murderous policies had been illegal from beginning to end. How did the newly formed West German judicial system go from having little power to investigate and try former Nazi criminals to launching one of the largest, longest trials in German history in 1963? A closer look at the attitude of the emerging West German state toward the Nazi past, and at the structure of the West German judicial system after the shift from Allied control, will help to answer this question.

Framing the Nazi Past

With the collapse of the Nazi regime in 1945, Germany had allegedly reached "Zero Hour"—*Stunde Null*—the point at which a break with the past occurred on all fronts. Germany was reduced to rubble, and its population was decimated and starving. The sole preoccupation of the majority of the people was to rebuild and to find food. Some contended that there would be no return to past political traditions, for Imperial Germany was long gone, the Weimar era had been an unmitigated political failure, and the Allies would do everything to prevent the renewed rise of National Socialist sentiment. As Gordon Craig puts it, "Before it was over and the Germans had been authorized to resume organized political activity . . . , old structures and elites had been demolished so completely that there was no possibility of building a new system upon them."[23] A completely new democratic system was the goal of the Allies and a few key political figures—particularly Kurt Schumacher, leader of the Social Democratic Party (SPD), Theodor Heuss, who became Germany's first president, Konrad Adenauer, Germany's Christian Democratic Union (CDU) leader and chancellor from 1949 to 1963, and Ludwig Erhard, chancellor at the time of the Auschwitz Trial— in what would become the new West Germany.[24] This democracy became one of the most successful new constitutional states in Europe, an "economic miracle," even after the devastation of the Nazi period and the troublesome legacy of Nazism's murderous policies.

How did politicians in the Federal Republic of Germany frame the Nazi period in the new democracy? How did politicians deal with the millions of German citizens who had been members of the Nazi party, or of the SS, and had in some way been involved in the "Final Solution"?[25] The historian Jeffrey Herf has examined the Adenauer period in the Federal Republic and found that post-occupation policies toward former Nazis were the direct result of disapproval of Allied policies. Specifically, with such a large number of former Nazis, denazification and harshly punitive trials were not popular. A large portion of the population "opposed any serious efforts at postwar judicial reckoning or frank public memory." Adenauer's main policy was to integrate rather than alienate ex-Nazis, because as many saw it, "one could have either democracy or justice but in the early days, certainly not both." Justice had been the pursuit of the Allies, in the seemingly endless investigations, denazification hearings, and trials between 1945 and 1949. Consequently, Adenauer made it his goal to focus on moving forward. Herf states that for Adenauer, "in order to avoid a renewal of German nationalism and Nazism, economic recovery and political democratization [had to] take priority over a judicial confrontation with the crimes of the Nazi past."[26]

Craig argues that Adenauer's ability to shift attention away from the depressing, devastating effects of Nazism was his greatest achievement and one of the main reasons for the success of the democracy and the economic miracle. Rather than continuing the purge instituted by the Allies, Adenauer proposed that it was time to pursue a policy of reconstruction, restitution to Jewish survivors, and reintegration of former Nazis. Continuing the denazification hearings, Adenauer reasoned, would backfire by making former Nazis into second-class citizens rather than integrating them as members of the new society. Endless punitive measures would invite a new kind of nationalism that would only make people nostalgic for the Nazi period. In Adenauer's view, says Herf, "forcing the Germans to face the Nazi past would only make things worse."[27]

Considerable debate surrounds the policy of Adenauer's government regarding the Nazi past. Many historians, including Herf, argue that Adenauer was not an apologist but a realist. He felt strongly that the architects of Nazism should be punished and presented to the German public as the faces behind the evil of Nazism. He was an opponent of Hitler, who had spent much of the Nazi period in hiding. Adenauer had an "emphatically non-military bearing" that made him the "ultimate bourgeois," a representative of the new Germany. Others argue that his policy of forgiveness for the majority of former Nazis paved the way for a rapid process of forgetting, as thousands of former Nazi party and SS members were integrated into society, culture, and politics. During the early years of postwar reconstruction, however, Adenauer's continued focus on the future and more immediate concerns—the cold war, entrance into NATO, and economic restructuring—made him a unifying force in an extremely fractured state with a "fragile popular psyche."[28]

During Adenauer's chancellorship, however, intense debate took place on what the West German state's relation to the Nazi past should be. The strongest opposition to Adenauer's policy of "integration" came from Kurt Schumacher, leader of the socialist opposition, and Theodor Heuss, president of Germany. Both Schumacher and Heuss were proponents of a democracy that would address the dark Nazi past and incorporate it into lessons for the future of the West German state. Adenauer had greater popularity, because of the large number of conservative voters to whom the idea of integration appealed, but Schumacher and Heuss also had a large following, which wished to promote justice and memory in the new democracy.[29] On the Left, confrontation with the past was a very important issue, and it achieved increasing prominence later in the 1960s, considerably weakening the Right.

In 1949, during his first address to the Bundestag, Adenauer outlined the policy of the Ministry of Justice toward former Nazi criminals: "The government of the Federal Republic, in the belief that many have subjectively atoned for a guilt that was not heavy, is determined where it appears acceptable to do so to put the past behind us. On the other hand, it is absolutely determined to draw the necessary lessons from the past regarding all of those who challenge the existence of our state whether they come now from right-wing radicalism or left-wing radicalism."[30] Adenauer's approach of "putting the past behind us," helps explain the decision of the new West German judicial system to prosecute Nazi criminals under the German penal code. Fritz Bauer criticized this decision, for he saw the early abandonment of judicial measures as a major impediment to any later investigation of Nazi criminals. Bauer maintained: "The extensive passivity of the administration of justice reflects the foreign and domestic policy of the Federal Republic" in general.[31]

After the Nuremberg trials, and in fact even during the trials, the German public lost interest in punishing the Nazi collaborators, as we have seen. This loss of interest was attributable in part to other concerns, like the cold war, in part to the recognition that many perpetrators already convicted of serious crimes were being pardoned, and in part to the Allies' having prohibited the Germans from trying anyone who had already been investigated by the Allied tribunals. Politicians and the public concentrated on building a democracy at any cost, and if they were to do that, ex-Nazis had to be reintegrated into society rather than castigated or alienated. Gradually throughout the early 1950s, they were welcomed back into society. Bureaucrats from the Nazi period were guaranteed pensions, and in general, "the West German government was preoccupied with mollifying the Nazi criminals."[32] By no means, though, were the courts empty of former Nazi criminals during the 1950s. The wheels of the young West German justice system were slowly set into motion, and investigations into Nazi crimes gained momentum throughout the 1950s.

Between 1951 and 1955 the new courts attempted to resolve the problems caused by the limitations of the German penal code. Rückerl states that during this time only twenty-one nonappealable sentences were recorded. Most sentences were extremely light (less than five years' imprisonment), and most acts of what would normally be considered murder were judged as aiding and abetting murder because of a restriction in the legal definition of the crime. In addition, many Nazi criminals had already been tried and convicted or released both by the Allies and in Eastern European courts; it did not occur to German officials to pursue them further during this period of reconstruction and preoccupation with contemporary crimes. An expanded sense of the possibilities of legal proceedings (especially given that the majority of crimes had been committed outside Germany) did not exist yet in the minds of fledgling prosecutors, who did not have much information about the Holocaust and often did not know where to begin to gather basic evidence. Older prosecutors were not always eager to investigate Nazi crimes, because many of them had been members of the Nazi party. Overall, these circumstances, along with the political climate during the Adenauer era, explain the general atmosphere of confusion and reticence within the German legal community with regard to Nazi crimes. Meanwhile, the Allies were also winding down denazification proceedings. In many ways, it was thought that the "goal of coming to terms with the past had now been reached."[33]

Finally, in 1955, the Transition Agreement between the United States, Great Britain, France, and West Germany included the stipulation that German courts could not investigate or prosecute anyone who had been investigated already by the occupying powers.

This had an unfortunate effect on subsequent investigations. Citing the example of the American trial of the commanders of the *Einsatzgruppen*, Rückerl notes that on the one hand, the main criminals in charge of the special killing commandos had all been released by the late 1950s and could no longer be investigated. On the other hand, many of their subordinates were tried in subsequent proceedings and often sentenced to life in prison.[34] The fate of the underlings caused some public resentment of the trials, for the majority of Germans blamed the architects and ideologues of Nazism for their program of destruction and saw themselves as victims who had had no choice but to comply. In hindsight these trials focusing on the role of subordinates as perpetrators and murderers were justified and necessary; however, in the West Germany of the early 1950s, this attitude had not yet formed.

The number of trials of former Nazis in the Federal Republic increased during the second half of the 1950s, often because individuals, usually survivors, had recognized camp guards or other Nazi officials on the street and pressed charges against them. This was the case with the initiation of the Auschwitz investigation, and also with the Ulm trial of 1958, when members of an *Einsatzgruppe* unit were tried. After one man appealed to the press to be reinstated in his job as police inspector, a survivor recognized him as the leader of a unit that had participated in mass killings in Lithuania in 1941. Such coincidences occurred more and more often as former Nazis were released from the East and made their way back to Germany.

As individual state public prosecutor's offices became apprised of the enormous number of uninvestigated crimes and suspects, they made a concerted effort to document investigations in a coherent manner. In October 1958 the ZS was established in Ludwigsburg through an agreement of regional judicial administrations and funded by all the states. It was dedicated to investigating Nazi crimes (primarily in the East) and collecting information, in the form of documents or eyewitness testimony, on perpetrators. This information would then be forwarded to the appropriate prosecutor's office for criminal prosecution. Whereas initially most information collected by the ZS came from previously collected documents and the Nuremberg trial records, new evidence began to appear and accumulate once the public became aware of the existence of the new office. In 1959 alone, the ZS initiated four hundred new investigations into crimes committed in the East by both the *Einsatzgruppen* and the guards at concentration and death camps.[35]

A new era of judicial investigation into Nazi crimes thus began, and by the late 1980s the ZS had launched investigations into at least 13,000 proceedings.[36] To be sure, many of these had to be closed owing to the death or disappearance of the suspects. By 1992 approximately 103,823 German citizens had been investigated for Nazi crimes. Of these, according to the legal historian Dick de Mildt, only 6,487 were prosecuted and convicted, 5,513 (85 percent) of them for "nonlethal" crimes of National Socialism—generally, aiding and abetting. Because racial hatred, identification of the ethnicity of the victims, and the program of racial annihilation were not elements central to a murder conviction, of all these convictions only a "little over 7 percent actually related to the mass killing of Jews." Of the 6,487 convicted defendants, 13 were sentenced to death (before the death sentence was abolished), 163 to life imprisonment (a murder conviction), 6,197 to temporary prison terms, and 114 to fines.[37]

In many ways, neither the Nuremberg statutes nor the West German penal code seemed satisfactory to the German public. Control Council Law No. 10, and especially the charge of "crimes against humanity," ignored the fact that those acts described as war crimes "should have been prosecuted as murder, manslaughter, grievous bodily harm, false imprisonment, duress, larceny and blackmail pursuant to the penal laws in force both then and now." This was the argument of the German judiciary and in many ways is part of the larger problem with the IMT. The crimes of the Holocaust had little if anything to do with war. However, once the German judicial system was completely independent again after 1950, German trials also had little to do with the Holocaust: they were run as regular criminal proceedings in which not the overarching Final Solution was on trial, but only the individual actions of each defendant. Neither the defendants nor the public was impressed with the outcome of regular criminal proceedings and the depiction of the people on trial, for "although they and their public might claim political victimization, they appeared in court as killers, rapists and thieves." It was virtually impossible to create a trial that could adequately deal with Nazi crimes and that would meet with public approval.[38]

I would argue that the use of the German penal code had in fact made the trials easier for the public to digest: it distanced them from the proceedings. By the very nature of the murder charge, the defendants had to be shown to be sadistic, twisted, malicious killers. Once this was proved, the public could look upon those convicted with disgust and read about them in the paper as the "other"—monsters and evil men, distinct from "ordinary Germans." Some West German state prosecutors may have wanted to find the best system to prosecute Nazi criminals properly—we shall see that the prosecution office in Frankfurt, led by Fritz Bauer, was determined to pursue these crimes rigorously and vigilantly—but the decision to avoid the Nuremberg statutes had unintended effects that may have weakened the public prosecutor's cases considerably.

The overall reaction of society, politicians, government, and West Germany on the whole has become part of a large historical discussion that functions as a second level of historical analysis regarding Nazism: Germany's confrontation with the past, or *Vergangenheitsbewältigung*. German historians such as Hans Mommsen, Norbert Frei, Ulrich Herbert, and Olaf Groehler have pioneered the historical inquiry into *Vergangenheitsbewältigung* in both East and West Germany. Frei has written extensively on the politics of the early Federal Republic in direct relationship to the preceding Nazi period. Herbert and Groehler have compared East and West German postwar confrontation with the past and explored whether either population engaged in meaningful introspection about the past or whether persistent authoritarian, nationalist, militaristic, and racist qualities that remained entrenched in the collective German psyche made the supposed *Vergangenheitsbewältigung* a superficial and imposed process. Jean-Paul Bier has examined the "strategies of oblivion" adopted by Adenauer's government—instituting reparations to Israel in 1952 as a psychological substitute for the equally important task of investigating and prosecuting the thousands of suspected murderers within Germany—as well as by the public, for whom the subjects of genocide, antisemitism, and concentration camps were "taboos which the new German society was trying to forget at all costs." Gotthard Jaspers argues that *Vergangenheitsbewältigung* in Adenauer's era was "half-hearted," especially judicially. Charles Maier has labeled the Nazi period Germany's "unmasterable past" and has examined the ways in which memory and historical dialogue about the Holocaust were affected and even distorted by the silence among historians that lasted until late in the 1960s. Nicolas Berg contends that the very historians who wrote the historical section of the Auschwitz Trial indictment—Martin Broszat, Hans Buchheim, and Helmut Krausnick—were guilty of selectively remembering the past, hiding some of their own questionable positions during the Nazi period, and ignoring the perspectives of Jewish historians. The conclusion that *Vergangenheitsbewältigung* has been incomplete, contradictory, and distorted will become further evident through an analysis of the Auschwitz Trial and the reaction to it.[39] But first, a brief examination of the independent West German judicial system, and the process by which it came into existence, demonstrates the foundations of the limitations that prosecutors in Frankfurt would face in putting Auschwitz on trial.

The West German Criminal Justice System

German law belongs in the greater central European legal family of continental law, in that five codes form the basis of its legal system: civil law in Roman law definition, civil procedural law, criminal law, criminal procedural law, and commercial law. This foundation stands in contrast to Anglo-American common law practice, and German criminal law shows three main differences from common law: first, it is an inquisitorial system—that is, the judge does the majority of questioning in trials. Second, the court is largely responsible for gathering and producing evidence, organizing the case, and deciding the course of the trial. Finally, Continental courts permit hearsay, whereas it is excluded by Anglo-American law. John Langbein remarks that the term "inquisitorial" should not be interpreted in a negative sense; it simply means that "the court inquires."[40] The German penal code (the *Strafgesetzbuch*, StGB for short) was established in 1871 with the founding of the Second Reich and existed throughout the entire Nazi period. Between 1933 and 1945 huge changes were made to the entire system of German law. No new constitution was instituted, but the law was either suspended or perverted by Nazi judges, who were party members implementing Nazi ideology. They simply issued many laws by decree. The rights of the individual were virtually negated, and the state (and the all-powerful police) became the absolute power that could determine treatment of individuals. After the demise of Nazism, some of the revisions made by the Nazis were repealed (although not all, as we shall see) and the old code of 1871 stood; in fact, the official name of the StGB is still the German Penal Code of 1871.

Despite these continuities, a new atmosphere of reasoning and interpretation of the law existed after the war, along with many new laws. For example, an important statute against genocide (paragraph 220a) was introduced in March 1954. The genocide law was clearly a result of the Nazi genocide of the Jews and an attempt to prevent the occurrence of another such catastrophe.[41] Unfortunately, paragraph 103 of the constitution (*Grundgesetz*, or GG—"basic law"), the ban on retroactivity *(Rückwirkungsverbot)*, made the genocide statute inapplicable in German postwar trials of Nazi perpetrators because of its ex post facto status. As we have seen, the German criminal code adhered to rigidly to the ban on retroactivity. It was also the subject of many major debates in the Bundestag. At the same time, any notion that the Nazi policy of murder was legal was not entertained, for the statute applying to murder (paragraph 211) stood throughout the entire Nazi period. The postwar court system was determined by a much more interpretive and precedent-based order. It was rooted in the greatest achievement of the immediate postwar period: the Federal Constitutional Court (Bundesverfassunggericht), which held (and retains) the power to overrule any laws which might be in breach of the constitution *(Grundgesetz).*

The Courts

Paragraph 92 of the GG creates the division between federal and regional courts, making for a highly specialized and decentralized court system.[42] The federal court (Bundesgericht), stands at the head of each of the hierarchies of the state courts (Landesgerichte), and is basically only used as a court of final appeal, which helps to define a uniform interpretation of law throughout the states of Germany. Each state is responsible for the administration of its own judicial system as defined by the GG and the court constitution *(Gerichtsverfassungsgesetz,* or GVG). There are ninety-three regional courts in Germany, based in larger towns and cities. (Smaller towns and villages have a system of local courts, or Amtsgerichte.) Within the regional court of each state exists a criminal chamber, which is divided into two sections: the small chamber *(kleine Strafkammer),* and the large chamber *(große Strafkammer).* For our purposes, the large chamber is relevant, as it is responsible for indictable offenses. For the most serious criminal cases, such as the Auschwitz Trial, the regional court creates within the large criminal chamber a *Schöffengericht* or *Schwurgericht,* which in English is known as a jury court or trial. In reality, the judges always participate in the actual verdict. During the 1960s the jury court had six jurors.[43] These lay judges are the equivalent of legal scholars in the North American context, as they need have neither professional legal training nor knowledge of the case before the actual trial and can issue judgments just like the professional judges.[44] The Auschwitz Trial was administered by the jury court at the regional court of Frankfurt am Main and was made up of three professional judges and six jurists.

The public prosecutor's office has exclusive control over the pressing of charges. The prosecution service, set up by the state, is a completely separate entity from either the police or the court. The prosecutor's office has the right to pursue an investigation begun by the police and generally works very closely with them, as police have the necessary expertise and capacity to gather evidence; however, prosecutors may also investigate on their own. They have the right to arrest suspects, subpoena witnesses and conduct searches, but they are not obligated to press charges based on police investigation or suspicion. The public prosecutor's office represents the public interest and must therefore always ensure that correct procedure is being followed, not only in the pretrial phase but also at the trial itself.[45] I shall return to the relation between the state and the court when I examine the German criminal procedure, which becomes relevant when the prosecution has decided to press charges and issue an indictment.

The Criminal Code (StGB)

The application of German criminal law and the shape of a trial are dictated by two separate yet equally important categories: substantive criminal law, as outlined in the StGB, and standard criminal procedure (StPO). The former sets up the actual requirements and details of crimes along with their punishments, and the latter determines the ways in which the StGB is enforced. The StGB, loosely based on the Second Reich's penal code, is divided into two parts: the general part *(Allgemeiner Teil)*, encompassing paragraphs 1–79, and the specialized part *(Besonderer Teil)*, dealing with paragraphs 80–358. The general part sets out the rules and regulations that apply to most criminal offenses, and the specialized part identifies the criminal offenses that make up the core of criminal law.[46]

Certain basic principles are outlined in the general part of the StGB; for example, paragraph 1 enunciates the principle of legality, which states that there can be no punishment without statutory legislation and there can be no crime without an offense. (In Latin, these are the principles of *nulla poena sine lege* and *nullum crimen sine lege*, respectively.) Paragraph 2 precludes retroactivity, insisting that "the punishment and its collateral consequences are determined by the statute which was in force at the time of the act."[47] This stipulation applies to laws implemented after 1945 and would have made it impossible to bring such charges as those of the International Military Tribunal at Nuremberg—of crimes against humanity, for example—in the German legal setting. Paragraph 2 is not to be confused, however, with the *Befehlsnotstand,* or defense of superior orders, used by many former Nazis, whereby their lawyers attempted to show that their clients had merely been doing as they were commanded and had therefore been acting legally. I will show in Chapter 2 that this claim was deemed inadmissible at Nuremberg, and again at the Auschwitz Trial, and therefore that the defendants were charged with crimes understood to be illegal during the time in which they were supposedly committed. Murder falls into the category of felonies, as outlined in paragraph 12 of the StGB, which creates a division between felonies and misdemeanors. Felonies constitute the focus of this investigation, for they are defined as indictable offenses carrying a punishment of one or more years.

In determining what constitutes a punishable crime, the general part of the StGB emphasizes three constituent elements that must be present: the existence of an offense, the unlawfulness of the offense, and the guilt of the offender. First, a punishable crime must fulfill the mental and physical elements in the statutory definition of an offense, or *Tatbestand.* Key to this finding is intent, which is defined as subjective mental reasoning. Paragraph 15 states that intentional behavior is always punishable, where negligent behavior is not. Intent is defined as the "knowledge that the behavior will have a particular result and the desire or will that this result should come about." Therefore, for example, a person is not guilty of murder because he pulled the trigger and killed another person, but because he pulled the trigger with the intention of killing the other person and succeeded in doing so.[48] This element of subjective intent behind a physical act will become crucial in the discussion of the limitations of the murder law and the determination of the motivation of the perpetrator.

The second element in the definition of the general concept of a punishable crime is unlawfulness *(Rechtswidrigkeit).* Simply, this concept means the act must be unlawful and, in cases such as murder, the offender must be aware that his action fulfills the definition of a crime *(Unrechtsbewußtsein)*. The third element of a crime is the guilt principle *(Schuldprinzip)*. The guilt principle is the basis for punishment of the offender as laid out in paragraph 46, and it incorporates social responsibility depending on the ability of the offender to choose between lawful and unlawful conduct. This is a complicated matter, determined largely by the specific charges brought against an offender.[49]

The General Part of the StGB also determines the parties to crime *(Teilnahme)*. This section is central to the Auschwitz Trial because of the division created between principal perpetrators and general participants. The numbers of the paragraphs were: 47—perpetrators and co-perpetrators *(Täter und Mittäter)*, 48—instigators *(Anstifter)*, and 49—accomplices *(Gehilfe)*. Paragraph 47 defines four types of principal perpetrators, all of whom would receive a life sentence if convicted: the immediate perpetrator *(unmittelbarer Täter)*, the perpetrator who acts through the agency of another *(mittelbarer Täter)*, the co-perpetrator, or *Mittäter*, and the collateral perpetrator, or *Nebentäter*. Paragraphs 48 and 49 define two types of participation: instigation *(Anstiftung)* and aiding and abetting *(Beihilfe)*. Paragraph 49, aiding and abetting, defines the behavior of an offender as someone who "intentionally renders assistance to enable another to intentionally commit an unlawful act."[50] Aiding and abetting is different from instigation, in that the offender is accused of having promoted or facilitated the commission of a crime, whereas a person accused of instigation is said to have occasioned the perpetrator's intent and resolve. Instigation is entirely different from and less serious than perpetration, which is the charge against the person or persons who willfully and intentionally commit a crime, with individual initiative. I stress the importance of the charge of *Beihilfe* here, and the distinction between aiding and abetting, on the one hand, and perpetrating, on the other, as the defendants in the Auschwitz Trial were generally charged with perpetration and the specific charge was murder (paragraph 211), but they were in the majority convicted of aiding and abetting murder. Despite the fact that the StPO held an accessory to murder liable to the same punishment as the perpetrator, it is difficult to find a case in which anyone convicted of aiding and abetting received a life sentence.[51] This holds true for the Auschwitz Trial. Only seven of the twenty defendants were convicted of perpetration of murder, while the rest either were convicted as accomplices with no "personal interest" in murder or were acquitted.

The reason for the large number of accomplice convictions was the interpretive flexibility of what it means to be a perpetrator or an accomplice. Different courts throughout Germany generally decided for themselves just how objective or subjective their definition of participation would be. This practice led to conflict among jurists in the postwar period, as they often had different notions about the nature of perpetration and culpability. Specifically, in the 1950s and 1960s legal theoreticians fell into different camps regarding the definition of perpetration *(Täterschaft)* as an objective or subjective act. This debate stemmed from what were considered by conservative jurists to have been very harsh sentences in the years immediately after the war, not only at Nuremberg but in West German courts. Some courts therefore chose to reject more objective interpretations of murder that were being put forth in favor of a precedent that had been set in 1940 in the Badewanne Fall (Bathtub case). As Henry Friedlander explains, the German Supreme Court ruled as follows:

> The female defendant had drowned her sister Maria's newly born illegitimate infant in a bathtub. The lower court had convicted her for murder. The Supreme Court reversed [this conviction] . . . The fact that the defendant had personally drowned the baby, and had thus actually committed the killing, is not relevant to determining the degree of participation. That is based on the motivation of the perpetrator: his or her personal interest in the success of the undertaking. Maria, the mother of the baby, had this interest . . . The defendant, her

> sister, did not have a personal interest in the outcome . . . She
> is therefore only an accomplice.[52]

This decision is a good example of a legal interpretation made during the Nazi period that would stand in the postwar period as well. Many jurists would return to this precedent and argue that the objective definition, which presented the perpetrator as the one who pulled the trigger, and was too narrow. Subjective theory had more complex explanations of perpetration.

Two important applications of subjective theory in relation to Nazi crimes were the dolus and the interest theories: the first defined perpetration as the result of malice aforethought and desire for an outcome (rather than negligence), and the second defined it by the presence of interest in the crime, whether carried out by the perpetrator or ordered by someone else.[53] Legal scholars attempted to find a way to mediate between these theories. Most influential in this debate were the writings of Claus Roxin, Werner Hardwig, and Jürgen Baumann.[54] Roxin proposed the theory of *Tatherrschaft*, or "mastery of the act," which combined the subjective and objective theories. In Roxin's definition, a perpetrator was anyone who was not under duress or dependent on someone else and could therefore demonstrate either physical mastery (having committed the act himself), willful mastery (having willed the act, also as a superior), or functional mastery (having been vital to the completion of the act).[55] Ultimately, not only such scholars as Baumann and Hardwig rejected Roxin's theories, but so did the German high court of appeals, which deemed Roxin's seemingly fitting theory inappropriate for Nazi trials. In its place the high court adopted Baumann's entirely subjective definition, which determined perpetration entirely by the will to obtain the outcome, regardless of whether the defendant physically committed the criminal act.[56] Precedent cases then reinforced this definition: a good example was the Staschynskij case, in which a KGB agent murdered two Ukrainian émigrés in Germany in 1962; he was convicted as an accomplice because the criminal motives were attributed to his superiors. In the case of Nazi trials, judges usually adopted a similar standard, and although they could still determine that a subordinate was a perpetrator, they had to be convinced, as the subjective theory required, that the subordinate had adopted the superior's criminal intent as his own. Prosecutors attempted to show that the lower-ranked defendants possessed the ideological motivations of their superiors (particularly antisemitism), and therefore the will to murder; but in the case of bureaucrats, camp guards, and murder squads this shared motivation was virtually impossible to prove: as Henry Friedlander says, "eventually most courts accepted the subjective interpretation of the Bathtub case."[57] This interpretation meant that prosecutors at the Auschwitz Trial had to contend not only with the restrictive definitions of perpetration, and the murder charge itself (as we shall see), but with the judge's interpretive inclination, based on his estimation of the severity of the crimes, his adherence to the high court's ruling, and his position on the legal debate on the motivation of the perpetrator that was going on throughout the 1950s and 1960s. Very few judges were inclined to challenge the norm, and the Auschwitz Trial judge was no exception.

Criminal Procedure (StPO)

The proper implementation of the German penal code is prescribed by the accompanying procedural law. This is basically the extensive statutory legislation that ensures the smooth running of the criminal process and complements the penal code, in order that substantive law and punishment will be correctly enforced. This means that the court plays a dynamic role during the pretrial and trial phases. The central element of the StPO for our purposes is state and court procedure, which is divided into three sections: the pretrial investigation (*Ermittlungsverfahren*), the interim proceedings (*Zwischenverfahren*), and the main proceedings (*Hauptverfahren*).

The pretrial investigation is conducted exclusively by the prosecutor, with extensive assistance from the police. The principle of officiality as outlined in the StPO states that only the prosecutor's office, not individual citizens, may bring public charges.[58] In this phase the prosecutor's office determines whether or not formal charges should be brought and initiates arrests of those under suspicion of serious criminal offenses. The suspects are placed in investigative detention as defined by the StPO in consideration of the risk of flight, the risk of the destruction of evidence, and the gravity of the offense. It is in this phase that the defense attorneys are brought in, for the trial cannot proceed without them. If the accused refuses to acquire an attorney, the court then makes the appointment. Also during this period a civil plaintiff *(Nebenkläger)* can press charges and therefore be heard within the criminal case rather than in a separate civil trial, as happens in common-law countries. The civil plaintiffs in the case of Nazi trials, and particularly the Auschwitz Trial, were often those victims who were not granted an investigation by prosecutors in their jurisdiction.[59] Once the prosecutors decide to proceed, they formally apply to the court responsible to commence judicial proceedings against a defendant or multiple defendants.

This is the beginning of the second phase of criminal procedure, the interim phase, in which the dossier of files is delivered by the prosecution to the court.[60] The court then conducts its own investigation, independent of the police or the prosecution, to determine whether the charges have validity and whether to declare a formal trial. The court cannot bring charges against a defendant independently; the public prosecutor's office must officially file the indictment. Once the charges have been filed, however, the court becomes involved in the investigative process and can therefore also recommend other charges it considers more appropriate. Only professional judges make these decisions; lay judges take part solely in the main proceedings, and do not have access to information from the pretrial investigations.[61]

Once the prosecution and the court have decided on the charges and the terms of the indictment, the final phase of the trial begins— the main proceedings. As determined by the StPO, this takes the form of an oral trial before the appropriate court. The prosecution reads charges aloud, and the accused can make a statement. The inquisitive nature of the criminal procedure of the German trial system is especially evident here, as the judges, particularly the presiding judge, play an enormous role in the courtroom. They are generally already very familiar with the facts of the case, and they ask a limited set of questions to determine whether the charges can be sustained. Most of the questions, in fact, come from the court, with very little cross-examination by the prosecution or the defense attorneys.[62] After hearing the evidence, the judges and the jury deliberate and make their judgment not on the basis of a unanimous decision but on the majority decision of two-thirds of the judges presiding. Following this stage the criminal code determines the punishment the defendants will face.

The pretrial files of the Auschwitz Trial consist mainly of communications between prosecutors, arrest warrants, and witness interrogations, extending over the relatively short period of the investigative process. The prosecutors officially informed the court only once they felt they had enough evidence for a large trial of those accused of crimes committed at Auschwitz. On July 12, 1961, the public prosecutor's office submitted the first motion to open the preliminary judicial inquiry" to the court in Frankfurt. The interim phase of the Auschwitz investigation began on August 9, 1961, with the court's formal declaration of the finding for an indictment and decision to begin the judicial inquiry. It is for this reason that the pretrial files of the Auschwitz Trial often contain two interrogations of the same witness: one conducted by prosecution attorneys and one conducted by the investigating judge, Dr. Heinz Düx. Often discrepancies between the two statements made the work of the presiding judge in the trial even more difficult. The discrepancies arose because the records of the pretrial interrogations were not verbatim transcripts, but protocols showing summaries by the police or judicial officials of testimony, which were then read and signed by the witnesses. We shall see that in the Auschwitz Trial, especially in the final stages of the pretrial investigations, the prosecutors continually reconstructed their cases and sought to press further charges against many of the defendants—to which the court did not always assent.

There was a two-year interim investigation in the Auschwitz Trial, during which charges were added or dropped and amendments were made largely on the basis of the court's findings. The main proceedings of the Frankfurt Auschwitz Trial commenced on April 4, 1963, when the indictment was filed. The trial began on December 20, 1963.[63]

Criminal Code Paragraphs 211 and 49

The murder law of the German penal code, paragraph 211, states that "1) The murderer shall be punished by imprisonment for life; 2) a murderer is anyone who kills a human being: from a lust for killing, to satisfy his sexual drives, from covetousness or other base motives, treacherously, cruelly, or by means endangering the community or in order to facilitate or conceal another crime." Such definitions are not uncommon in Continental and common-law countries. Motive is always central to the charge of murder and distinguishes it from manslaughter, which is applicable, states the StGB, to "anyone who kills a human being under circumstances not constituting murder." The attempt to define the motivation, however, as a subjective inner disposition such as sadism or sexual desire is unique to the German criminal code. It considerably narrows the spectrum of criminal behavior that the prosecution can validly try as murder. Interestingly, before 1941 the murder statute had been defined as "intentional killing accomplished with premeditation." In 1941, however, the Germans adopted the language of other European countries, particularly Switzerland, and a premeditated killing now became "particularly reprehensible," the definition of which is spelled out rather specifically in the code, as we have seen.[64]

The German lawyer Alfred Bongard has closely examined the murder charge in conjunction with deficiencies in Nazi trials and has determined that the charge can be applied only with difficulty to Nazi crimes and cannot easily be manipulated or interpreted to convict Nazis of murder. Adalbert Rückerl confirms this finding in stating that "it is virtually only the criteria thirst for blood, base motives, maliciousness and brutality which come into question in connection with the prosecuting of Nazi war crimes."[65]

Bongard points out that the Bundesgerichtshof (BGH) had determined that the phrase "base motives" in the case of Nazi trials would be defined as racial hatred and antisemitism or would apply to anyone who killed Jews and used ideological brainwashing as a defense in the hopes that it would preclude him from being held criminally responsible for the act. "Base motives" could also apply to someone who made himself "Lord over life and death, while believing that those over whose life he decided were less than worthy, not even humans."[66] As a consequence, the federal high court had made interpretive decisions that allowed for antisemitic Nazi ideology to be included as a valid part of the murder charge; however, the prosecution was rarely able to prove base motives, and murder convictions grounded on the charge were surprisingly rare. In addition, the detection of base motives, particularly racial hatred, was often the determining factor in whether a defendant was considered a perpetrator or an accomplice.[67] Interestingly, the BGH has been criticized for concentrating too narrowly on the question of racial hatred and therefore letting other possible motives go unexamined. Bongard states:

> Whoever had in any way "reasonable," although objectionable, yet still prosecutable motives for killing, could not be in a worse position than someone who killed out of totally empty motives. The BGH maintains that the defendant "after all didn't have these base motives [race-hatred] himself, but only obeyed orders as a police officer or SS member, even though he recognized them as criminal." The BGH does not consider the possibility that the defendant himself may also have possessed these base motives when he carried out the killing.[68]

Thus, early decisions by the BGH determined that base motives of race and Jew hatred existed only among the lawmakers or desktop murderers of the Nazi regime and therefore could not apply to the lesser personnel on trial for individual murders at the camps. It was virtually impossible to prove the personal antisemitism of the defendants at the Auschwitz Trial, as they could always insist that they were not ideologically driven but were simply following orders.

Proving that a defendant had acted "treacherously" was also difficult in the case of Nazi perpetrators. In Bongard's opinion and in the ruling of the BGH, killing someone who was both "defenseless" and "harmless" was treacherous behavior. Of course, most victims of the Holocaust qualified as defenseless, or at least "seriously limited in their ability to resist"; however, the BGH yet again did not always rule for defenselessness, particularly in the case where the victims killed were prisoners of war.[69] Even defendants who killed the most "harmless" of prisoners, the ill, were often convicted only of manslaughter or aiding and abetting because of the other limitations inherent in the murder law.

The stipulation of cruelty is another good example of a loophole the defense could use to exonerate their clients. The BGH defined a perpetrator as cruel if he intentionally tortured or inflicted pain, either emotionlessly or joyfully, for an extremely long period or with excessive force. This qualification applied to what has become known as excess perpetrators, some of whom were certainly on trial at Auschwitz. Implicit in this definition is evidence of individual initiative inherent in random, unsolicited acts of cruelty. Such extreme sadists could be and were convicted of murder; however, as Bongard scornfully states, "the mere mass liquidation of victims was not considered cruel treatment by the courts."[70]

As we have seen, the problem of individual initiative was obvious not only in the murder statute, but in the laws determining level of participation. Individual initiative tended to be the determining factor in differentiating between perpetration and aiding and abetting. Here the decision to apply the subjective theory, to emphasize the "inner disposition" of the defendant, became crucial, much more so than the overall nature of the crime. A perpetrator was someone who committed an offense "of his own will," demonstrating the will to perpetrate, whereas an accomplice simply committed the offense. The "individual initiative" clause was applied very liberally in trials of Nazi criminals; even if defendants killed someone with their own hand, they were generally convicted of aiding and abetting rather than murder because a certain degree of "lack of will" could almost always be proved. Or at least with those who did not visibly demonstrate excessive force or commit violent acts without being ordered to, individual will could very rarely be shown. Instead, the profile of the defendant as "entangled in national socialist ideology" or "part of the state power apparatus" very often led to a lesser conviction.

Bongard shows that the BGH handled such decisions entirely differently in "normal" criminal procedures. The introductory statement of a regular criminal decision runs: "He who kills a person with his own hand is fundamentally considered a perpetrator, even if he does it under the influence, in the interest, or in the presence of another."[71] This standard was obviously not always applied to Nazi criminal trials, and in final judgments the BGH often decided on convictions of aiding and abetting rather than murder, especially in the court of appeals. It appears that this practice was the result of a tendency to treat Nazi criminals leniently, as Bongard maintains; these trials were not "ordinary" criminal trials, and precedent shows that despite the best efforts of prosecutors, judges often chose the lesser convictions when interpretation would allow it.[72] In many ways, the prosecution had no way of proving individual initiative if a defendant could not be found to have the subjective, inner desire to kill, as outlined in any of the stipulations of the murder statute. Those who acted only on orders and without excessive force or cruelty could always insist that they felt no personal malice, no individual antisemitism, and therefore no particular will to murder. If no witness could conclusively and explicitly contradict this defense through precise evidence, it was impossible to show intent.

Rückerl reiterates the distinction between a perpetrator and an accomplice by describing the latter as "anyone who fulfilled the legal characteristics of murder by virtue of his action but thereby completely obeyed the wishes of a third party without taking any interest in the accomplishment of the crime." With reference to the Auschwitz Trial, although the "order defense" could not be used on its own, as the Nazi state had been ruled illegal, its organizations criminal, and its orders therefore invalid, this defense could still be used to demonstrate that the defendant had not carried out individual acts of cruelty (to make the cruelty clause of paragraph 211 inapplicable), had not demonstrated personal antisemitism (to make the base motives clause inapplicable), and had not acted on individual will (to make perpetration inapplicable, although aiding and abetting might be). The disappointing result was that defendants who had selected victims for death in the gas chambers at the platform or had carried out ordered executions at the "Black Wall" or had reluctantly given lethal injections at the camp hospital were not convicted of murder: "The jury courts often punished persons accused of aiding and abetting murder where they had in fact objectively committed an act of murder pursuant to Paragraph 211 of the Penal Code by virtue of their action but where the courts were unable to prove that they had been actuated by their own wishes."[73]

The Debate on the Statute of Limitations

Adding to the prosecution's frustrations and inability to punish the Nazi criminals on trial fully was the *Verjährungsdebatte* (debate on the statute of limitations) that took place throughout the 1960s in West Germany. Beginning in 1960, the public and the parliament became aware of the limitations on certain statutes, and it soon became obvious that changes had to be made for the special case of Nazi trials. Rückerl explains, "Limitation rules out judicial punishment of a criminal act . . . All crimes become statute-barred after a certain period of time has expired. Pursuant to Paragraph 67 of the Penal Code . . . the limitation of crimes liable to a life sentence was twenty years; for criminal acts liable to a term of imprisonment of more than ten years (manslaughter), a period of fifteen years; and for other criminal acts, ten years." The limitations meant, of course, that after 1960 defendants could not be charged with manslaughter for crimes committed during the Nazi period. After 1965, murder would be invalid. The charge of aiding and abetting is a peculiar one. Fritz Bauer says that *Beihilfe zu Mord* initially fell into the fifteen-year limitation span that applied to manslaughter. It was only in 1943, with a change to the StGB implemented by the Nazis themselves, that aiding and abetting became punishable with a maximum sentence (under the Nazis the death sentence, but under the general penal code a life sentence) and therefore subject to a twenty-year limitation. Paradoxically, the zeal of the Nazis for harsh punishment worked against them after the war.[74]

In the late 1950s and early 1960s, members of parliament began to debate the fundamental problem of limitations on the prosecution of Nazi crimes. Certainly, given that information on alleged perpetrators only trickled in very slowly from Eastern countries, there was no way to investigate many suspects until long after the crimes had been committed. The SPD gave the first official utterance to murmurs about the need for change, when the party presented a draft law in March 1960. This bill proposed that the limitations on murder be extended by four years, allowing Nazi murders to be tried up until 1969.[75] The logic for the extension was ingenious: West Germany did not have the facilities to try criminals within its own court system until after the withdrawal of the Allies in 1949. Therefore, technically, those four extra years from 1945 to 1949 should not count toward the span in the statute of limitations. The SPD pointed to the gravity of the crimes, the disadvantages of a hasty investigation, and also the political responsibility of the generation following National Socialism to take these acts seriously. The Bundestag, however, rejected the proposal. A series of parliamentary and public debates began on the matter. The political scientist Peter Steinbach thinks that public opinion on the 1960 debate was best represented by the words of one Freie Demokratische Partei (FDP) member of parliament: "Hear nothing, see nothing, know nothing."[76] The debate at the time heralded the larger issue of how to deal with collective, national, and individual guilt, and the policy of silence was still very much official, especially among members the older generation both in parliament and in the country at large.

Members in favor of extending or even removing the limitations looked to the stipulations in the law—paragraph 69 of the StGB—that permitted an interruption of the limitations in special circumstances—for example, if the jurisdiction of a suspect could not be determined. In some cases the prosecutors managed to stall and obtain more time to gather information and prepare a case. Sometimes, however, stalling also worked against the prosecutors in their bid for an interruption. For example, in November 1964, six months before the limitations on the murder charge would officially have taken hold, the federal government called for any unknown documentation of possible crimes to be brought forward for examination, including files from U.S. World War II investigations, and especially Polish evidence from the main commission in Poland investigating Nazi war crimes. The federal government, according to Rückerl, "assumed at the time that it would not prove possible for constitutional reasons to extend the period of limitation beyond May 1965."[77]

The opposite proved to be true. Enormous quantities of documentation and incriminating evidence about Germans suspected of Nazi atrocities poured into Germany. Officials of the ZS in Ludwigsburg examined the evidence and determined that there was far too much information to process by May 1965. The government initially cited this finding as a reason not to interrupt the limitation period, which, it claimed, would be virtually endless. Writing in 1964, Fritz Bauer pointed to the chaos created by the looming limitation and argued that no prosecutor could adequately compile the information that was accumulating rapidly with each new investigation. The realization caused enormous pressure on public prosecutor's offices everywhere in West Germany. As Bauer insisted at the time:

> There cannot be any discussion of the possibility that we have dealt judicially with the past. In many trials new "crime complexes" are surfacing, and new suspicions are being brought against new perpetrator groups. Berlin recently conducted a very comprehensive proceeding against the functionaries of the RSHA [the Reichssicherheitshauptamt, the Central Security Department of the Reich]; thousands of suspects were

affected by this. It should not be a foregone conclusion, despite the strained efforts of Berlin and the support of the public prosecutors of the Federal Republic, that they will have
managed to either name the perpetrators or bring forth concrete accusations within the allotted time span.[78]

Bauer went on to list some of the difficulties prosecutors faced not
only in Berlin but throughout West Germany and particularly in
Ludwigsburg, before any trial had been initiated. There was little
time, for example, to investigate the claims of family members that
particular suspects were dead. If further investigation had been possible, it would surely have shown that many of these characters were
hiding outside Germany or were living in states that were not very
determined to investigate and prosecute their Nazi criminals. The
Auschwitz Trial provided proof of this problem, for time constraints
were a large part of the reason that out of eight hundred investigated,
only twenty were brought to trial in 1963.

Finally, in February 1965, the federal minister of justice forwarded
a report to the Bundestag stating that serious undetected crimes by
unrecognized criminals holding high public office might still come
to light after May and it was therefore imperative to announce an extension.[79] Finally, on March 25, 1965, after heated debates in parliament, both the SPD and the CDU voted on the Statute on Com-
puting Periods of Limitation in Criminal Law. The new act passed,
decreeing the period from May 1945 to December 1949 to be excluded from limitation. In essence, a technicality helped extend the
murder statute until 1969. Nothing, however, was done to amend
the fifteen-year limitation on manslaughter, as the limitation had already come into effect and could not be altered retroactively. Aiding
and abetting was subject to the discretion of the individual court,
and mostly lighter sentences were imposed for this offense. In October 1968 the Ministry of Justice revoked the statute of limitations on
aiding and abetting, but this ruling did not apply retroactively and
therefore did not apply to the Auschwitz Trial.

It is interesting to note the preoccupation with the illegality of retroactivity in postwar West German legal discussion. Just as the 1954 genocide statute could not be applied to the Nazi case, despite its extraordinary nature, the limitations laws also could not be changed retroactively. Fritz Bauer pointed to the 1964 Warsaw conference of East-Bloc jurists regarding the statute of limitations. This conference adopted the standard of the Moscow Declaration of 1943, and the Statute on International Military Tribunals of August 8, 1945, which declared Nazi acts to have been criminal under Allied Control Council Law No. 10. In simple terms, the Warsaw declaration, citing article 2, paragraph 5 of Control Council Law No. 10, determined that "in a criminal proceeding the defendant cannot use the statute of limitations, as long as the time span of January 1, 1933–July 1, 1945 is in question."[80] Bauer believed that this possibility still existed also for the federal republic. He clearly felt that such an exception should be made for the Nazi period; however, as he conceded, arguments would prevail among jurists and politicians that such an exception would weaken the constitutional ban on retroactivity. What seemed to be simply a question of justice to Attorney General Bauer was actually a question of political motivations, particularly anticommunism and anti-Nuremberg sentiments.

On November 26, 1968, the General Assembly of the U.N. passed its Convention on the Non-Applicability of the Legal Limitation Provision on War Crimes and Crimes against Humanity. Paragraph 4 of this convention "obliged the signatory states to annul retroactively a limitation which had already begun."[81] The annulment would require the investigation and prosecution of thousands of suspects who had slipped through the October 1968 ban on limitations for aiding and abetting especially. Germany refused to accede to the U.N. requirement, despite the fact that the 1969 deadline was looming and some parties to the debate were once again calling for overturning the murder limitation. The Bundestag referred to its March 1965 debate, in which it decided unanimously that any form of retroactivity would infringe on basic law. This decision was clearly a product of the bitterness over the victors' trials at Nuremberg and the use of ex post facto law to convict many Germans of international war crimes. West Germany had deliberately avoided the adoption of international war crimes charges, in order to demonstrate its ability to deal by itself with the criminal Nazi state.

As the limitation on murder approached in 1969, while many suspected Nazi criminals were still at large, the debate resurfaced. The federal government proposed a bill annulling the limitations on murder and genocide that was approved by the Bundestag on June 26. This lengthened the investigatory period to thirty years rather than twenty. Only in 1979 did all Nazi crimes become immune to limitations in Germany. The centrality of the *Verjährungsdebatte* to the issue of Nazi crimes has led many historians to argue that the German government was foolish in not adopting international war crimes charges. Still, the district courts of the West German states were bound to the Penal Code of 1871. It was from this starting point that investigations slowly began into the activities of ordinary men and women living inside and outside Germany who had participated in Nazi crimes on every level. Although many of these proceedings throughout West Germany were lackluster, the investigation that became the Frankfurt Auschwitz Trial was anything but. In the next chapter we shall see why.

CHAPTER 2

Pretrial Investigations

E VEN ONCE the investigations into the Auschwitz perpetrators
were initiated at the end of the 1950s, it took five long years for
the trial to begin. Why? To begin proceedings against suspected
criminals, the courts had not only to investigate the accused themselves but to determine the reliability of the sources bringing complaints. We can begin to understand the intricacies of such a drawn-
out trial and the length of time it took before the trial began by
studying the twists and turns of the pretrial phase and examining the
role of a few key players. Although the 1950s have commonly been
considered the period of silence and of "lying low" that preceded the
opening of the investigation in 1958, we have seen that in fact considerable investigation of Nazi crimes and many trials had already
taken place by the beginning of the Auschwitz investigation. We
have also seen how the West German judiciary came to try Nazi perpetrators under the national penal code. The prosecutors at the trial
of Auschwitz perpetrators in Frankfurt had the ambitious aim of putting on trial the entire illegal system of mass murder at the camp; but

legal constraints would make this goal virtually impossible. To meet the challenges imposed by these constraints, Fritz Bauer and his prosecutors in Frankfurt undertook as early as the preinvestigative phase to fit the Auschwitz complex into the legal context.

The Investigation Begins

On March 1, 1958, Adolf Rögner, a prisoner in the Bruchsal penitentiary convicted of fraud who was serving a two-year sentence imposed by the jury court at Stuttgart, wrote a letter to the prosecutor's office in Stuttgart "regarding the distribution of medication" and referring to Wilhelm Boger, a camp guard at Auschwitz who was known as a terrible sadist. In a letter which began with a plea for heart medication that had supposedly been promised to him, Rögner continued:

> Urgent: In addition, I ask you to pass this on to the responsible prosecutors:
>
> In 1946, former SS-Oberscharführer Boger escaped from an extradition transport and fled to Poland. The transport was compiled from the War Crimes Camp 29 at Dachau. Boger is most gravely incriminated by the crimes against humanity he committed at Auschwitz (mass murder, selections, manslaughter, forced confessions with and without the use of the Boger swing, etc.).
>
> I myself was at Auschwitz from May 6, 1941, until January 16, 1945, as prisoner number 15,465. I have furthermore learned that:
>
> A Boger supposedly hid in Unterrath bei Schwäbisch Hall until 1948. He then resurfaced. He is married and now lives in Weil im Dorf. Since approximately 1956 he has, supposedly, been working at Heinkel, an engine factory for cars, in Zuffenhausen.
>
> Insofar as this is the same Boger, I hereby today press charges against him for mass murder. I will immediately pro-

> vide proof and witnesses; similarly, the International Ausch-
> witz Committee (IAC), Vienna 10, Wiegandhof 5, and the
> Central Council of German Jews in Düsseldorf, can certainly
> provide ample evidence . . . the head of the Auschwitz Com-
> mittee in Vienna is Hermann Langbein, also a former camp
> prisoner.[1]

As a result of this seemingly banal letter requesting medication, the public prosecutors in Stuttgart found themselves contemplating a serious criminal charge against someone in their jurisdiction, made by a criminal whose credibility was in doubt (owing in part to his repeated filing of trumped-up charges against the Hohenaspern penitentiary where he had previously served time) but whose accusations, because of their seriousness, could not be ignored. Rögner contended that he had been a prisoner at Auschwitz and knew very well that Boger had interrogated and murdered many inmates on his so called Boger swing—a torture device on which prisoners were beaten to death. Rögner's mention of Hermann Langbein of the International Auschwitz Committee (IAC), who was conducting investigations of his own on Boger and other former Auschwitz guards, made Rögner's assertions all the more credible.[2] For these reasons, the prosecution decided to pursue the allegations. There followed an extensive series of investigations into Rögner's character by both the junior judicial officer in Stuttgart, Wasserlos, and the main police detective, Brunk, which were intended to determine whether Rögner should be heard as a witness and interrogated officially by prosecution lawyers.

Again and again the officials who questioned Rögner characterized him as an unreliable witness. Wasserlos reported that although at first Rögner gave the impression of being a calm, thoughtful man, he became extremely agitated when he saw a picture of Boger and heard him mentioned. Rögner began to accuse the public prosecutors themselves of being implicated, stating that the officials treated him just the way the guards at the prison had; they used "Gestapo and camp methods and wouldn't let him speak, because they [the prosecution] sympathized with these people that he had a lot to complain about." Wasserlos reported on the peculiarity of Rögner's testimony, in which certain facts, numbers, and details were astoundingly accurate, although the witness was unable to come up with a chronological narrative for the activities he reported. Wasserlos surmised that "his comprehensive and detailed knowledge of the occurrences at Auschwitz can possibly be explained by the fact that he had large amounts of material at hand with which he was obsessed during his time in prison." Wasserlos reported that the guards at the prison had stopped bringing Rögner material on the camps and war crimes trials, as his accusations and attempts to press charges against former SS officers became so insistent that it could only be assumed he had obtained his information from his readings and not from personal experience.[3]

Wasserlos concluded that Rögner was an irrational, untrustworthy man who got pleasure from derailing the prosecutors by busying them with false charges and accusations. The officer's statements were corroborated by a report from the Bruchsal Penitentiary regarding Rögner's requests to be moved from Bruchsal to Munich and his threat to press charges against the prison. The head of the prison in Bruchsal also portrayed Rögner as a troublemaker: "In countless, unfounded complaints about supposedly lacking medical care, insufficient physician's supervision, etc . . . [Rögner] repeatedly reminds us that he could be the "chief witness" and contribute a great deal about the crimes committed at Auschwitz. On this point I would like to note that he tenaciously attempted to obtain the report tapes from the Nuremberg trials while in prison in Hohenasperg. He also wrote the International Auschwitz Committee in Vienna attempting to get information."[4] This same report mentioned what was probably a greater cause of unease for the prison authorities and for the prosecution—Rögner's leftist leanings, his membership in the Communist Party, and his dislike of West German parliamentary politics. The tension between East and West German political ideologies was palpable, and it surfaced again, in more overt fashion, during the trial itself.

Rögner's reliability was highly questionable, then, because of his background as someone convicted of fraud, his relentless focus on the happenings at Auschwitz, his continuous complaints against the prisons where he had served time, and his legal charges against the medical workers, compounded by his Communist leanings during the early phases of the cold war. Nevertheless, two months after Rögner filed the charges, the prosecutors decided to hear him in an official interrogation, thereby signaling the opening of the case against Boger. In a memo by prosecutor Weber dated May 13, 1958, his ambivalence was clear: "The interrogation conducted by Judicial Officer Wasserlos (as per my instructions) was necessary, because on one hand, the clear evidence of the previous charges he has filed show the plaintiff [Rögner] to be an attention-seeking psychopath; on the other hand, the serious nature of his charges against Boger cannot be discounted, but demand scrupulous investigation."[5]

One can assume that the prosecutors decided to pursue the investigation of Boger based on the fact that Rögner had indeed been a prisoner at Auschwitz as a so-called *Berufsverbrecher*, or professional criminal. In addition, correspondence with Hermann Langbein and the IAC corroborated the charge that Boger was guilty of murder and torture at Auschwitz between 1942–45. Such an example helps to demonstrate that the stalling and hedging of the German court system often had much less to do with a will to keep the past in the past and much more to do with legal red tape and the need to establish the credibility of a witness. For despite the prosecution's obvious disdain for the plaintiff and his political leanings, his charges were eventually taken seriously and eventually led to the largest trial of Auschwitz perpetrators ever.

From Stuttgart to Frankfurt am Main

Following the lodging of complaints by Rögner, six months passed during which, seemingly, little was done to investigate Boger. Langbein, as head of IAC, was already aware of Boger's activities at Auschwitz through the recollections of survivors who had worked in the

Political Department and had become members of the IAC after the war. He began putting pressure on the prosecution, expressing great dissatisfaction with Stuttgart's slow response to his requests that Boger be arrested. After what he called a "sluggish correspondence" between the prosecutor's office and the IAC, Langbein wrote to Stuttgart in September of 1958:

> After my short discussion with prosecutor Weber on the ninth of September, I am under the impression that up until now, you still have not exhausted all possibilities in order to gain approval for the arrest of Wilhelm Boger. In relation to this, I should like to remind you that already in a letter of May 9, 1958, our committee brought attention to the fact that Boger committed serious crimes at Auschwitz . . . In a letter from August 30, we named five witnesses to the public prosecutor's office who could give testimony about Boger's crimes . . . On the 3rd of September we provided two more witnesses. But in our conversation of September 9, I established that none of these witnesses had yet been interrogated, not even the three from West Germany . . . We realize, Sir, that before arresting someone all necessary and sufficient materials must be collected; however, we also realize that the public prosecutor's office has not shown any initiative to get these materials.[6]

It is difficult to establish whether Langbein was justified in his complaints that the prosecutors in Stuttgart were dragging their feet. It is certainly possible that some involved in the investigation feared public reaction to the arrest of someone who had lived there peacefully, without a pseudonym, for ten years. Prosecutors might also have feared public outrage at such *Nestbeschmutzung* (befouling the nest). However, there is little in the actual pretrial files to demonstrate that the prosecution did not take the accusations of Rögner and the IAC seriously, except perhaps the prosecution's inclination to give more recent crimes priority in their investigations. Whatever the case, Langbein was quite certain that after his letter of September 1958 the prosecution felt obligated to act and, because of this pressure, filed a "proposal for an arrest warrant" for Wilhelm Boger on October 1, 1958.[7] The warrant was issued (by the district court) the next day.

The police brought Wilhelm Boger into investigative detention on October 8, 1958. The six-day lapse created frustration on the part of the IAC, whose members felt that speedier action was necessary. The arrest of Boger and the ensuing investigation spawned a series of further inquiries. In the next six months the IAC received a flood of letters from survivors they had contacted regarding the Boger investigation; former Auschwitz prisoners accused many others of committing crimes at the camp and relayed remarkable details. The IAC then passed this material along to the public prosecutor's office.[8]

Many explanations are of course possible for the passage of thirteen years before an investigation of this scope could take place within West Germany. Apart from the problems explored in the previous chapter, one purely legal reason stemmed from the standard federal criminal procedure (StPO). Under the StPO, public prosecutors and courts were responsible only for crimes committed within their respective jurisdictions. This restriction created an obvious problem: the crimes of Auschwitz had been committed in Poland. To make matters more complicated, although the Polish courts had responsibility for the crimes, those who had committed them were no longer in Poland, nor were they for the most part Polish citizens. This left the hands of both countries' legal systems tied, each system being left with half the necessary jurisdiction.

In Poland immediately after the war major trials had taken place, as a result of which some top officials at Auschwitz were tried and executed. In Kraków, in December 1947, Arthur Liebehenschel, the former commandant of Auschwitz, Maximilian Grabner, former head of the Political Department, Hans Aumeier, also of the Political Department, and Arthur Breitwieser, the "disinfector," were all sentenced to death, in a trial of some forty Auschwitz perpetrators.[9] The commutation of Breitwieser's death sentence to life in prison and then to time served left him free to return to Germany. He was rearrested in Germany in December 1960 and was one of the three acquitted of the twenty defendants in the Auschwitz Trial. Oswald Kaduk, who was considered one of the worst sadists at Auschwitz and convicted of murder at the Auschwitz Trial, had also been previously sentenced to death by the Soviet courts, in 1947.[10] It is unlikely that the West German authorities knew that such trials had even occurred, let alone who the defendants were and what judgments had been made. Such information trickled down to them slowly through various channels—either from survivors who had testified at these trials and came forward again during the Auschwitz investigation, or through difficult and frustrating communications with the hostile Communist countries. It was then the job of the German prosecutors to locate those defendants who had been exonerated, if they were in Germany at all, and arrest them again under German criminal procedure.

The constraints of jurisdiction were relaxed in the early 1950s when the German supreme court amended the StPO to make it possible for German prosecutors to arrest suspects as long as they had been born in that jurisdiction or had at some time lived there.[11] This change made possible the arrest of many of the suspects—in all the states of West Germany—who would later be tried at Frankfurt. By the time of the move to Frankfurt, four suspects had been arrested; after that point, all those arrested were transported from various prisons to Frankfurt and the arrest warrants became the responsibility of the state of Hesse.[12]

A few timely coincidences were crucial to the case and to the dedication with which it would be pursued in Frankfurt. Increasing public curiosity about the fate of leading Nazi criminals led the federal Ministry of Justice to open the ZS in 1958; between December 1958 and February 1959, the ZS and the IAC in Vienna were in constant contact, sharing information that revealed the names of many other Nazis suspected of participating in genocide at Auschwitz. Owing to the recollections and reconstruction of events by (mainly Polish) survivors, Langbein was able to inform the ZS of the charges against various doctors, dentists, block captains, even the main camp pharmacist, and often their whereabouts in or outside Germany. The survivors who got in touch with Langbein on hearing about the investigation became pivotal figures in the trial itself and provided the courts and the public with the most important facts we have about the Auschwitz concentration camp. Former prisoners surfaced all over in Europe and North America and offered information (both solicited and unsolicited) throughout the five years leading up to the trial. By April 1959 survivors had brought enough evidence to the IAC, and through that committee to the ZS, that the public prosecutor's office in Stuttgart was able to issue arrest warrants for three more suspects (Hans Stark, Klaus Dylewski, and Pery Broad) and file further charges against Boger.[13]

The pretrial investigation moved to Frankfurt in June of 1959. This change of venue was the product of a fortuitous discovery by Fritz Bauer, the attorney general of Hesse. A man named Thomas Gnielka made contact with Bauer in January, claiming to have some documents that might be of historical or legal interest to the prosecution; his decision to pass these documents on to Bauer was merely a logistical one: Gnielka lived in Wiesbaden, the capital of the state of Hesse. He had little knowledge of the activities of Bauer or of his previous involvement in punishing Nazi crimes, particularly in the Eichmann case. On January 15 Gnielka wrote Bauer a letter:

> Here, as promised by telephone, are the reports of the commanders of concentration camp Auschwitz to the SS and Police Court in Breslau. These documents were given to me personally in confidence by Mr. Emil Wulkan . . . on January 14, 1959 . . . Mr. Wulkan, former camp prisoner, today a member of the Frankfurt Jewish Council, was temporarily in Breslau with other prisoners directly after his liberation and took these papers, as a "souvenir," from the burning police court of Breslau. Until today, it didn't occur to him that this material could be of legal significance.[14]

The documents enclosed with the letter to Bauer were records made by the administration at Auschwitz in August 1942 of the "Shooting of Fleeing Prisoners." Accompanying the list of names of dead prisoners and their tattoo numbers was a list of SS officers suspected of shooting these prisoners; the documents appear to have been investigative reports to the SS and police court in Breslau of "corrupt" SS officers. Why these officers were charged with a crime is not clear from these documents; however, a few explanations are possible. In the "official" death certificates of the hundreds of thousands who were either worked or tortured to death at Auschwitz (this does not include those who were gassed immediately upon arrival, as they were not tattooed), "shot while fleeing" was often given as the standard cause of death for a prisoner, along with various maladies such as heart failure and dysentery. Such a report then, to the police court at Breslau, may have been written using false causes of death to document the activities of SS officers who were considered corrupt by transgressing against the hierarchical chain of command for the camp and murdering prisoners without an official order. The Nazi courts investigated SS men and women who acted on their own initiative frequently, as we shall see later. The false causes of death were used as a flimsy cover allowing the SS to maintain the perception that its crimes would not be discovered or that their magnitude would at least be lessened, should death certificates for the millions missing be requested. In addition, it was standard bureaucratic procedure to document the death of inmates as a way of keeping track of the work force and determining how many new workers were needed. Therefore, the murder of "fleeing" prisoners was also recorded in an effort to keep track of available labor. In general, however, countless baffling examples of the use of protocol and painstaking bureaucratic policy are evident in the everyday world of Auschwitz. A mania for record keeping characterized the whole of Nazi policy.

Whatever the explanation for such documents, in January of 1959 they landed on the desk of Fritz Bauer. He then passed them along to the ZS in Ludwigsburg, as was customary with suspected Nazi crimes. The ZS had already received reports about approximately thirty suspected perpetrators from Auschwitz and saw the potential for a large-scale legal proceeding. Because the ZS had been established by the federal government, the matter was turned over to the federal Supreme Court (Bundesgerichtshof) for a ruling. With the cooperation of the ZS, the public prosecutor's office in Stuttgart, where the investigation had begun, and Fritz Bauer, the Supreme Court ruled to move the "Auschwitz investigation" to Frankfurt am Main, where evidence would be gathered for a trial exclusively pertaining to crimes committed at Auschwitz.[15] The ZS from that point on forwarded all the information it received or collected regarding Nazi crimes at Auschwitz to the public prosecutor's office in Frankfurt. This included investigations of at least thirty criminals from Auschwitz—former prisoners as well as SS officers—conducted by the IAC and by various public prosecutor's offices throughout West Germany, including Munich, Stuttgart, Frankfurt, Darmstadt, Hamburg, Berlin, Hannover, and Braunschweig. In mid-July the public prosecutor's office in Frankfurt submitted a request for transfer to Frankfurt of three suspects already in detention (Boger, Stark, and Broad) and further called for the arrest of Oswald Kaduk, Franz Hofmann, and Heinrich Bischoff. One week later, on July 21, all three men were arrested.[16]

Fritz Bauer and the Prosecutor's Office in Hesse

Fritz Bauer was the decisive force shaping the trial. Bauer, a German Jew who had lived in exile during the Nazi period and who led the public prosecutor's office in Frankfurt after the war, made it his lifelong mission to bring the perpetrators of the Nazi genocide to justice. Bauer's intentions were not strictly judicial but more broadly historical as well. Quite explicitly, beyond his concern with individual cases, Bauer wanted to bring to task a whole era, an entire ideology. He saw this trial as something quite removed from a normal criminal trial. Indeed, it would have been most difficult for anyone following the pretrial investigations and the proceedings themselves to view this as a typical trial, for sitting on the defendants' bench were twenty men involved in mass murder and genocide, in state-sanctioned and state-ordered systematic killing at a death camp.

Bauer saw the trial as an opportunity for Germany to confront its past and to examine its relation to the Nazi period. During the trial Bauer declared,

> One of the most important tasks of this trial is not only to present the horrendous facts [of the Final Solution], but also actually to teach ourselves something, that we here in Germany have completely forgotten in the course of the last one hundred years . . . You must worship God more than human beings . . . That's why it is the be all and the end all of this trial to say: "You should have said no." I think that in Germany we must all recognize that there are limits that everyone sees and feels. Watch out for your fellow men, such things cannot happen again, you must not go along with it! . . . And if something is to be learned from this trial, then it is the meaning of the fight for equality, which must be taken seriously, the meaning of tolerance, care, and recognition, and the understanding that hate . . . leads to such things as Auschwitz.[17]

Bauer's sense of right and wrong and his approach to the meaning of this trial, made his task clear. It came down to his view of the basic tenets of the Bible, those upon which the German state was supposedly based. For Bauer, most important was the commandment "Thou shalt not kill," and any "order" to the contrary was worthless. Bauer called upon every individual to be mindful of human equality and to understand that any orders or laws negating this were illegal. Anyone who had voluntarily subscribed to Nazi ideology and helped realize its goals was thus also suspect. Immediately before the trial opened, when asked how he would judge the defendants on the stand, as murderers or simply accomplices, Bauer replied:

> I personally believe that the question can be answered only if we ask it this way: Were those who were present at Auschwitz there because they were convinced Nazis or not? By and large, especially for those at Auschwitz, one has to answer this in the affirmative . . . This was no strange or foreign crime,

the perpetrators were largely people who were at that time convinced they were doing the right thing, namely pursuing their National Socialist worldview to victory. In my eyes, those men are simply perpetrators, together with Hitler, committed with Hitler to the "Final Solution of the Jewish Question," that they believed to be right . . . For me, they are all accomplices.[18]

Bauer's sense of universal morality called for Germans to police themselves. He was especially critical of the *alte Kämpfer* (old fighters), those convinced Nazis who believed completely in the validity of the Final Solution. In discussing the "superior-order defense" used by lower-ranking Nazis to excuse their participation in mass murder, Bauer stated unequivocally, "There is no question, at least not for myself or for the prosecutors in the Federal Republic, that there was a long list of people who didn't act only on orders, but who acted as they did out of real conviction that what they were doing was right."[19]

Bauer was well aware that the public prosecutors were bound by the StPO and obligated to begin an investigation when punishable behavior was suspected; however, the Auschwitz Trial was also intended to serve as a sort of "political enlightenment." By this, Bauer meant that such a trial was important not only as an attempt to uncover facts but also as a way to "ask the question why, because without the answer to why, without questioning the roots of evil and the roots of disease, there can be no healing."[20] Bauer even viewed the rather late date of the Auschwitz Trial as a positive development, for he believed that the trial could serve as a much better lesson in the 1960s than it could have directly after the capitulation, when Germans had focused more on securing material necessities than on confronting the atrocities of Nazism. According to Bauer, then, trials of Nazi criminals in West Germany, which began again in the late 1950s and gained momentum throughout the 1960s, had to teach lessons, for before this period, understandably, Germans were little inclined to "beat their own breasts in search of the historical, political, sociological, and psychological roots of the worst criminality of the years of the illegal state." Bauer urged Germans to understand their inner responsibility and not to take the easy way out, to practice and teach tolerance, and to see the trials of former Nazi perpetrators not as an assault on newly democratic German society or as befouling the nest, but as an attempt once and for all to "clean the nest."[21]

Such were the motivations and intentions that drove Fritz Bauer and the prosecution in Frankfurt; such were the guidelines he set for the attorneys he put on the case.[22] Bauer himself did not participate in the pretrial investigation or the court proceedings. He had as his team Dr. Hans Großmann, chief prosecutor, and Joachim Kügler, Georg Friedrich Vogel, and Gerhard Wiese. They were all young, dedicated lawyers whose professional careers had begun after 1945 and had not been tainted by Nazism. Could the trial really serve as a lesson and a thorough housecleaning? Was such a noble goal attainable, in light of the legal system that bound the prosecutors? Was everybody involved in this enormous trial dedicated to the same goal, or did some feel it was their duty to stick to the guidelines of the StPO and the StGB? The answers to such questions become clearer through an investigation of the evolution of the trial and the problems faced by the prosecutors in achieving this goal.

Developing the Case in Frankfurt

How did the prosecution determine which witnesses were most reliable, had the most accurate memories, and had justice and truth as their motivations rather than revenge? How did the prosecution decide which investigations to pursue, which to postpone, which to drop? More than four hundred survivors and former SS officers were interrogated, and with each new statement came a new suspect to be located, summoned, interrogated, and investigated. At one point the investigation involved an unmanageable eight hundred suspects. The prosecution had to create the strongest case possible, which meant dropping witnesses who could not give accurate, specific information. The charges and testimony by Adolf Rögner, for example, did not appear in the indictment, largely because overwhelming evidence against Boger had since been gathered and many witnesses with far more detailed and accurate accounts of Boger's activities—witnesses without criminal records or therefore credibility problems —had come forward. However, Rögner did testify briefly at the trial.

Beginning in October 1959, the prosecution in Frankfurt cast its net all over the world, looking for survivors to testify. A form letter was sent to a wide variety of newspapers internationally, requesting that witnesses come forward.[23] This call, along with the efforts of the IAC and various other survivor and human rights organizations, had an enormous effect; survivors living in Canada, France, Israel, Argentina, and a host of other countries wrote to Frankfurt offering themselves as witnesses. The choices the prosecutors made in Frankfurt regarding which investigations to pursue and whom to arrest were largely dependent on the prosecution's ability to determine whether the accused was still alive, whether that person had already been tried, and whether he or she could be located. A letter from the German-based organization the Alliance of the Persecuted of the Nazi Regime (Vereinigung der Verfolgten des Naziregimes) aided the prosecution immensely from October 26, 1959, on, in referring to seventeen former Auschwitz guards who "move freely about the Federal Republic of Germany."[24] This letter led to the immediate issuing of arrest warrants for a further four suspects, including Victor Capesius, the camp pharmacist.[25] the prosecution patched together such pieces of information, along with the testimony of survivors, and established a general pattern in which the most heavily incriminated suspects kept reappearing. Rarely did suspects help in any way to incriminate fellow camp guards, and therefore the prosecution gained most information through a process of elimination.

To understand the extraordinary detail the prosecution needed to arrest a suspect and make a formal investigation, it is helpful to look more closely at the testimonies within the pretrial files. It is difficult to convey the grisliness and brutality of the accounts that the survivors of the camp gave; it is even more astounding to read such accounts and recognize the precision of the witnesses' recollections, considering not only the amount of time that had passed but also the horrifying nature of what they had experienced. Most witnesses were interrogated twice in the pretrial stage—once by the prosecution and once by the court. Such testimonies ranged from two to twenty pages. Generally, the interrogators permitted each witness to speak freely but without frequent breaks. Sometimes the survivor or an interpreter wrote up the testimonies. Often the testimonies were translated into German. Such details merit scrutiny because of the importance they later came to have at the trial; for example, in the trial setting, the judge or attorneys often interrupted the witness and asked for more specific information on each detail or terrifying experience of twenty years before. This led to discrepancies between pretrial and trial interrogations and generated confusion over the actions of each defendant. In addition, problems arose as a result of the translation of certain testimonies, in which witnesses often insisted in court that their pretrial testimony had been misinterpreted by the transcriber. Such difficulties would generally not surface until the trial itself, for the prosecutors and the court took pretrial testimony very much at face value.

From these pretrial files, two survivors groups emerge. First, there were the prisoners employed as caregivers and doctors in the prisoners' hospital (the Häftlingskrankenbau, or HKB) which occupied Blocks 19 through 21, and its subsidiaries: the experimentation block (Untersuchungsblock, Block 10), and the emergency block (Ambulanz, Block 28). Second, there were the secretaries in the Political Department, an extraordinary group, in that they were predominantly Jewish women who had been allowed to survive. The great majority of witnesses at the trial were not Jewish, for the simple reason that Jews were not generally given important posts but were sent immediately to the gas chambers. The testimonies of these two groups of witnesses formed only a small part of the crucial testimony given about all the defendants, but they provide invaluable accounts of the everyday workings of the Auschwitz camp, as the secretaries had a good knowledge of various different sections and administrative departments and retained their positions for fairly lengthy periods. These witness groups can serve as a focus for the pretrial testimonies in general and their pivotal role in illuminating the crimes committed at Auschwitz.

The Men of the HKB and Its Subsidiaries

Dr. Tadeusz Paczuła, a Polish surgeon, was one of the first survivors to approach the IAC. He had come to Auschwitz as a political prisoner in one of the first transports to the camp, in December 1940, and became prisoner #7725. He remained there until September 1944 and was employed first in the documentation office (Schreibstube) of the HKB and then as the main report writer (Rapportschreiber) in the HKB of Auschwitz I. Paczuła's testimony derived entirely from pretrial interrogations and his own recollection of events twenty years later, in contrast to that of some other witnesses, who wrote contemporaneous accounts of their experiences. In the first months of 1959 Paczuła wrote to Frankfurt and declared himself "prepared to give exact details of the crimes of the SS men before the German courts."[26] Rather than being interrogated in Poland with German prosecutors present, Paczuła went in October of 1959 to Frankfurt, where public prosecutor Vogel questioned him. Paczuła's description ran to more than twenty-five pages, starting with his arrival at Auschwitz before the selection process had been implemented. After two years in a work unit, Paczuła contracted a lung disease and was sent to the HKB in Block 21. Prisoners dreaded such a transfer and avoided it until the last possible moment, for illness was usually a death sentence. More often than not the HKB was a place of experimentation and murder and certainly not a place for healing. Paczuła, however, was determined to use his medical skills to his advantage, and soon after arriving he began to conduct the "fever curves"—graphs documenting the levels of fever in the patients. The Nazi doctors and orderlies in the HKB noticed his work, and he was allowed to remain and work in the office of the HKB.

Paczuła had a unique opportunity not only to observe the atrocities that went on in the HKB and experimentation blocks, but also to scrutinize the actions of the Political Department. It was his duty to update the death books *(Totenbücher)* of the HKB constantly. During the capture and execution of the Russian prisoners of war in 1941–1942, he documented the name, number, date of death, hour of death, and cause of death of those who perished. As always, the cause of death was falsified and listed as an ailment—hence the deaths of approximately fifteen thousand Russians, actually by shooting, were recorded as "heart attacks" and "strokes." Paczuła directed the prosecution at this time to the existence of these death rolls at the Auschwitz museum, where they were stored after having been smuggled out by fellow report taker and witness Jan Pilecki. The courts later obtained the death rolls and used them as important evidence in the trial. The logic behind the meticulous documentation of the illegal slaughter of Russian prisoners is again difficult to grasp; however, as Paczuła states, it was absolutely mandatory: "It was out of the question for even one dead prisoner to be left out of the book. One thing always had to be correct in the camp: the prisoner number. It is totally impossible that I received false data about the number of dead prisoners. It may have happened once or twice that an incorrect prisoner number was documented; but this was already considered a 'crime' in Auschwitz." Paczuła made it his mission to document the true cause of death for all the prisoners he entered into the death books, and did so with various secret symbols representing either gassing, phenol injections, shooting or hanging. Unfortunately, not all of the death books could be recovered and these entries were therefore not available to the courts.[27]

Paczuła's role in the office of Block 21 gave him extraordinary insight into the gruesome crimes committed at the Black Wall between Blocks 10 and 11, as he could see directly into this courtyard from the second floor window of Block 21. His testimony on this matter is particularly convincing because of his detailed descriptions of the room itself from which he made his observations. He described it as the treatment room in which a small surgery unit was installed, with a three-story bunk bed from which he could look out the window. His descriptions of the type of window, the forty-five-meter distance to the Black Wall, and his ability to see such events were all corroborated by an on-site examination of Auschwitz that took place during the trial. It was from this location that on March 19, 1942, Paczuła observed the execution of three hundred women, whom he understood to be French Jews. They were shot at the wall because the facilities for mass gassings were not yet completed. His testimony included an exact depiction of how this execution took place. He stated:

> All the women were brought into the bunker, where they had to undress completely. They had arrived at the camp around noon, in buses. The shootings began at approximately 2:00 PM and were completed in around three hours. The women were led in groups of two by the *Bunker-kalfaktor* [caretaker] to the Black Wall, where SS-Oberscharführer Gehring shot them with a small-caliber gun. For the period that I was watching, Gehring was all alone. I myself couldn't watch the execution to the end, because an SS orderly came into the room and I had to disappear . . . While I was at the window, about twenty to twenty-five women were shot to death. I can't say whether Gehring shot all the women by himself; generally the SS-men would relieve each other or shoot two at a time. The corpses of the women were thrown into the left corner of the court-yard by the corpse bearers. The women all went very quietly and without any delays to the Black Wall, although the next two in line always had to see the bodies of the two executed before them. All shootings were conducted by *Genickschuß* [a shot to the neck]. After the evening roll call the corpses of the women were taken by truck to the crematorium and burned.[28]

Such details, although they did not incriminate any of the defendants, nevertheless demonstrated the extent of Paczuła's credibility and found corroboration in the testimony of others and in the on-site inspections. In the early phases of the investigation of Auschwitz, such detailed descriptions served to flesh out an accurate, detailed, and credible picture of camp atrocities.

In the spring of 1944 Paczuła, having become the report writer for the entire HKB, began entering the daily patient numbers for Blocks 9, 19, 20, 21, and 28. Here he was in constant contact with the head of the corpse-carrying unit *(Leichenkapo)* and his corpse bearers. They had to give him the list not only of prisoners shot at the Black Wall but of all who were taken into the "corpse cellar." Paczuła was often in the cellar in Block 28 and therefore also saw the bodies of the executed. It was there that he witnessed the results of the most heinous crimes committed by defendant Josef Klehr, the orderly in charge of injecting prisoners with phenol. In a second interrogation conducted by the public prosecutors in Frankfurt approximately one year later, Paczuła gave a detailed characterization of Klehr—his personality type, his favorite sadistic activities, and more specific accounts of crimes he committed. Paczuła described Klehr as a "typical primitive despot-type, who had to show everyone what kind of a 'personality' he was." Klehr especially liked to assert himself when his superior, the camp doctor, was absent, and assume the role of the main medical authority in the HKB. On such occasions Klehr would order a few prisoners to attend to his "needs"—one would wash his motorcycle, another would take off his boots and wash his feet, and at the same time yet another would polish his fingernails. While smoking his pipe and being tended to, he would order eight or so other prisoners to dance for him; as Paczuła said, "he behaved just like a pasha."[29]

Klehr's delusions of grandeur also extended to performing the lethal injections *(Abspritzen)* himself. He would walk through the HKB proclaiming, "Today I am the camp doctor, and the illness notices *(Krankenmeldungen)* will be presented to me."[30] He then performed selections of newly admitted patients and injected them himself to cause their death, although this was not his duty. It is important to note here the emphasis Paczuła placed on Klehr's insistence on doing jobs not within his jurisdiction or authority. This was crucial to the prosecution's case, in determining and proving perpetrator motivation. It was Paczuła's depiction of Klehr as a sadist and a lusty killer who acted with individual initiative and in fact *against* the regulations of the camp that led to Klehr's conviction for perpetrating murder rather than simply aiding and abetting. In particular, one incident that Paczuła described and other witnesses corroborated demonstrated Klehr's willingness to act on his own and kill without direct orders, thereby making him a suitable candidate for the murder conviction under West German law. Paczuła stated:

> I would like to describe a selection that remains fixed in my memory, owing to its particular emotional cruelty. It was Christmas Eve—December 24, 1942—when Klehr appeared around noon in the HKB, selected approximately two hundred prisoners, and injected them immediately. As the camp doctor had already made his rounds in the morning at around eight or nine, we felt certain, in fact we knew, that he had thereafter left for the Christmas holiday. Everything was already in the Christmas spirit, and everyone had somehow prepared himself for this day and wanted to have a little Christmas celebration. In this atmosphere Klehr burst in and murdered the prisoners. I don't think I need to describe what kind of poverty of feeling and coldness is needed to carry out this activity on such a day.[31]

Various other witnesses would repeat this testimony throughout the pretrial period and during the trial itself, and the story provided the courtroom with one of its most chilling and upsetting moments. Such details, although seemingly almost trivial in the context of large-scale murder and cruelty, stirred the hearts of the judge, jury, and audience most deeply because of the horrible dissonance that all could recognize—between the symbolism of the Christmas holiday and inhuman cruelty. Klehr's insistence on committing an act of particular brutality on that day convincingly demonstrated his sadistic impulse.

The importance of Paczuła's testimony is evident in entirely different example, his assessment of the testimony of a fellow prisoner and survivor, Walter Scheerer. In this interesting incident, the court found itself addressing perjury of a peculiar kind. Scheerer was by

Defendant Josef Klehr, December 20, 1963. Klehr was said to have injected as many as twenty thousand prisoners with phenol, a poison that killed them instantly. He was convicted of more than four hundred charges of murder. SOURCE: DPA/LANDOV.

no means a denier or a revisionist insisting on the innocence of any of the defendants. Rather, he distorted the facts and reported false incidents that would seemingly make little difference to the case itself. The prosecution noted inconsistencies in the discrepancy between Scheerer's description of the camp setup and that of other survivors from the HKB.

Scheerer, who testified in September 1959, reported that after being sent to Auschwitz in April 1943 as a German Communist political prisoner, in May 1943 he became an orderly in the HKB at the request of the main camp doctor at the time, Dr. Entress. Most of Scheerer's testimony recounted the activities of Klehr and his crimes with phenol injection. However, when the testimony was shown to Paczuła (and other survivors of the HKB) it became clear that Scheerer was falsifying his account. As Paczuła observed, "First of

all, the block numbers given by the witness are completely wrong
. . . I was also working in the HKB at the time witness Scheerer was
supposedly active there. In my opinion he was at most a janitor there
. . . It is out of the question that he was the head orderly and boss of
all other caregivers."[32] A fellow orderly, Dr. Stanisław Kłodziński,
corroborated this information and indicated that Scheerer was attempting to pass himself off as a man of greater importance in the
prisoner hierarchy than he had actually been.

Paczuła's refutation of Scheerer's testimony further pointed up
other bizarre falsehoods and holes in his account. Scheerer reported
that Klehr had injected his victims with Evipan, a tranquilizer to in-
duce sleep, before killing them with phenol. This information was
incorrect. In addition, Scheerer reported that victims were injected
on an operating table; according to Paczuła and Kłodziński and others, this was rarely the case. Victims were made to sit on a chair and
hold their left arm above their head. Scheerer's accounts of witness-
ing executions at the Black Wall through a window in the wash barrack were also untenable, according to Paczuła, for "unless he stood
on the chimney, the wash barrack was only one floor and there was a
wall between Blocks 10 and 11 of almost four meters in height."[33]

Finally, Paczuła claimed that Scheerer's account of a mass shooting of forty prisoners by the Sonderkommando in the corpse cellar
of Block 28 was impossible, for people were not shot in the cellar;
they were simply brought there afterward.[34] The prosecution needed
to assess such details in meticulous detail in order to present a valid,
factual case concerning the actions of each defendant. Scheerer
exemplified a peculiar type of witness, a survivor who would falsify
stories and tell tales that resembled the truth and seemed to incriminate the defendants. In actuality, his testimony worked against the
prosecution. Whether Scheerer intended to help or hinder the case
is difficult to determine, but this example shows the problems in establishing accurate and reliable testimony and building a large case.
It also indicates one reason the trial took so long to begin.

Another interesting example is the case of defendant Herbert
Scherpe, a medical orderly (Sanitätsdienstgrad, or SDG) in the

HKB who often worked as Klehr's representative. Almost all witnesses who reported on the activities of the defendants in the HKB testified that Scherpe had helped inject prisoners; some knew through hearsay that he had taken part, and some through more concrete experience. One incident, however, is especially important, in that it both implicated and exonerated Scherpe. As Paczuła described it, in 1943 Scherpe took over the injecting of prisoners when Klehr was absent. Two transports came in from the Polish town of Zamość carrying young boys, approximately ages thirteen to fifteen. Scherpe killed the first group of about sixty on the first day; however, on the second day, Paczuła said, "Scherpe almost had a breakdown and could not go on. The 'injections' were then carried out by another SDG whose name I no longer remember."[35]

Another witness at the trial, Stanisław Głowa, prisoner #20017, described in chilling detail the day on which the first group of boys were murdered. Głowa was in Auschwitz from August 1941 to August 1944. Having became ill with diarrhea in October 1941, he was brought to Block 20, where he stayed on afterward as a caregiver of sorts. Głowa stated that "on the first day there was a panic among the children, because they noticed that those boys who were taken behind the curtain in the hall never came back. They therefore had to be brought with force into the treatment room." Głowa could recount this because he was ordered by the guards to help bring the boys into the room to be murdered. Głowa remarked after this testimony: "I have to make it known right now, that as a prisoner one could not refuse to do such a job, because one would then also have been injected."[36]

The witness Kłodziński also recalled this event. Kłodziński, a Polish prisoner brought to Auschwitz in August 1941, worked first as an orderly and then as a doctor in the HKB until its evacuation. He was also a member of the international underground resistance at the camp, acting as the liaison between the movement in the camp and the illegal underground in Kraków. Because of his political motivation he was especially concerned with observing and documenting the crimes committed in the HKB. As a doctor, he became aware of

Klehr's phenol injections, and it was clear to him that healthy prisoners were also being murdered in this fashion, not just the inmates of the HKB. As an example he cited the incident with the Polish boys from Zamość, and stated, "I want to note that SS-SDG Scherpe refused to undertake these injections."[37] Finally, Hermann Langbein, who provided some of the most important corroboration in this case through the sheer weight and credibility of his personality, stated that he remembered with certainty that Scherpe had been excused from his duties in the murdering of the boys, which was then taken over by the defendant Hantl.[38]

This incident and the witness reports describing it demonstrate a crucial issue for the prosecution's case. On one hand, the testimony of several witnesses showed that in all likelihood Scherpe had indeed participated in the injections. On the other hand, the testimony also showed a certain reticence on the defendant's part which the defense could use to show that Scherpe did not have murderous intent or sadistic motivation and most certainly did not demonstrate individual initiative in this action as Klehr had in the incident at Christmas 1942 discussed earlier. Therefore, the prosecution would have great difficulty finding sufficient grounds to charge Scherpe with murder. This kind of problem frequently confounded the prosecution, and it flew in the face of Fritz Bauer's initial hopes that those who killed at Auschwitz would be punished for murder, no matter whether they disliked their work or not. The simple goal of putting the Auschwitz complex on trial and prosecuting the people who had worked there became more and more problematic, as the West German criminal justice system increasingly seemed to be totally inadequate to this extraordinary case of state-sanctioned genocide.

The Superior-Orders Defense

Bauer's goal and the difficulties in achieving it led to another element in this particular count against Scherpe, one that would aid the prosecution in throwing out the *Befehlsnotstand* defense, based on the claim by the accused of having been obliged to follow orders.

Over and over, witnesses reported that certain guards had refused to carry out certain tasks, whether selections at the platform or executions at the Black Wall or, as in this case, injections in the HKB. The witnesses, both survivors and former SS officers, all stated that none of the people who refused were punished by either the camp authorities or the camp administrators in Berlin. Defendant Scherpe, for example, was allowed to be relieved of the duty of shooting the Polish boys and continue his work as an SDG.

The mounting evidence of the possibility of refusing to murder contradicted the testimony of nearly all the defendants, not only in this trial but in virtually all Nazi-criminal trials, that the defendants had had to follow orders because if they had refused, they would have been marched to the gas chambers. The argument of "doing my duty" and "only obeying orders" was a familiar one, with which all postwar courts had to contend when attempting to prove that the Nazi state was an illegal one and that therefore its orders were invalid and also illegal. This proof was eventually achieved by establishing that the StGB—and in particular the murder paragraph—had been in effect throughout the Nazi reign. However, in determining the validity of the defense citing a perceived threat of punishment for refusal to follow orders, the prosecution had to dig more deeply into Nazi files.

To accomplish this aim, the prosecution summoned various expert witnesses who were specialists dedicated to researching the Nazi period—historians familiar with the Nazi documents who could elucidate the system as a whole. The most famous of these experts were researchers at the Institute for the Study of Contemporary History in Munich: Martin Broszat, Helmut Krausnick, and Hans Buchheim. Their investigations into all aspects of Nazi criminality led to the most illuminating and important revelations about the SS system, and their research and testimony in support of the indictment and at the trial resulted in publication of *The Anatomy of the SS State*. Many other experts were called too, however, and one of the first crucial reports was provided by Dr. Hans-Günther Seraphim, senior lecturer at the University of Göttingen.

On July 1, 1958, Seraphim submitted a report to the jury court at

Ulm for the famous trial of ten members of the *Einsatzkommando Stapo* and SD Tilsit, a subgroup of *Einsatzgruppe* A accused of murder and aiding and abetting murder in the summer and fall of 1941 in Lithuania. (This was also a West German trial.) The report dealt with the following question posed by the court: "whether SS leaders or SS-men who *refused* participation in the 'cleansing actions' or other 'annihilation measures' that were ordered by the rulers of the Third Reich could expect harm or damage to life and limb." Seraphim established early in his report that it was preposterous to assume that the members of the SS lived in fear; indeed, they were perpetrators and creators of the system. Seraphim stated sardonically, "These men didn't live in fear; they themselves spread it across the land through their activities." In fact, Seraphim asserted, the Criminal Code of the German Army *(Wehrmachtstrafgesetzbuch)* remained binding for the SS despite special jurisdiction, and so did the key paragraph 47, which forbade the carrying out of criminal orders.[39]

Seraphim turned to the documents of the subsequent Nuremberg trials—most particularly the trial of Otto Ohlendorf and the *Einsatzgruppen*, in which he acted as an historical expert for the defense—to prove his argument that no SS officer was ever punished for disobeying orders. Time and again the defendants referred to the refusal of many of their subordinates to commit the murders, and Ohlendorf claimed, he was accustomed to sending those who would not follow orders back home. Other superiors too, to show themselves decent and sympathetic men, stated that they had never punished any of their men for not performing executions. Such facts are by now well known among Holocaust scholars and have been demonstrated most succinctly by Christopher Browning in his study of Police Battalion 101.[40] Inthe West Germany of the late 1950s, however, this evidence came as quite a surprise to a nation convinced of the "totalitarian terror" of the Third Reich.

Seraphim conceded that SS men were threatened with the possibility of being transferred to the front if they refused to follow orders; this argument appeared in the Nuremberg Trial against concentration camp supervisor Oswald Pohl, and it was used often thereafter. That the SS-men who worked voluntarily in a death camp like Auschwitz used this as a defense was, Seraphim pointed out, an added insult to the victims and demonstrated only the perpetrators' cowardice and weakness of character. He stated that "a transfer to the front or anywhere else cannot be seen as danger to life and limb . . . there just cannot be any doubt of that."[41]

Seraphim concluded his study decisively: "In more than ten years of research focused particularly on the history of the SS and related police organizations, this expert witness has not found one case that resulted in 'damage to life and limb' when an SS officer refused to carry out an 'annihilation order.' On the contrary, the results of my research show that when refusal to obey an order became known, neither was there an investigation by the SS police courts nor was any other serious form of punishment considered."[42]

Seraphim's research extended in this regard to a close analysis of the Nazi "worldview" as described in Himmler's speeches and orders to his SS-men, which supposedly proved that following criminal orders was a duty and demonstrated the necessary "loyalty" and "obedience." Seraphim remarked that it could be concluded that refusal to participate in the Final Solution, even in the words of Himmler, qualified not as a sign of disloyalty but rather only as "character weakness," and "spent nerves."[43] In every regard, then, Seraphim demonstrated that the superior-orders defense was untenable.

But what of the perceived threat of punishment, transfer to the front, or death in the gas chambers? Many defendants at the Auschwitz Trial claimed that they had become aware of the possibility of refusal only at the trial itself, that although there might have been no punishment for refusal, the threat was still very real. The case of the defendant Scherpe contradicts this contention. Such acts of refusal were rare, vocal, and therefore public knowledge. The camp functioned as a rumor mill in which any news traveled very quickly throughout the various channels and hierarchies of prisoners and guards. Other guards could and did deduce from his hesitation that they would not be punished if they declined to follow orders. Some did: some even chose the alternative of going to the front, rather than kill another innocent victim in Auschwitz. These resisters were, however, exceptions.

The Women of the Political Department

During the course of their pretrial investigations, prosecutors discovered an extraordinary group of survivors, thanks to the IAC, a group that came to shed the most light on the activities of the Political Department of the Auschwitz I camp and particularly on the crimes committed by Wilhelm Boger. These were the women who worked as secretaries (Schreiberinnen) in the Political Department, of whom at least eight made themselves available to the courts for interrogation. A few factors made this group unique. First, they had a high rate of survival, for prisoners with so much insider information about the camp. These women wrote the death books for the HKB, the crematoriums, and the Political Department, they witnessed the methods of "interrogation" used by Boger, which came to be called intensified interrogations (verschärfte Vernehmungen), they saw his infamous Boger swing and the unrecognizable state in which most prisoners appeared after being brutalized on it. The numbers of murders and acts illegal even by Nazi standards that these survivors witnessed, along with the secret information to which they were privy, made them perfect candidates for the kind of short work cycle allotted to the Sonderkommandos of the crematoriums and corpse cellars. However, these women seemed to be oddly favored, especially by Boger. They were usually allowed to live, even if they committed indiscretions or small acts of resistance, as they almost all did on a regular basis—providing food or water to prisoners who had been beaten, lying to superiors in order to improve the conditions many prisoners had to endure, smuggling out letters, and performing other acts of solidarity and kindness toward the inmates. Only those who were openly disobedient were killed.

Second, these women were all Jewish. It was highly irregular for

Jews to be given positions of relative security at Auschwitz, or jobs that enabled them to witness in detail the activities of the SS. Virtually all those who worked in the HKB as capos, or as secretaries in other sections, were either political prisoners of Polish or Ukrainian descent or German criminal prisoners. In general, the vast majority of Jews were marched straight to the gas chambers without being given numbers and tattoos. Only healthy men and women were selected to work, and they were given the most grinding and agonizing jobs, which usually led to a quick death. For a group of Jewish women to be selected for secretarial work and allowed to survive to the end was highly unusual. It is unclear why Boger and the others had a soft spot for them, but frequently these witnesses reported exactly that. Their higher level of educational attainment—their reading, writing, and typing skills, as well as knowledge of more than one language, including very often German—may have also contributed to their "lucky" situation.

In the search for evidence about Boger's crimes, Maryla Rosenthal, a survivor who had recently moved from Israel to Berlin, was one of the first women the central office in Ludwigsburg called upon. She was interviewed on March 2, 1959 by the State Criminal Investigation Department of the state of Baden-Württemberg (the Landeskriminalamt, or LKA, a subsidiary of the public prosecutor's office dedicated to investigating criminal matters brought before the prosecution for trial). Before being captured by the Nazis in April 1942, Rosenthal had lived in Kraków and worked as a secretary and a translator of Polish, German, English, and French. In July she was brought to Auschwitz and initially delegated to work in the sandpits at Birkenau. This work was extremely taxing and caused her to fall ill from both hunger and abuse. She was quite aware that being ill meant certain death in the HKB and was therefore terrified of the roll calls, which often lasted four hours and were virtually impossible for her, with her swollen legs and fever. She therefore took a huge risk and spoke up on one occasion, lying about her language abilities when an SS *Aufseherin* (female guard) asked for someone who could speak Czech to act as a translator in the Political Department. In this way she became the official translator for the Political Department and worked very closely with Boger.[44]

Rosenthal's main duty with Boger was to translate his "interrogations" of Polish prisoners. Because these interrogations were usually brutal and deadly, Rosenthal witnessed and later reported atrocities that were inexpressibly gruesome; however, she had very little negative to say about Boger, and especially his behavior towards her and the other Jewish women in the Political Department. She stated:

> Boger was very nice to me, and I cannot complain about his actions toward me. He even went as far as to regularly give me a portion of his own food, which would be left on his plate, under the pretense that I should wash his dishes. He also got clothing for me from the Birkenau camp. I remember these things quite well, as Boger often put himself in danger of being punished if he were found out. He was also very nice to the other Jewish female prisoners who worked in the Political Department, and we all liked him very much. This may sound unbelievable, but I still remember this very well, and I have to tell the truth. I also remember that Boger didn't have any real, outspoken hatred for Jews. In contrast, however, he would always tell me how he hated the "Polacks."[45]

Rosenthal's impression of Boger as a "nice man" lacking in antisemitic sentiment was all the more striking because he qualified as one of the worst sadists at the camp, one who certainly exercised gratuitous violence in his treatment of prisoners brought into his interrogation room, whether they were Polish, Jewish, or German. It will be obvious throughout this book that there was enough evidence of Boger's crimes to convict him of murder beyond any doubt; however, in his own defense, he could turn to the testimony of a Jewish prisoner to prove that he was not only free of ideologically driven hatred of Jews but capable of acts of great kindness. Rosenthal's Boger was kind, sensitive, and sometimes even regretful when he had to interrogate prisoners.[46] She never saw him mistreat anyone. She was willing to admit that Boger was one of the most feared men in the camp and was known as the Devil of Birkenau, and that prisoners often spoke of the massacres that would occur after he had entered the men's camp at Birkenau. She was always quick to follow such admissions with conditions: "I never knew anything exact about this. Boger never spoke to me about such things . . . For this reason I cannot, with the best intentions, say anything about where or when Boger shot people."[47] Rosenthal constantly alluded to her bad memory and her forgetfulness regarding any specific detail about Boger. In response to questions about the Boger swing, she admitted to knowing of the existence of such an instrument of torture but insisted that it was never referred to as the Boger swing but only as the swing, or more often, the talking machine. She recalled vaguely one instance in which Boger used it and the prisoner was so badly beaten she was sure he was near death. However, she again gave no precise details and spent more effort in her testimony recalling Boger's apology to her, his shame, and his explanation that he had been obliged to carry out such acts because the RSHA had ordered that he get information from political enemies in any way possible. When asked if she knew whether Boger had conducted executions without an order from the RSHA, but rather on his own initiative, she could not respond directly, but considered it unlikely that he would have done so.

In her recollection of a famous case of a Slovakian Jewish prisoner named Lilly Tofler, Rosenthal again defended Boger. Tofler was also a secretary, and she had attempted to smuggle a letter out to her lover in the Birkenau men's camp. Rosenthal thought that either Grabner, the head of the Political Department, or Kirschner, another guard there, had discovered the letter. Boger then interrogated Tofler and later shot her to death. Rosenthal stated: "Boger was very sorry about the imprisonment of this Slovak and told me that if the letter she wrote had not been put into the hands of Grabner or Kirschner, this situation could have been dealt with differently."[48]

The other women in the Political Department told this story very differently; in fact, it becomes clear upon closer assessment that they did not agree with Rosenthal in her positive opinion of Boger at all.

Her reasons for painting an almost benevolent picture of Boger were initially unclear, for nobody else who came into contact with him did so. However, throughout her testimony she gave indications that she had been profoundly traumatized by her experiences at Auschwitz and was in fact still quite fearful. At one point she stated: "It has just been pointed out to me I can actually only say very little about the occurrences in the Political Department. This is to be blamed, first of all, on my bad memory and the huge holes in my recollections, as I have already mentioned. On top of that, because of my disposition I am a very frightened person, and I was always very reserved."[49] It became painfully clear to the prosecution in Stuttgart from a letter three months later by her husband, also a survivor, that overwhelming fear was the motivating factor behind her reticence about Boger's actions. He wrote:

> I told you my thoughts about this before the interrogation on the telephone and, unfortunately, they proved to be correct. As a consequence of the interrogation (I must assume), my wife had another serious gallbladder attack. I would therefore like to stress again, as I already discussed with police detective Weida, that under no circumstances can a further interrogation about the Boger case, or an appearance by my wife in court occur . . . The detective assured me that my wife's name—maiden and married—will not appear in public. You will certainly understand, sir, that my wife cannot be put in danger of becoming the object of slander of the undoubtedly still existing SS organizations.[50]

Rosenthal's testimony about Boger, however vague and unhelpful, was clearly influenced by paranoia about the man almost fifteen years after the end of the Holocaust. In the end, her words worked in favor of the prosecutors because they showed the terrifying influence of Boger and the effect he had on those working around him.[51] Although the psychological effects of his behavior on his secretary would not qualify as concrete evidence of his murderous actions, the court noted her reactions as part of the case against the accused.

The other women called upon by the prosecution were in general much more prepared to address the crimes of the men in the Political Department. Three, Sylvia Normann, Jenny Schaner, and Raja Kagan, had in fact written their memoirs and had books on their experiences published; Dounia Wasserstrom had written pamphlets in French and had distributed them in France. The women's recollections often made such an extraordinary impression on the prosecution and the court that they became quasi-legendary: as Auschwitz stories that would come to signify the brutality of the camp, they would be retold by many survivors in an almost folkloric manner. Some witnesses from the Political Department were rather vague in their pretrial testimonies and then told much more detailed and horrifying stories in the courtroom, leaving the prosecution baffled. This intensification of the testimony then led to further investigation, in which only witnesses' accounts given in the courtroom itself would have to be verified down to the smallest detail.

A good example of this was the testimony of Dounia Wasserstrom, a survivor residing in Paris who was interviewed in March 1959 by the West German embassy in Paris using a strict list of questions prepared by the Ministry of Justice of Baden-Württemberg in March 1959. In Auschwitz, Wasserstrom had been an interpreter in the Political Department, working chiefly for SS-Rottenführer Draser, but also for the defendants Boger and Broad. Wasserstrom made a strong impression on the interrogators in Paris, who described her as very calm and composed, while at the same time warm and sensitive; they in fact decided not to ask her about the Boger swing because it was clear to them that she was able to control her emotions only with the greatest of effort.[52] In her testimony Wasserstrom reported having seen countless times the beating and torturing of prisoners by many of the defendants and stated that in most cases these prisoners died as a result of the abuse. Her statements were generally quite vague, and she mentioned only cursorily an incident in which she remembered Boger beating and then shooting a Russian prisoner. She always referred to the pamphlets she wrote on the subject of Auschwitz for further proof of her experiences at the camp. Correspondence between Hermann Langbein and the central office in Ludwigsburg after her interrogation showed that the prosecutor's office was quite unhappy with the results of her interview.[53]

Despite the vagueness of her pretrial testimony, Wasserstrom was called as a witness at the trial itself, owing to the nature of her position at Auschwitz. The decision to put her on the stand was a wise one, for her recollections proved to be some of the most important and sensational in the entire trial. In her cross-examination by some of the defense attorneys, Wasserstrom suddenly related a story of the utmost brutality:

> There is one incident I can never forget: it must have been around November 1944. A truck, carrying Jewish children, drove into the camp. The truck stopped by the barracks of the Political Department. A boy—he must have been about four or five years old—jumped out. He was playing with an apple that he was holding in his hand. Boger came with Draser to the door. Boger took the child by his feet and smashed his head against the wall. Draser ordered me to wash the wall after that. Later I was called in to do some translation for Boger. He was sitting in his office eating the boy's apple.[54]

The defense attorneys naturally pounced upon this new piece of testimony, questioning Wasserstrom about why she had not related something so important in her pretrial testimony or in any of the numerous pamphlets she had written after the war. Her response was simple: "That is a very private matter. Since that moment I have no longer wanted to have children."[55] The judge and the public prosecutors also repeatedly questioned her about her silence in the pretrial phase. In her responses, she always alluded to the fact that she found it embarrassing that she could no longer look at children without crying and no longer wanted to have a child. For this reason she had withheld the information.

This story was of course picked up by the press because of its sheer emotional and sensational impact; the rather tasteless and shocking headline in the *Frankfurter Rundschau* the next day read, "Witness:

Boger Splattered a Child on the Wall." The paper reported on the eerie silence and horror in the courtroom as Wasserstrom testified. It also reported one of Boger's extremely rare retorts in his own defense. Replying to the judge's inquiry whether he had anything to say, Boger calmly replied: "To the matter of the child I have nothing to say. That is a ridiculous invention, maybe something for the press."[56]

The story had to be verified by virtually every other woman in the Political Department who had contact with Wasserstrom after the war. In his interrogation of Raja Kagan, Judge Hofmeyer referred to the incident in an attempt to determine when exactly Wasserstrom had first mentioned it to the others, for if it was only a subject of conversation directly prior to the trial, it would have to be discounted. Kagan, however, backed up Wasserstrom's story, repeating it as her friend had told it to her. Hofmeyer then asked her:

H: When did she tell you the story?
K: Around 1947, in Paris.
H: This is a very serious matter; we need the truth— Wasserstrom never told the story before the trial, so we need to know when she told it to you.
K: Nineteen forty-seven, with certainty.[57]

Such discrepancies between pretrial and trial interrogations demonstrate the dilemma the court faced in its attempt to get the "whole picture" of the activities of the defendants at Auschwitz and Birkenau. They also show the extraordinarily delicate nature of witness testimony and the varying traumatic effects of the experiences of each person who survived to testify. The hope for clear-cut, straightforward testimonies about the specific actions of each individual defendant was already waning long before the trial began and proved frustrating within the confines of the Federal German Criminal Code.

The testimony of Raja Kagan in both the pretrial interrogations and the courtroom itself was indispensable for its meticulous, detailed accounts of life for women in the Political Department. Born in Russia and raised in Vilna, Kagan was arrested by the Gestapo in 1942 while she was studying in Paris. She was transported almost immediately to Auschwitz, and within two days of her arrival there was sent to work in the prisoner registry of the Political Department because of her language abilities. Kagan was determined to recollect to the best of her ability all that she could from her experiences at Auschwitz; in both her pretrial and her trial testimony she stated that it was her driving purpose in surviving to bear witness to the crimes of the SS guards at Auschwitz.[58] The courts used her 1947 memoir, "Hell's Office Women," extensively, and sections of it appeared, translated from the Hebrew into German, in the pretrial files. Her memoirs provide the first real glimpses into the stories of Lilly Tofler, mentioned earlier, and Mala Zimetbaum, who was publicly hanged for attempting to escape. These two women were among the very few female workers in the Political Department who were killed for acts of resistance.[59]

The prosecution was largely interested in the details she could provide about Boger, and her memoirs include many specific descriptions of his actions. As if she were telling a story, Kagan recounted how she first became aware of the Boger swing:

> One day Henny [a fellow secretary] came to us and reported to us about uninterrupted noises, screaming, and beatings in the investigation room. "I have already told you that they are abusing the prisoner," whispered the Frenchwoman, and in order to muffle her voice, she turned on the water faucet. "Boger is training Bauer, this handsome, dark-haired young lad. He issued the order to have something demonstrated in the room." Henny bent over my ear and whispered, filled with horror: "He ordered [him] to demonstrate a 'swing.'" I decided to verify the correctness of the story personally. In the morning I asked Leo to send me into the blockhouse with some sort of memo . . . I felt ashamed that I had come to see their [her fellow prisoners'] torture, and I hurried into the

blockhouse. Screams and cries of pain filled the air . . . I stood as though nailed down, my legs as heavy as lead, my heart as though it had been hollowed out. Suddenly, the door to my left opened, and I thought quickly enough to move back, just as a body came flying out of the room and then lay motionless on the ground. Before the door closed again, I cast a glance into the room. A low trestle stood there, with an iron rod on its back; there was a person tied to the rod by his hands and feet, and his head was hanging down.[60]

This account was translated and provided to the ZS by 1959, one of the first pieces of concrete information amassed for the investigation of Boger, and therefore invaluable information of the infamous swing. Such details were new to the investigating authorities. Kagan's descriptions laid the foundation for a history of torture and atrocity that is now the basis of common knowledge about the crimes committed at Auschwitz.

Kagan's testimony in her interrogations by both prosecutors be-

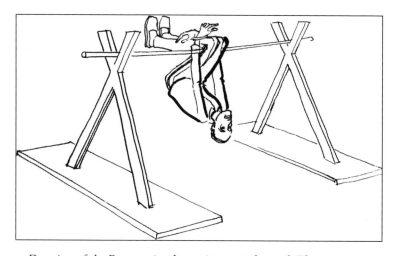

Drawing of the Boger swing by a witness at the trial. The swing was the invention of Wilhelm Boger, who used it to torture prisoners. SOURCE: SCHINDLER/DPA/LANDOV.

fore the trial and in court were vital to the prosecution of Boger. However, as was true of many other witnesses also, Kagan was not allowed access to the room in which Boger conducted his "interrogations" and therefore did not actually see whether anyone died on the swing. She stated, however, that "because of the catastrophic conditions in the camp, I consider it out of the question that any prisoner had even the slightest chance of coming out [of such an interrogation] with his life."[61] Kagan could list the names of those widely known by the secretaries of the Political Department to have been executed by Boger, in particular the unit in charge of peeling potatoes (*Kommando Kartoffelschälerei*), accused of attempting an uprising in the fall of 1943; among them was the adjutant of Marshal Pilsudski. Again, Kagan did not witness this execution herself, but stated: "I looked into their files after their death and could confirm that Boger personally conducted this investigation and carried out the 'interrogations.' "[62]

Such were the pieces of evidence provided by the women of the Political Department. While often specific, detailed, and exact, their evidence was also sometimes excluded because it failed to conform to the tests posed by the rules of evidence. It was clear to the prosecution and later to all who heard the stories recounted by these women in the courtroom that the actions and crimes that they had seen must undeniably have resulted in the death of tens of thousands at the hands of many of these defendants. Owing to the stipulations of the murder laws, however, such imprecise accounts often did not suffice for a conviction. Determining where to draw the line between invalid testimony and important evidence in the trial itself was very often up to the judge; for as presiding Judge Hofmeyer stated tersely in a rebuttal to a defense attorney, "this is why we must ask many people for hearsay: in order to create a picture of the circumstances as they were there . . . because the dead can no longer speak."[63]

In retrospect, does the period between 1945 and 1963 represent a shameful period of silence in West Germany? Is it, as Hannah

Arendt contends in *Eichmann in Jerusalem*, the result of an extreme reluctance on the part of the government, the Ministry of Justice, local courts, and the German public to try the "murderers in their midst"? We have seen in Chapter 1 that during and immediately after the Nuremberg trials, West Germany was not permitted to try Nazi criminals and, for many complex reasons, did not adopt and the four international criminal charges.

In addition, and perhaps most important, the limitations of the German criminal code and of the murder statute in particular made prosecution extremely difficult and required the prosecutors to make painstaking efforts to gather huge amounts of specific evidence against each possible suspect. This requirement in turn led to another delay in prosecution, whereby logistics and evidence gathering, along with a rapidly expanding list of perpetrators, extended the pretrial period immeasurably. Hannah Arendt contended that the dismal record of investigation of Nazi criminals was the direct result of indifference and even distaste for such prosecutions and that only the Eichmann capture had acted as an impetus to turn the wheels of justice in Germany—for all the wrong reasons. This interpretation reflects a certain level of ignorance of the largely confidential investigations that were already going on in Germany long before the Eichmann trial. A particularly good example is the case of Richard Baer, arrested coincidentally after the beginning of the Eichmann prosecution. Arendt saw the arrest as a clear indication that "Eichmann's capture would trigger the first serious effort made by Germany to bring to trial at least those who were directly implicated in murder." It may be correct that the Eichmann investigation uncovered new evidence about uninvestigated perpetrators who belonged to Eichmann's unit, of which Baer was a member. It may also be true that many local courts were indeed uninterested in moving quickly to prosecute and punish Nazi criminals, as many judges and lawyers worried about their own culpability as former members of the Nazi party; however, the argument that the entire West German justice system was tainted with a malaise regarding Nazi crimes is too simplistic. Certainly, the dedication and thoroughness of the public prosecutor's office of Hesse in the Auschwitz Trial is testimony to the contrary. In order to understand the outcome of the trial and the disappointing results of most German trials, it is necessary to recognize the limitations of the criminal code as the main barrier to effective justice. Arendt's contention that "the reluctance of the local courts to prosecute these crimes showed itself only in the fantastically lenient sentences meted out to the accused" is unsatisfactory and does injustice to the efforts of the Frankfurt prosecutors.[64] The main impediment to effective justice in Nazi trials was the law, and its contemporary interpretation in Nazi trials.

CHAPTER 3

The Indictment

THE FRANKFURT AUSCHWITZ TRIAL opened on December 17, 1963, at the Römer courthouse in the medieval center of the city. It began with the motion to open a preliminary judicial inquiry *(Antrag auf Eröffnung der gerichtlichen Voruntersuchung)* on July 12, 1961, and culminated in the motion to open the main proceeding: the indictment *(Antrag auf Eröffnung des Hauptverfahrens: Anklageschrift)* on April 24, 1963. The 1961 motion was the court's first involvement in the investigation process. That investigation process, which had begun four years before with the complaint of a prison inmate, was officially comprehensive enough for the prosecutors to turn it over to the district court (Landgericht) of Frankfurt am Main. Approximately one month later the court agreed to open the investigation, with its decision on the opening of the preliminary judicial inquiry *(Beschluß über die Eröffnung der gerichtlichen Voruntersuchung)*.

The indictment is a seven-hundred-page document consisting of two parts: first, a historical overview of the SS, the concentration camp system, and Auschwitz itself; and second, the charges against the defendants. On the one hand, the public prosecutors in Frankfurt, and particularly Attorney General Fritz Bauer, sought to put the entire Auschwitz complex on trial, as we have seen. On the other hand, because of the limitations of the German penal code, the prosecutors felt obliged to prove that the defendants had acted on their individual initiative and with some specific subjective inner motivation such as sadism, desire to kill, or other "base motives." To do this, the prosecution had to turn to the laws of the camps themselves and use them to elucidate which defendants had acted on their own, exceeding the orders of the SS in Berlin. As a consequence, SS guards and commanders who had participated in ordered selections for murder at the platform entrance of Auschwitz were not as easy to convict as those who had acted on personal initiative.

Legal constraints created a paradoxical situation in which the prosecution initially attempted to put Auschwitz on trial, but instead had to use some of the laws of the Nazi regime—particularly camp regulations—to show the personal initiative of the defendants and convict them of murder. In attempting to indict the Nazi system as a whole, the prosecution was limited to trying to show that the actions of the defendants had been conducted on their individual initiative, whether out of race hatred and base motives or excessive cruelty and sadism. To do this, in their historical overview prosecutors used Nazi documents to demonstrate which actions had been ordered, and they set up the charges to prove that all alleged crimes had in their opinion been undertaken partly out of personal initiative. In citing the camp regulations to show which defendants had exceeded them, the prosecution attempted to demonstrate individual initiative. Thus, the second goal, to prove that the defendants had broken Nazi camp rules, negated the first, which was to show that the entire SS system was corrupt. I would argue, though, that the inclusion of the historical overview in the indictment created a new historical awareness of the crimes of the SS and introduced new information about the Nazi system and Auschwitz, information that has remained central to our understanding of the concentration camps.

During the pretrial investigative phase *(Ermittlungsverfahren)*, evidence gathered by the prosecutors had, after only two years, grown almost unmanageably. The list of suspects rose to approximately eight hundred at one point and had to be whittled down to a realistic number for the trial. Throughout the pretrial phase numerous updates, memos, and addenda were introduced. This process continued until as late as October 1963, six months after the official announcement of the indictment. The prosecution and the court continually changed the list of suspects, dropped some investigations, and took up others. A chronicle of the events involved in the preparation of the trial demonstrates this fluctuation: suspects were regularly arrested and then released, rearrested and then dismissed from investigation either by the prosecution or (more often) by the court. Many suspects could not be located, or they had already been tried or executed or had died of natural causes. Others were relegated to separate files, in order to be tried at a later date, and still others simply had their cases closed and discarded because of concerns about their identity.[1] Mainly, the prosecution and the courts were making tactical decisions about what would constitute the most effective trial. The court wanted to have a manageable process without too many defendants, so that the proceedings would not fall apart or become disjointed. The prosecution wanted to put on trial the defendants who could most easily be convicted. They therefore kept returning to the most obvious cases of criminal behavior. Defendants against whom they had no watertight case threatened to become a burden to the prosecution and a waste of time and money.

Motion to Open the Preliminary Judicial Inquiry

After the pretrial investigation phase, the prosecution had to file an official request with the district court to begin proceedings against the perpetrators at Auschwitz. This was not yet the actual indictment, but a motion that the court should seriously consider indicting these suspects. This step followed the West German procedural code as described in Chapter 1, and it represented the investigation's move into the interim proceedings phase *(Zwischenverfahren)*. On

July 12, 1961, the public prosecutor's office presented the district court in Frankfurt with the motion to open the preliminary judicial inquiry. It contained the names of twenty-four suspects.[2] The men named in the motion were accused of perpetration and of aiding and abetting murder *(Mord und gemeinsame Beihilfe zu Mord)*, under paragraph 211 of the German penal code (StGB). The charges included a brief discussion of the unique and abhorrent circumstances of the concentration camps. They also mentioned criminal activities at other camps, for at this time the investigation was not limited to crimes committed at Auschwitz. Richard Baer and Alois Staller, for example, were charged with crimes committed not only "in Auschwitz and vicinity" but also at the concentration camps Neuengamme and Flossenburg in Germany. The motion addressed the greater crime of the Nazi extermination of the Jews, an indication of the attempt to keep this aspect of the crimes on trial at the forefront of the court's deliberations. The preliminary remarks at the beginning of the document stated:

> Along with the millions of people who died on the battlefields and in the bombed cities during the Second World War, there were millions of others who lost their lives as part of the systematic extermination policy of the National Socialist regime. From the invasion of Poland in 1939 until the collapse in 1945, countless people were shot, hanged, drowned, poisoned, gassed, and tortured to death in Germany and the occupied territories. The victims chosen for extermination had to endure a cruel death, after terrible degradation and the worst physical torture. The gas chambers of Auschwitz have become a symbol of the mass extermination program of the so-called Third Reich . . . In Auschwitz, there were primarily two groups of people who suffered death: Jews, who were brought there for extermination from Germany and the occupied territories, and prisoners who were incapable of work, who were imprisoned in Auschwitz for various reasons. The extermination of the Jews is outlined in the framework of the "Final So-

lution of the Jewish Section" (see under section B II), and for its realization, transports of Jewish men, women, and children from all over Europe were brought to Auschwitz and in large part gassed to death immediately upon arrival, without any registration in the camp . . . A large number of those responsible for these crimes have already been sentenced in foreign courts immediately after the collapse, and some also through German courts. The proposed proceeding is directed against those suspects who could be investigated in the last few years, and whose involvement in the crimes committed at the extermination camp Auschwitz weigh so heavily that an open interest in their criminal prosecution exists on the principle of justice.[3]

The remarks continued with a lengthy passage on the "development of the persecution of the Jews" and the Final Solution. The inclusion of such background information about the circumstances and the crimes to be prosecuted (and their political and ideological foundations) distinguished this from regular criminal proceedings despite the fact that it was to be conducted as one. Such important historical description was not uncommon, however, in West German trials of Nazi criminals. The prosecution wanted to bring to the fore the extraordinary nature of these crimes for two reasons: first, the proceedings themselves would have to adhere strictly to the criminal code, and the prosecution (particularly Fritz Bauer), feared that the law might overshadow the larger picture of the circumstances of Auschwitz (and that, as I shall discuss in Chapter 4, is exactly what occurred). Second, it was necessary information, as the basis for the definition of "base intentions" in paragraph 211.

Some sixty pages of the motion described the organizational structure of the camp system and the particular characteristics of Auschwitz itself. This information was gathered both from historians at the Institute for Contemporary History in Munich and from witness testimony. The form in which the background information appeared in the motion is important because it contained crucial new information about the Nazi system, especially in relation to the concentration and death camps; for example, one section explained the internal chain of command in the camps, beginning with the commander and ending with the prisoners. This guide is still useful, for it demonstrates the complex hierarchy within the camp and shows which camp guards had more authority or information about the Final Solution.[4] This chart refuted some of the defendants' claims that they had occupied positions of no importance in the camps. The prosecution's motion laid the groundwork for an extensive, comprehensive trial of the functionaries of Auschwitz.

Because the prosecution was obliged to charge the defendants according to the German penal code, the passages giving an introduction to those accused included an explanation of the ways in which their actions satisfied the definition of the murder charge. In particular, the prosecution dealt with the subjective motivations for cruelty *(Grausamkeit)*, treachery or malice *(Heimtücke)*, and desire to kill *(Mordlust)*, or sadism *(Sadismus)*. Treachery was explained as follows: "the definitional element of 'treachery' is fulfilled because the victims, who were gassed immediately after the arrival of the transports, mostly under the pretext that they were being transported to work, and needed to be disinfected, were in fact brought into the gas chambers, where instead of undergoing a disinfection, they were killed with gas."[5] Desire to kill and sadism were also in evidence, according to the prosecutors:

> 2. The accused in the proposed proceedings were all at the Auschwitz concentration camp as participants in the execution of a centralized extermination program. Their activities are therefore considered to be correlated punishable offenses per paragraph 13 of the StPO. This thematic connection enables and justifies the collective investigation of all the accused and their collective judgment in *one* trial. The accused had varying duties in different capacities, but they were all a part of the extermination machinery of Auschwitz with which the planned killing of prisoners was carried out. In this capac-

ity, the majority of the accused used this [situation] to realize their general aim of torturing people to death out of sexual drive for killing and sadism.[6]

In many ways, the basis for bringing a presumed perpetrator to trial, already at this early phase, was the maltreatment of prisoners and excessive cruelty leading to death, rather than murder per se. It became a trial of sadists and reprobates, often referred to as excess perpetrators *(Exceßtäter)*. The specific descriptions of subjective motives in the penal code made the presence of excessive brutality a necessity for the murder charge. This created two problems. First, the legal limitations led to a public portrayal of Auschwitz guards that was quite distorted, as the majority of the guards at Auschwitz did not demonstrate excessively violent behavior. Many were like defendant Scherpe: hesitant killers who completed their tasks anyway. To convict the accused of murder and arouse public indignation about their behavior, it was necessary to emphasize extreme cruelty. Otherwise, the punishment of these people was not a matter of urgency to the general public. Hannah Arendt wrote on this very subject that "the attitude of the German people toward their own past, which all experts on the German question had puzzled over for fifteen years, could hardly have been more clearly demonstrated: they themselves did not care much one way or the other, and did not particularly mind the presence of murderers at large in the country, since none of them were likely to commit murder of their own free will."[7] Second, the prosecution made no distinction between the psychological motives of former SS guards and those of former prisoners of Auschwitz who were under investigation. All were charged equally with possessing the subjective motivation or inner disposition of sadism. The prosecution did not differentiate in the cases of Emil Bednarek and Alois Staller, whose psychological makeup as long-term prisoners of concentration camps was entirely different from that of the SS-men. The law makes it clear that psychological motives had to be cited, but the circumstances surrounding the sadistic behavior were not taken into account.

These were problems at the very core of the trial conducted under the German criminal justice system. It was immensely difficult to prove that these men would be dangerous murderers—or a threat to society—outside the concentration camp setting. The special circumstances of Nazism had created an atavistic world in which murder was not only justified but ordered. The focus of the prosecution could not be limited to the lawlessness or the danger posed by the defendants, as those would be almost impossible to prove in cases where individual sadistic initiative was not shown. The prosecution's task, then, which could be accomplished only in the indictment, was twofold: to indict the camp system and to indict the defendants. To convict the Auschwitz functionaries of murder, the prosecution would have to show that their crimes satisfied the definition of murder used in everyday criminal proceedings. The prosecutors wanted to establish that the camp setting itself was immoral and illegal, and that it could therefore not be cited as justification for the violent behavior of the accused. Unfortunately, the indictment provided one of the last opportunities to make the point, as the activity in the courtroom would be dominated by attempts to establish the specific actions of the defendants. This is one of the main reasons that so much attention was paid in the courtroom (and outside it) to the excess perpetrators. They were easier to convict.

This dilemma did have one positive by-product. The charges in the motion demonstrated the individual guilt of each defendant. Each man was held personally responsible for his actions. In the motion, for example, the accused Kaduk was indicted for the following crimes, among other charges:

I.(a)   In countless cases [he] undertook selections in the bathroom and hospital of the Auschwitz I camp, in which the selected prisoners were loaded onto a truck and transported for gassing. In the selections conducted by the accused, the prisoners Horowitz and Kolawski from Antwerp, and the prisoner Oboka Löwenstein, who suffered from prostate cancer, underwent death by gassing; . . .

II. [He] trampled to death Rabbi Weiss, who had collapsed from exhaustion after the evening roll call; . . .

V. In early 1942, in Block 8, more than once, and often in a drunken state, he beat prisoners and then strangled them. He would lay a walking cane over their necks and stand on it. In this manner he killed, among others, the diamond handler Moritz Polakewitz, the former secretary of the Antwerp Jewish council, Teidelbaum, and another unidentified prisoner from Block 8.[8]

The specificity of the charges and the actual naming of victims had a profound effect later in the courtroom. Individual defendants, Kaduk included, were often accused of killing more than one thousand people; Stark was suspected of murdering more than eleven thousand prisoners, and Klehr allegedly had almost twenty thousand victims to his name. The scale of the murders at Auschwitz was precisely what captured public attention and has preoccupied historians. It seemed almost incongruous to focus on the individual acts of the guards, especially their being "in a drunken state" became a primary aspect of the charge against them. This focus was especially jarring in a period when the "machinery of destruction" was for the first time being examined as an enormous, complex, bureaucratic structure.[9] However, this focus on the crimes of individual guards is precisely what the trial accomplished, and it can be seen as one of the more constructive aspects of the proceedings. People who died at Auschwitz came into focus as individuals, with names and occupations and not just numbers. All of this information was gathered from the witness interrogations in the pretrial files. In this sense, witness testimony was crucial both in according individuality to these representatives of the millions of victims and in demonstrating the individual responsibility of the defendants.

The charges in the motion addressed the problem of individual initiative, which was a recurring issue for the prosecutor's office because the defense always insisted on the superior-orders *(Befehlsnotstand)* defense, and in many cases, the protests were legitimate. A

good example of this dilemma can be found in the prosecution's attempt to address the topic of death sentences at Auschwitz. It was
easiest for the prosecutors to prove that a defendant was guilty of
murder if he had taken part in an execution or a murder that was not
somehow ordered in advance by the RSHA or the WHVA (Wirt-
schafts- und Verwaltungshauptamt), the SS Economic and Administrative Office, in Berlin.[10] Suspects Max Lustig and Klaus Dylewski
were accused of having carried out death sentences unbidden. The
prosecution contended that Lustig

> regularly took part in the "court-martial hearings" (Stand-
> gerichtsverhandlungen) against the so-called police prisoners,
> led by SS ieutenant colonel Rudolf Mildner in Block 11.
> These court-martial hearings occurred over an approximately
> four-week period. During such a hearing, a hundred or more
> police prisoners, whose every basic right of defense was de-
> nied, would be sentenced to death in a one-minute-long ille-
> gal proceeding . . . The sentenced police prisoners were shot
> shortly thereafter either at the so-called Black Wall between
> Blocks 10 and 11 or at an unknown location, or they were
> openly hanged near their own barracks. The death sentences
> were objectively illegal, and the accused, as a party to the
> court-martial, knew this. Through his knowledge of the over-
> all circumstances—for example, the use of pro forma death
> sentences—he knew that these "hearings" were a complete
> farce, designed to liquidate the police prisoners.[11]

In sum, Lustig was being charged with participating, without direc-
tives from Berlin, in false, ad hoc hearings constructed within the
camp, at which prisoners were issued false death sentences and
immediately shot. He was also implicated as a perpetrator because
of his knowledge of the illegality of the act (Unrechtsbewußtsein),
which demonstrated individual initiative. The description of certain
kinds of death sentences as a "farce" necessarily leads to the conclusion that for the court in Frankfurt, some death sentences executed
at Auschwitz must also have been "valid." A mass execution, ordered

by camp officials in Berlin and carried out at the Black Wall at a designated time and following procedure, would ostensibly not have had the elements necessary for a conviction of murder, even though the prisoners were almost certainly innocent victims who had been labeled political or police prisoners. The hypocrisy inherent in this legal dilemma was not lost on the prosecutors, but it was beyond their control. It was the product of paragraphs 211 and 49, which made individual initiative and a sense of the illegality of the act requirements for a successful murder charge. These could not be proved if the accused argued that he was acting under superior orders (or if the prosecution could not disprove that he had not).

On August 9, 1961, the district court in Frankfurt am Main released its decision on the motion to open an official judiciary inquiry. It was agreed that the courts, in preparation for an official trial, would investigate the twenty-four men accused by the public prosecutor's office of various crimes at Auschwitz. In Chapter 2 I examined the two-year interim phase that followed the motion, along with the pretrial investigations in general. The pretrial proceedings that began with Adolf Rögner's letter in 1958 and resulted in the indictment of 1963 continued from 1961 to 1963, and during this time both the prosecution and the court conducted new interrogations of witnesses. These interrogations resulted in the indictment of the Auschwitz Trial.

Motion to Open the Main Proceeding

The indictment consisted of seven sections, which listed the defendants, the charges against them, the paragraphs in the StGB that applied, the evidence, and the "essential results of the investigation." The indictment functioned on two levels: as a historical account of Nazism, the SS, and Auschwitz; and in its traditional role as the list of charges against the defendants. This dual function was a product of the prosecution's (and especially Fritz Bauer's) initial goal: the public exposure and trial of the Auschwitz complex, not just the individuals who worked there. The indictment succeeded in bringing together and exposing the crime of Nazi racial ideology as a whole and the crimes of the "small men" who carried out its horrific aims.

The Historical Overview

The introductory note to part 4, "The Concentration Camps 1933–1945," in *The Anatomy of the SS State*, states: "The following account, produced as expert evidence for the Auschwitz Trial in Frankfurt, is not itself a fully comprehensive history of the National Socialist concentration camps, but it perhaps provides the framework for one. Its primary aim is to describe the chronological development of the concentration camps, the structure of their organization and leadership, and their function, importance and effects, which underwent a considerable change during the twelve years of National Socialist rule."[12] This book is a significant text, describing in minute technical detail not only the concentration camps but also the hierarchical system of the SS, including its racial worldview, its relationship with other Nazi organizations and the police, and the important ideological training behind the superior-orders mentality. The book, which became the first comprehensive scholarly text to examine the entire Nazi machinery, had as its blueprint the Auschwitz Trial indictment.

Nowhere is the judicial and moral condemnation of the entire Nazi SS and concentration camp system more evident than in the two-hundred-page overview in the indictment. The background of the SS and concentration camp systems in both the indictment and the judgment from the trial (where the background appeared again, in similar form) provided an authoritative summary of the criminal structure of Nazi society. Interestingly, though, this was not the first time such background had been provided. Beginning in 1958, trial judgments (and presumably also indictments) included some relevant information about either the surroundings in which the crimes were committed or the hierarchical system that had ordered them. Even then, such information was not standard or included in all trials. For example, on August 8, 1958, the judgment from the Ulm trial of ten members of the Einsatzgruppe Tilsit charged with murder in Lithuania included sections titled "Development of the Jewish Question," "Organization of the Police in Lithuania," and "Education of the Einsatzgruppen."[13] For two years thereafter, no such historical background was given in the documents for the various trials that took place. Then, in the Sachsenhausen trial at the district court of Düsseldorf, the judgment of October 15, 1960, included some information on the structure of the guard system at the camp, and where the defendants (three former male guards) fit into this structure. No explanation of the Final Solution or the Nazi war against the Jews appeared in the Sachsenhausen judgment.

Only beginning in 1961 did the indictment and judgment for each trial contain some form of background information. The first instance was the trial of a man accused of having rounded up twelve Jews in the town of Oelde and helped in their deportation to the Riga ghetto. The judgment of March 8, 1961, at the district court of Münster, included introductory information on the Final Solution and "Jewish policies" *(Judenpolitik)*.[14] For no other trial, however, was the background information as extensive or definitive as the documentation included in the Auschwitz Trial indictment and judgment. In many ways, the expert testimony by the historians of the Institute at Munich provided a sense of history, a graphic image of the scope of SS ideology, that had been lacking until that time.

One aspect of SS ideology absent from the indictment of the Auschwitz Trial was a discussion of the superior-orders defense *(Befehlsnotstand)*. Although testimony on the inadmissibility of this defense appeared in the pretrial files, and although Hans Buchheim discussed it on the stand on day sixteen of the trial (directly after the opening interrogation of all of the defendants), mention of the defense was not present in the historical overview of the camp system or the charges themselves. In fact, none of the German trials of Nazi perpetrators included such a discussion in the indictment. Although the orders defense may seem central to the trials of former Nazis, it was actually irrelevant to the charges against the defendants. The superior-orders defense might shed light on the mentality of the SS guards at the camp and the illegality of the orders on the whole, but it did not affect the murder charge. To prove each defendant guilty of murder, the prosecution had to show the presence of the subjective elements examined earlier: sadism, desire to kill, base motives, and so on. To show perpetration of murder (as opposed to the less serious aiding and abetting of murder), prosecutors had to prove individual initiative and knowledge of the illegality of the act, which went beyond the following of orders.

One could argue that the entire historical background given in the indictment was irrelevant to the charges, and in many ways, it was; however, it makes sense that the courts decided that some form of explanatory overview was necessary for trying crimes of this nature. These facts about the SS and the camps were being unearthed for the first time and had not yet been absorbed into public consciousness. The evolving understanding of the crimes of the Nazi regime paralleled the genesis of the trial process. The more that became known about the ideological war against the Jews and about the centrality of the extermination program, and the more the West German courts were allowed to investigate (beginning with German nationals only and going on from there to "end phase crimes" to the Holocaust), the more the Final Solution became permanently recorded in the trial proceedings.

The historical documentation of the SS system and the Auschwitz camp is divided into four sections. Section A, the preliminary remarks, is identical to that which appeared in the motion and is quoted earlier in this chapter. Sections B and C, "Organization and Tasks of the SS," and "The Concentration Camps," respectively, were the work of the historians at Munich. Section D, titled "The Auschwitz Concentration Camp," was a combination of documents from the pretrial files, witness testimony about the murderous activities in each section of the camp, and the testimony of the historians.[15] The indictment placed heavy emphasis on the role of the guards who were on trial in Frankfurt and whose role had been of the utmost importance. The types of criminal activities they engaged in, and the methods of murder each employed were set forth at length in the historical account. Former SS officers were not the only people on trial, however. The distribution of work at the camp was depicted in order to deal with the lone prisoner on the stand, who was a barracks capo accused of murder, and whose guilt had to be proved.

The portion of the indictment dealing with the SS organization began with the history of the SS starting in late summer 1925, when the group was officially formed in Munich. Its duty was spelled out in the indictment as the "protection of Hitler and the other high party leaders, as well as the defense of the party and the Führer against attack through precautionary measures."[16] Going on to explain the relationship between the SS and the police as it evolved, this section used quotations from Hitler to illustrate his goals. This section of the historical overview gave exceptionally detailed descriptions of the SS, the police, the security police, and the Gestapo, and the specific roles of the each of the main offices. For example, the overview described the WVHA in particular (its origins in 1939 and its official designation by Himmler in 1942 as one large office for Economic Administration, headed by SS lieutenant general Oswald Pohl), because it was the central administrative body for the concentration camp system. The section also explained the SS army and the military structure of the SS "special-assignment" troops *(Verfügungstruppen)* and "Death's-head units" *(Totenkopfverbände)*, in reference to their connection with the concentration camps. Going on to explain the educational process that SS guards underwent in the camps, the historians delved into the ideological training the guards received and the intensity of their racist convictions. In this way the indictment set up the historical background for an understanding of the defendants and their voluntary role at Auschwitz. Such detailed information about the administrative organization of the camps and of the SS system in general was not available to the public until this time. Its inclusion there demonstrates the way in which this trial altered the perception of history and of the Third Reich in the mind of those involved in the trial and later, in the comprehension of the general public. The background on the SS was an important introduction for the next section of the overview, dealing with the concentration camps first, and then specifically Auschwitz.

The history of the first camps within Germany, their role as enforcers of the National Socialist policies, and the role of punishment in Nazi society were central to the prosecution's argument about the criminality of the Auschwitz complex and were therefore explored in depth in the indictment. The majority of the documents used to prove these findings came from the Nuremberg trials; for example, the historians cited Nuremberg documents written by Hermann Göring and Hans Frank on the reasons for imprisoning "enemies of the state," particularly communists, in the concentration camps. According to the General Gouverneur (and lawyer) Hans Frank in the *Zeitschrift der Akademie für Deutsches Recht* (Journal of the Academy of German Law) in 1936: "Throughout the world people are always reproaching us, because of the concentration camps. They ask: Why do you arrest people without judicial arrest warrants? They should place themselves in the situation of our people! They forget that the whole, big, still unshaken world of Bolshevism will not let us forget that we thwarted their final victory over Europe."[17]

The abundant use of Nuremberg trial documents demonstrated the prosecution's attempts to incorporate the fundamental criminal aspects of Nazism into the indictment. Although the illegality of the Nazi state had already been established at the Allied trials, the prosecution consulted many of the expert witnesses from Nuremberg on this question for the Auschwitz investigation. The new West German state had backed away from any possibility of using international criminal charges for trying Nazi defendants. As a consequence, the aims of the Nazi war, including the extermination of the Jews, could not be subjected to legal inspection or prosecuted in any way. Still, the indictment managed to include many passages that, in their explanation of the SS and camp system, harshly condemned not only the defendants but National Socialism itself.

One of the ways that the expert witnesses could show the guilt of the defendants was to turn to the camp regulations themselves. Because the prosecution had to establish "subjective inner motivation" and individual initiative in order to get a murder conviction, the inclusion of the official Nazi camp policies early on in the indictment could show which of the defendants' actions constituted perpetration of or aiding and abetting murder. The indictment therefore included a statement on October 10, 1933, by Theodor Eicke, who was at that time the commander of Dachau concentration camp. In 1934 he was promoted to inspector of concentration camps. The statement read:

> In the framework of the existing camp instructions, the following penal regulations are issued for the preservation of discipline and order in the domain of the Dachau concentration camp (KLD).
>
> These regulations apply to all prisoners of KLD from the time of arrival to the hour of release.
>
> The executive power is in the hands of the camp commander, who is personally responsible for the execution of the camp instructions issued by the political police commanders.
>
> Tolerance means weakness. Acknowledging this means there will be ruthless seizure, where it becomes necessary in the interest of the Fatherland.[18]

The excerpt went on to list various regulations regarding not only the crimes that would lengthen or intensify the term of imprisonment at Dachau, but also the punishment that would be inflicted. This statement ran counter to the StGB, which was still very much in force during the entire Nazi regime. For example, paragraph 6 stated: "With eight days strict arrest and with twenty-five cane lashes at the beginning and the end of punishment, the following crimes are to be punished: 1) whoever makes critical or mocking remarks to an SS officer, or purposely fails to salute, or through any kind of behavior makes it know that he will not submit to the force of discipline and order."[19] The paragraphs also included more serious crimes, and crimes such as the instigation of political insurrection (11) and mutiny or sabotage (12) were to be punished by hanging or shooting. Paragraph 19 of this statement of camp regulations was most pertinent to the Auschwitz case, as it listed the types of punishments that were enforceable in the case of "criminal" behavior within the camp. These punishments, which applied to prisoners who were sentenced to death or solitary confinement, clearly fell within acceptable Nazi practice of "intensified interrogations" *(verschärfte Vernehmungen)* and therefore would presumably not have been considered sadistic, excessive behavior or individually initiated criminal activity. The paragraph stated:

> Arrest will be carried out in a cell, with harsh conditions, and water and bread. Every four days the prisoner will get warm food. Work detail includes hard physical labor or especially dirty work under special supervision.
>
> As extra punishment the following can be considered:
>
> Exercise drills, corporal punishment [beatings], withholding of mail, deprivation of food, confinement to quarters, tying to a post, reprimands, and warnings. All punishments will be recorded.
>
> Arrest and hard labor will prolong protective custody by not less than eight weeks; secondary punishment will prolong protective custody by not less than four weeks. Prisoners in solitary confinement will not be released within a foreseeable period.[20]

These special regulations introduced by Eicke at Dachau became standard for all of the camps. The inclusion of these rules within the indictment gave the courts a model of what was considered acceptable in the camps; for, according to Martin Broszat, "the object of [these] regulations was to lay down in writing and to stress that caning could not be carried out arbitrarily by individual guards and that it was a regular form of punishment. Because the caning was carried out by several SS men the ill-treatment became impersonal and anonymous and every member of the guard formations was accustomed from the beginning to this act which he might at any time be ordered to perform."[21]

Why did the SS commanders stop at a certain level of brutality? Why were guards held accountable for excessive cruelty? The explanation lies in what was theoretically the strict chain of command and authoritative rule of Nazi society and the SS system. Disobedience and breaking the chain of command were not supposed to be tolerated. In fact, sometimes breaking the rules in favor of more violent behavior was punished more harshly than refusing to carry out a task at all. A certain level of "decent German behavior" *(anständiges deutsches Verhalten)* prohibited the guards from sinking to the level of depraved sadists.

More relevant to the Auschwitz investigation was what the inclusion of these documents meant in the courtroom in Frankfurt. We know that the defendants and their attorneys could not have recourse to the superior-orders defense. The prosecution used them purely to show that the actions of the defendants on the stand had been undertaken on their individual initiative and in the knowledge of the illegality of the actions, and that these could therefore be tried and punished as perpetration of murder. Whether or not the SS leadership strictly enforced these regulations was not important in the Frankfurt proceedings, only that they existed. Thus the ironic situation arose in which the standard of the Nazi state was adopted in the courtroom in Frankfurt to try the very crimes committed under that state. To convict the defendants on the stand, Judge Hofmeyer had to refer to Nazi documents and Nazi regulations to determine who had exceeded what the regulations permitted. The absurdity of this situation was not lost on the judge, whose exasperation with (and yet adherence to) the rigid interpretations of the law I will address in the discussion of testimony on the stand in Chapter 4.

The overview of the concentration camps continued with a description of the intensification of the persecution of different elements of society, from "asocials" to Jews. On January 2, 1941, Reinhard Heydrich issued a statement placing the camps in four different categories, depending on their functions. Level I *(Stufe I)* which included Dachau, Sachsenhausen, and Auschwitz I, was reserved for "all security prisoners with minor charges who are definitely capable of improvement, and for special cases and solitary confinement."[22] Clearly, this was an early designation for Auschwitz, before the official implementation of the Final Solution and before the creation of a system of slave labor camps and death camps.

The next document in the overview, however, points to a significant change and a blatant expression of a new program. From the files of former Reich justice minister Otto Thierack came the following memo:

> A discussion with Reichsführer [Himmler] on September 18, 1942, in his field quarters in the presence of StS [Secretary of State] Dr. Rothenberger, SS Lieutenant General Strecken-bach and SS Lieutenant Colonel Bender.
>
> 2. Handing over of asocial elements for execution of court-imposed sentence to the Reichsführer SS for EXTERMINA-TION THROUGH WORK. There will be tireless handing over of security-risk prisoners, Jews, Gypsies, Russians and Ukrainians, Poles with prison terms beyond three years, Czechs and Germans with prison terms beyond eight years according to the decision of the Reich justice minister.[23]

This now infamous letter transferred the persecuted minorities and political prisoners from the authority of the legal system and courts into the hands of the SS and the police. The concentration camps were thus given full jurisdiction over the Jews and the extermination policy (at this phase still through "work") was officially sanctioned. The project was of course already under way, however, and gas chambers existed by this time at Auschwitz, Majdanek, Chelmno, Belzec, Sobibor, and Treblinka.[24]

The overview went on to describe more precisely just who the victims of the camps were. According to the experts, the Gestapo was responsible for four groups of undesirables: political adversaries, criminals (including homosexuals), asocials and members of "inferior races," and the "racially/biologically inferior." Among these groups also a hierarchy existed, with criminal prisoners—particularly German professional criminals (Berufsverbrecher)—at the top

of the list. The historians, calling this a system of self-rule, stipulated: "This is to be understood as: what the SS leaders wanted is
what occurred."[25] This system of self-rule applied also to the hierarchy among the prisoners who were given roles of authority (*Häft-
lingsfunktionäre*), meaning German, Polish, and Ukrainian prisoners. As mentioned earlier, Jews in the camps very rarely became part
of this system, as they were immediately sent into the "extermination
through work" program—if they were registered at the camp at all.
The vast majority went straight to the gas chambers without registration or tattooing.

The most extensive and detailed portion of the overview dealt
specifically with the Auschwitz concentration camp. Together with
some initial historical background gathered by the experts in Munich, this section is a collection of documents ranging from excerpts
of the death books to extensive testimonies from survivors. The table
of contents from this section is most illuminating, for it traces the
range of information about Auschwitz presented to the court. It began with such subheadings as "National Socialist Policies in Poland"
and then described the different camps of Auschwitz, including
Auschwitz I, the main camp; Auschwitz II, or Birkenau; Monowitz
and other subcamps; and Auschwitz as an extermination camp.
Thereafter, it gave comprehensive accounts of the specific forms of
torture and murder practiced in the camp. Some examples of subheadings in this category include "Cap Throwing," "Interrogation
Methods: The Swing," "Killing through Injection: *Abspritzen*," and
"Walking into the Barbed Wire." The inclusion of the last subhead-
ing demonstrates the prosecution's attempt to condemn all aspects
of Auschwitz. This mode of suicide (the wires were electrified) was
explained in the overview as "the last way out," the only wish left
to many inmates who could no longer bear the living conditions in
the camp.[26]

Included in this section was a description of the "hospital" blocks
at the camp by former prisoner Dr. Władysław Fejkiel, who had
been the "camp elder" (*Lagerältester*) at the hospital and was at the
time of his interrogation a professor at the University of Kraków.[27]

His description of the building of the hospital blocks and the conditions within them is extremely graphic. He described the first operation that took place there (an appendix extraction with stolen Polish surgical instruments in November 1940) and explained clearly that it was a shoddy operation, performed without anesthesia on a prisoner who was tied down to a table. His narrative went on to depict the incarceration of the "Muselmänner" in Block 20 of the hospital. They had clearly been brought there to die, as they were given fewer rations than regular prisoners or other "patients."[28] Dr. Ella Lingens, another prisoner-doctor who worked in the hospital buildings also gave testimony about those prisoners. Details were important to the prosecution because they made it possible to provide more concrete examples of the activities of the defendants within the camp structure.

One important topic dealt with in this section is "self-justice through the prisoner-functionaries." This was a sensitive issue for the prosecution because it concerned prisoners who performed their duties under threat of death, a danger that did not exist for the SS guards. Prisoners who were capos and block leaders had more privileges—better clothing, more food, warmer shelter, and less crowded conditions—and saw the fulfillment of their duties as their only chance for survival. Those who refused to obey orders were subject to death or a severe beating. It seems that the German courts took this threat into account in their investigations, for only a tiny minority of people investigated and tried were former prisoner-functionaries. It was understood that many prisoners in roles of authority had little choice in their actions, and certainly much less than the SS guards did. It was even clearer to the prosecution that it would be extremely difficult to prove individual initiative or base motives for many of these people. Research into the camp hierarchy and the wanton brutality at Auschwitz did, however, show that many of the functionaries had been extraordinarily cruel and vicious with the prisoners under their control. Countless stories of prisoner atrocities appear in the scholarly literature about the camps and in survivor memoirs.[29] For this reason the public prosecutors in Frankfurt had two prisoners on their list of accused, Alois Staller and Emil Bednarek. (Staller, as we shall see later, was dismissed from the investigation, but Bednarek was eventually convicted of fourteen counts of perpetrating murder.)

In the overview of "self-justice," Staller's pretrial testimony was used to explain this phenomenon. He stated:

> I never submitted to an SS officer's wish when he hinted to me that he no longer wanted to see a prisoner. This was the way that the SS let it be known that they wanted a fellow- prisoner to kill another prisoner, or that they would at least tolerate it. Of course, it happened, in fact very often, that a prisoner would kill another prisoner. There were a variety of methods, which I saw not only in Auschwitz . . . Often prisoners killed other prisoners to create extra eating portions, because the prisoners would be killed before food was given out and then reported dead only the next day. The extra portions of food would be divided among the most efficient prisoners, also those the SS was considered to have given the best beatings.[30]

In such cases, former prisoner-functionaries were generally not charged with murder. In the case of Bednarek, however, sadistic individual behavior could be demonstrated. These complex cases of prisoners who committed crimes merit further investigation. It was much harder for the prosecution to show individual initiative, even in the most sadistic of activities, if it was possible that the accused had acted under the orders of an SS guard. For such cases as Bednarek's and Staller's, specific witness testimony was crucial. The prosecution's decision to try these men shows the eagerness to condemn the system itself, and therefore to condemn all those who had participated in murder at Auschwitz. The prosecutors were more successful with some than with others, as the judgment will show.

Despite the limitations of the law, the prosecution naturally tried to prove that all deaths at Auschwitz were a form of murder—including suicides (when prisoners were driven to it, as described above), fatal beatings, and "standard" methods of torture and killing that were practiced by all the SS guards, whether on their personal initiative or not. For this reason the prosecution took great pains to describe the many different camp punishments *(Lagerstrafen)* that were either immediately or eventually fatal. These included "doing sports" *(Sportmachen*—excessive, prolonged, difficult exercise that exhausted prisoners to the point of death), corporal punishment, hanging by the arms, standing cells, punishing work commandos, starvation, and hanging. The prosecution had gathered many documents from the camp that pertained to these forms of punishment. The SS meticulously recorded the definitions and acceptable forms of punishment. For example, beatings *(Prügelstrafe*—beatings with canes, sticks, or whips), were ordered when a prisoner misbehaved, as prisoner Calvo had on November 11, 1944. He allowed a gold tooth to be extracted in exchange for food. The prescribed forms of beating were explained in this way in an early Nazi memo: "Blows with a leather whip in quick succession, in which the blows are counted, is allowed; undressing of prisoner or of certain body parts is strictly prohibited. The prisoner may not be tied down but is to lie on the bench voluntarily. He can be hit only on the behind or the upper thigh." A memo of April 4, 1942, from the WVHA, Administrative Section D, signed by SS Lieutenant Colonel Liebehenschel, at the time head of the central office and later commander of Auschwitz, ordered that a new policy on corporal punishment would go into effect: "The Reichsführer SS and the chief of German police has ordered that during the execution of corporal punishment (for both male or female protective-custody prisoners), when the word 'intensified' *(verschärft)* is added, the punishment should be carried out on an unclothed behind. In all other cases, proceed as already ordered."[31]

These documents demonstrated that strict rules and regulations were in place, and constantly revised, regarding the nature of punishment in the camps. Limitations were put on the type of beating that was acceptable, the ways in which prisoners were to be hanged, and who could carry out the punishments; for example, a memo from the same office on November 8, 1942, made the execution of corporal punishment by other prisoners "legal," as long as an SS guard was present. The typical images of concentration camp life— a chaotic and brutal existence on the one hand, the *anus mundi* where sadism and excessive violence were the norm; and efficient, disciplined, orderly murder in the gas chambers on the other hand —do not necessarily represent the reality of the camp. The SS had extensive, written regulations on all manner of SS and prisoner activities, and many kinds of punishment and violent behavior were officially sanctioned by the WVHA. But the very formulation of these rules meant that much behavior was not formally acceptable and would not be officially tolerated. The extent to which the regulations were enforced depended on the personality of the camp commander, the stage of the Final Solution, and other circumstances. The prosecution deemed actions taken by SS guards and prisoners that were either not ordered or strictly forbidden acts of individual initiative, regardless of whether the regulations were enforced. The prosecution tried to convict the defendants of murder regardless of whether they had been under orders from Berlin or from the camp commander, because of Fritz Bauer's stated goal to put the Auschwitz complex on trial and show the illegality of all killing in the camp. In the courtroom, however, these documents made the difference between a conviction for perpetration of murder and one for aiding and abetting murder.

The overview of life and death in Auschwitz included a twenty-page section titled "Participation of the Political Department," focusing specifically on the ways in which prisoners were tortured and murdered by members of the central administrative body at the camp. The role of the Political Department was ostensibly to interrogate prisoners who were accused of political insubordination and insurrection outside and inside the camp. The indictment states, however: "The members of the Political Department, who were in charge of interrogating prisoners, used raw violence in many cases, to make the prisoners speak. This happened especially when they were supposed to make statements about escape attempts, escape preparations, and resistance groups. These prisoners were beaten, kicked, or in other ways physically abused."[32] This section dealt more pointedly with the defendants themselves, because in the Political Department they were known to have their own peculiar forms of torture.

The most infamous example was Wilhelm Boger and his Boger swing *(Boger Schaukel)*. The overview used witness testimony to describe the swing, a primitive contraption consisting of a long wooden stick which rested on two supports. The prisoner was tied to the stick under his arms and under his knees, and the stick was placed on the supports so that the prisoners hung in the air, suspended, and could easily be beaten.[33] For the purposes of the indictment, the swing was crucial because the prosecution could show that it was an invention of Boger's sadistic imagination and was therefore solid proof of his guilt as a murderer. A document from the Chief of the Security Police and SD (Gestapo), Lieutenant General Heinrich Müller, on June 12, 1942, demonstrates the illegality of the swing. The memo regarding intensified interrogations, addressed to all leaders and commanders of the Gestapo and specifically directed at the Gestapo inspectors, read:

> 1. Intensified interrogations can be employed only when the results of a preinvestigation demonstrate that the prisoner can give new information about important communications regarding associations or plans that are hostile to the State of the Reich, but who is unwilling to reveal his knowledge, or it could not be established through investigation.
>
> 2. Under these conditions, intensified interrogations can only be employed against communists, Marxists, Jehovah's Witnesses, saboteurs, terrorists, members of resistance movements, undercover agents, asocials, Polish or Soviet-Russian work resisters (slackers), or vagrants.
>
> In all other cases my earlier memo prevails.
>
> 3. Intensified interrogations cannot be employed to bring about confessions of individual crimes. Moreover, this

method cannot be used against people who have in the meantime been transferred for other investigations by the legal system.

4. The intensification, depending upon the situation, can comprise:

- the most basic rations (bread and water) under harsh conditions,
- darkened cell
- sleep deprivation
- exercise to exhaustion
- the dispensing of canings (a doctor must be present if there are more than twenty lashes).[34]

Clearly, the SS had very specific regulations for interrogations in the Political Department. The chief of the Gestapo defined them in such a way that they could not be interpreted as torture. The indictment showed, however, that many members of the Political Department engaged in extreme torture leading to death, and that their interrogations "far exceeded this directive from the chief of the Gestapo in both recklessness and brutality."[35] Countless examples came from witness testimony, including the relentless beating of one prisoner because he had an extra piece of bread, and the execution of members of the Polish intelligentsia and Russian prisoners of war at the Black Wall. The testimony of Jan Pilecki, block clerk on Block 11 from 1942 to 1944 (the Black Wall was located between Blocks 10 and 11), included eyewitness accounts of executions there. He stated explicitly that all prisoners were ordered to undress before being shot at the wall, an order that was clearly against SS regulations as defined by Müller. In addition, as the person in charge of the prisoner registry in this block, he was responsible for carefully controlling and then entering the tattoo numbers of the prisoners who were shot. That certain prisoners were shot immediately, without being registered—the lack of procedure and the total anonymity of the prisoners—indicated that their deaths could not have been ordered.

The execution of the intelligentsia, according to the indictment, was an attempt to "liquidate" this section of Polish society entirely. Because they were not listed as people to be interrogated, let alone shot, in Müller's memo, the prosecutors could use this information to charge defendants from the Political Department with murder. An important piece of evidence came from SS lieutenant colonel Grabner, the chief of the Political Department. An SS investigation headed by SS judge Konrad Morgen investigated Grabner and convicted him of corruptionin 1943. Grabner wrote: "The so-called liquidation of the Polish intelligentsia was ordered by Höss in my time and afterward. Whether he got an order from Berlin or did so independently is unknown to me. This happened in the following way: the protective custody commander [Schutzhaftlagerführer] was put in charge of this. Because Höss had put him in charge of this action, he took care of it and made lists."[36] The tenor of the indictment made it increasingly clear that the absence of an order from Berlin was crucial to the prosecution's case. On the one hand, the prosecution was exposing the crimes of the SS at Auschwitz in their entirety by examining them closely and making them public in this section of the indictment. On the other hand, the requirement for the prosecutors to work within the narrow confines of the law made them dependent not only on witness testimony that certain defendants had acted independently, but also on the Nazi documents that laid out these draconian and unjust regulations.

Indirectly included in the indictment was a discussion of the *Kommissarbefehl* of June 6, 1941, ordering the execution of the commissars of the Soviet army. This order applied to Auschwitz in 1941 because the camp had a large population of Soviet prisoners of war (POWs). The evidence at Nuremberg included some of the key orders given regarding the Soviet POWs, and among these was one from Heydrich on July 17, 1941, for the commanders of the security police and SD in Administrative Section 4, regarding the segregation of civilians and prisoners in the POW and transit camps, known respectively as Stalag and Dulag. Special commandos (comprising one SS leader and four to six subordinates) were responsible for sorting out the prisoners into groups, such as important state and party officials, people's commissars and their deputies, all former Red Army political commissars, Soviet intellectuals, and Jews (among others).[37] These commandos then had to decide which among these "suspects" were dangerous and therefore subject to execution. The memo stated clearly that "the executions may not be carried out in the camp or in its immediate vicinity. If the camp is in the General Gouvernment or near its border, the prisoners should be brought to the former Russian-Soviet territory for "special treatment" [*Sonderbehandlung*, a euphemism for mass execution]."[38] The Political Department was generally in charge of the execution of these POWs, and many of the charges against these defendants included the murder of Soviet soldiers in 1941–1942. Interestingly, the overview included a memo from Admiral Canaris, head of the Foreign Office and Counterintelligence. Canaris expressed his reservations about the *Kommissarbefehl*, because it broke international law and would lead to voluntary abuse and killing, as well as growing resentment and resistance among the native populations of the occupied territories.[39] In the case of the Soviet POWs, then, the prosecution attempted to show that the entire order was illegal, not simply the actions of the defendants who exceeded the orders. In the end, according to the expert witnesses, at least ten thousand POWs were executed in 1941 at Auschwitz, and hundreds more were worked to death.

The list in the indictment of arbitrary executions and death sentences was extensive. The indictment also contained a further examination of the court-martial hearings, ruled to be ad hoc proceedings clearly undertaken at the whim of the SS guards. Witness Jan Pilecki described at length the procedure followed, in which at least a hundred alleged political adversaries were tried and sentenced to death within an hour. Initially, such prisoners were executed immediately at the Black Wall, but when their numbers became too great, they were taken away by truck, presumably to the gas chambers.[40] Sometimes ordered by Berlin, sometimes carried out on the initiative of the SS guards themselves, most mass killings in the Political Department at Auschwitz followed some sort of regulated procedure. Though more difficult to prosecute as such, these murders were nonetheless described in the indictment; the prosecution sought to demonstrate the depravity of the system as a whole, while showing that certain specific actions of the defendants had been undertaken with "murderous intent."

The indictment also dealt with the grisliest of crimes at Auschwitz, the medical experiments. Included in this section was witness testimony on such procedures as "urine tapping," "typhus infection," the collection of human skeletons, and, most relevant to the Auschwitz case, death by injection. The last began as an experiment, in which first water or air, then gasoline, Evipan, and finally phenol were injected into either the arm or the chest of the prisoner. These experiments were conducted in order to find the quickest way to kill "patients"—the speed being for the benefit of the medical orderly conducting the injections, not the prisoners themselves. Generally, this form of death was administered to prisoners who, having been worked to the point of exhaustion and disease, were no longer useful. Children were also subject to injections. According to the estimates of survivor Dr. Stanisław Kłodziński, who witnessed the injections, approximately twenty-five to thirty thousand prisoners were murdered this way between the fall of 1941 and January 1945 in Block 20. Of these, ninety to ninety-five percent were Jews.[41] The indictment did not include orders either from Berlin or from the SS commanders regarding the injections.

In the historical overview in the indictment, the drafters examined Auschwitz as a "mass extermination plant" (*Massenvernichtungsanstalt*) which explored the "Final Solution of the Jewish Question," the use of Zyklon B, the selections at the entrance platform, and the liquidation of the Theresienstadt and Gypsy camps. Most of the information on the policy of exclusion and extermination of the Jews came from Nuremberg documentation, including documents and the testimony of various defendants. Beginning with the first policies of discrimination in 1933, the indictment included a relatively comprehensive history of the Final Solution, from the Wannsee Conference in January 1942 to the murder of the Hungarian Jews at Auschwitz in the spring and summer of 1944. The prosecutors were aware of the limitations of both the law and their knowledge of the subject matter; for example, they stated that "it is not the task of this investigation to determine with any certainty the total count of Jews murdered in the extermination sites of Majdanek, Chelmno, Belzec, Sobibor, Treblinka, and Auschwitz. But with certainty we can say that of all the extermination sites, Auschwitz was by far the biggest in the framework of the 'Final Solution to the Jewish Problem.' "[42]

The treatment of children is one of the most gruesome topics in the indictment, one that functioned as a fitting ending to the overview and introduction to the charges against the defendants. The prosecutors used graphic witness testimony to show the reckless disregard for innocent life. Presumably, the murder and torture of children would get a murder conviction, as paragraph 211 specifies "malicious intent" as one characteristic of murderous activity. Malicious intent, according to historian Ingo Müller, could mean "that the killer exploited a situation in which the victim was unsuspecting and defenseless."[43] The indictment presented the murder of children as abhorrent and illegal and did not add much in the way of interpretation or explanation of why such acts exhibited the characteristics necessary for conviction. However, the witness statements that appeared in this section did show particular defendants' excessively cruel behavior or their comprehension of the illegality of this act. Dr. Ella Lingens, for example, was quoted here: "Once, in the summer of 1944, I got as close as I could to Crematorium II . . . I saw a large fire on the ground, but I cannot say if it came out of a pit or not. I could see that small children, who were still alive, were being thrown into this fire. Obviously it was too troublesome to take them all the way to the gas chambers. Because it was dark, I cannot say if the men who did this were wearing uniforms."[44]

In another passage, defendant Stefan Baretski's testimony was used to demonstrate that even he understood that this was entirely outside the law. In many ways, this admission sealed his fate as a murderer. He stated that "often, sometimes two to three times a week, we were told by the SS officers that the occurrences in Auschwitz were legal, because the prisoners who were transported there had been active saboteurs. There were also other reasons given for the killing measures introduced. I, personally, though, was of the opinion that all of these things were illegal. After all, what kind of sabotage could children have participated in?"[45] The murder of children was looked upon as a much more serious offense than any other crime. Still, in cases where individual initiative could not be shown, a murder conviction was not self-evident. The case of defendant Scherpe, who allegedly killed at least ten boys attests to this: he was convicted of aiding and abetting murder and sentenced to four and a half years prison.

The Charges and the Evidence

The list of accused in the indictment who were charged with murder and aiding and abetting murder was slightly different from the one presented in the motion. Seven suspects were dropped from the proceedings, and five were added. These changes occurred through a typical process during the interim proceedings in which the court conducted its own investigations and could make changes to the charges as it saw fit, with the cooperation of the prosecutor's office. Some of the accused could not be identified, for example, or had been confused with other suspects of the same last name. Some who did make it into the indictment were too sick to stand trial. Others could simply not be found.

The motion included one very important figure at the camp, Commander Richard Baer. Baer was the great find of the prosecutors, who hoped that his capture and prosecution would bring widespread public attention to the trial and to the crimes of the Nazis. He was the last commander at Auschwitz before January 1945, after a brief period of command by Arthur Liebehenschel. Baer was much less famous than the notorious Rudolf Höss, who had immediately preceded Liebehenschel; however, the prosecution hoped to prove that he was as brutal as Höss, if not more so. To the prosecution's dismay, he died a few weeks before the beginning of the trial proceedings, a turn of events that initially seemed a great blow to the prosecution's case. In fact, the media coverage was nonetheless extensive, and Baer's absence did not diminish public curiosity about the trial.

A few suspects not included in the motion were added later, among them Herbert Scherpe, Karl Höcker, Dr. Franz Lucas, Franz Neubert, and Bruno Schlage. The decisions that finally brought them to the trial itself were not extraordinary but rather resulted from further investigation and accumulating evidence. What was extraordinary was the decision, two months after the indictment was issued, to drop four defendants (Alois Staller, Kurt Uhlenbroock, Jacob Fries, and Bernhard Rakers) from the proceedings. The process that led to the dismissal of these cases merits more intense scrutiny before I examine the final list of charges in the indictment.

Countless witnesses accused Jacob Fries, Bernhard Rakers, Kurt Uhlenbroock, and Alois Staller of murder. All remained untried, following a court decision on July 8, 1963, in the "Decision on the Indictment" ("Eröffnungsbeschluss"), to discontinue the proceedings.[46] Some confusion existed about all these suspects, despite the mountain of evidence against them. By April 1963, sufficient doubt already existed that they could be convicted of murder, and four months later their cases were officially dismissed.

Uhlenbroock's case was somewhat of a scandal for the prosecution, for he was described by many witnesses and cited by the prosecution as a garrison doctor (*Standortarzt*) at Auschwitz between July 17 and September 6, 1942, after which he was replaced by Dr. Eduard Wirths and demoted to regular camp doctor. In that position he remained until, having been infected with typhus, he was allowed a recovery vacation until November of the same year.[47] Uhlenbroock, however, insisted that he was in actuality a prisoner there. A letter written to the prosecutor's office by Uhlenbroock and present in his case files stated: "I deny that I am guilty of that of which I am accused in the arrest warrant. I was never the garrison doctor at Auschwitz and never gave orders to the camp doctors. I was in Auschwitz as a prisoner."[48]

A report by the prosecution described the interrogation of Uhlenbroock in November 1960 in Hamburg. During his interrogation at the police station the suspect asked to be allowed to retrieve some papers from his home that would help to exonerate him. He went there, accompanied by two police officers and public prosecutor Kügler. The report stated:

> We went first into the master bedroom, where the suspect retrieved a brown leather briefcase in which some of these papers he sought supposedly were. The briefcase was not taken from the suspect; he was given the opportunity to get the papers out himself. The suspect then went with this briefcase into the bathroom, where the police observed him. They could see that the suspect took out a letter, crumpled it and hid it in his left hand. (The suspect then tried to escape.) Once in the bedroom the suspect was asked by attorney Kügler to stand still, turn around and open his hands. The crumpled paper was still in his left hand and was taken from him. It was a letter written by the suspect to the garrison doctor [Standortarzt] at Auschwitz asking for a four week "recovery vacation," dated "KL Auschwitz, Sept. 21, 1942."[49]

Two years after the August 1961 "Decision on the Opening of the Preliminary Judicial Inquiry" (Beschluß über die Eröffnung der Gerichtlichen Voruntersuchung), a fairly long and detailed memo appeared in the pretrial files regarding updated investigations, in which Uhlenbroock was still described as having been a garrison doctor for a short time at Auschwitz. His contention that he was there as a prisoner in a sort of "officer's detention" was at the time of this memo unequivocally refuted as false, "as a result of the investigation."[50] Evidence had been gathered from witness statements appearing earlier in the pretrial files—including statements from Hermann Langbein, Stanisław Głowa, Dr. Stanisław Kłodziński, and other reliable sources—as well as from important diaries and reports written by fellow SS officers, particularly the diary of Dr. Kremer. The court's decision to drop the charges against Uhlenbroock, with the explanation that "there is insufficient suspicion that the accused, during his relatively short stay at Auschwitz, took part in the mass murder of prisoners in any punitively relevant way," remains an enigma.[51] This case reflects the tensions that existed between the prosecutors and the court, for certainly Fritz Bauer and the public prosecutor's office, acting on their own, would never have allowed Uhlenbroock to go untried.

Alois Staller, a prisoner cited by countless witnesses as a sadistic killer, admitted to the most brutal of acts but insisted that in order to survive, he had had no choice but to carry them out. Prosecutors issued Staller's arrest warrant in November 1959, charging him with the murder of "an uncertain number of prisoners through beatings with a club, asphyxiation with a rod placed on their necks or drowning in the water pits." After much confusion about his identity, the court decided to drop the charges against Staller in June 1963. The final statement by the court about the closing of the investigation ruled that "on both counts it is not to be ruled out that the witnesses confused the identity of the suspect."[52] In fact, there seemed little doubt that the prosecution had found the right man, but the court decided that the evidence was too tenuous to proceed.

The dismissal of the charges against Rakers was also a peculiar process. It was discovered late in the investigation that Rakers had already been charged with crimes committed at Auschwitz, not once but twice. Rakers had initially been arrested on July 24, 1950, in Lingen, and was indicted by the district court of Osnabrück on August 20, 1952. He was charged with murder and bodily harm leading to death. On February 10, 1953, he was convicted of murder, attempted murder, and aiding and abetting murder in five cases and sentenced to life in prison plus fifteen years. Four days before the judgment, the courts decided to separate one charge from the proceeding. This was the charge that as the *Rapportführer* at Monowitz (a satellite camp of Auschwitz) between 1944 and 1945, Rakers had beaten a French prisoner to death.[53] Given that the StPO allows for the reinvestigation and retrial on new charges of persons already convicted of crimes, the courts in Osnabrück took up this charge again in 1958. On June 19, 1958, the district court ruled that the proceedings against Rakers should be discontinued for lack of proof.[54] The statement of the court revealed that there were trustworthy witnesses with accurate recollections of Rakers, but their statements did not amount to enough for a conviction. When witnesses testifying for the Auschwitz investigation began to mention his name, Rakers was arrested again in relation to the new proceedings because he was already on the books as a Nazi criminal. But in the end, just before the beginning of the trial, the prosecution again found itself on shaky ground and declared the case too tenuous to proceed. He was dismissed from the proceedings in July, 1963. He remained in prison for the rest of his life.

Jacob Fries exemplified the most extreme case of these questionable dismissals. At least five survivors testified in their pretrial interrogations about the activities of Fries, who was asserted to have beaten and shot many victims during the selection process. He was always described as one of the more brutal guards at Auschwitz. In an interrogation conducted by the ZS, the interrogator's notes indicate that Fries "did not appear very credible" and that he gave the impression that "he can't be bothered to make clarifications on this case."[55] The interrogators were clearly exasperated with Fries's denial of any form of participation in or knowledge of killing at Auschwitz. In the end, though, the prosecutors did not feel that they could prove more than aiding and abetting murder, for which he had already been convicted in 1952 by the district court in Nuremberg-Fürth and received a thirteen-year sentence. Fries appeared as a witness at the trial, but he was still under investigation for having participated in murder at Auschwitz. He could therefore refuse to answer many questions, and his testimony was virtually valueless because of the limitations on the questions that could be asked and the suspicion surrounding him. His testimony was not accepted and he was not sworn in.[56] The prosecution clearly felt that he should have been on trial with the rest of the defendants, but the court did not.

There are countless examples of such decisions, many of which permitted mass murderers to live out their lives as ordinary citizens

in postwar West Germany. In effect, the often arbitrary process of selecting defendants defied explanation. This fact of political, cultural
and judicial life must be recognized as part of Germany's confrontation with its Nazi past and kept in perspective as an important backdrop to this trial.

The twenty-four defendants charged in the indictment were:

1. Richard Baer: SS major and camp commander from May
   1944 to January 1945
2. Robert Karl Mulka: SS first lieutenant, captain, and adjutant to Commander Rudolf Höss from February 1942 to
   March 1943
3. Karl Höcker: SS first lieutenant and adjutant to Commander Baer from May 1944 to January 1945
4. Wilhelm Boger: SS staff sergeant and investigator in the
   Political Department from 1942 to 1945
5. Hans Stark: SS corporal/staff sergeant and head of the registration office in the Political Department from the end of
   1940 to December 1941 and from March 1942 to November
   1942
6. Klaus Dylewski: SS corporal/staff sergeant and investigator
   in the Political Department from 1941 to 1944
7. Pery Broad: SS private and investigator in the Political Department from January 1941 to 1945
8. Johann Schobert: SS private/corporal and member of the
   Political Department from 1943 to the end of 1944
9. Bruno Schlage: arrest supervisor in Block 11 of the main
   camp at Auschwitz from 1942 to 1943
10. Franz Hofmann: SS captain and protective custody com-
    mander in Auschwitz I, and camp leader in Birkenau from
    January 12, 1942, to June 1944
11. Oswald Kaduk: SS corporal and block/reporting officer
    from 1942 to 1945
12. Stefan Baretski: SS private and block officer in Birkenau
    from 1942 to 1945

13. Heinrich Bischoff: SS private or corporal and block officer from 1942 to 1945

14. Arthur Breitwieser: SS private and "disinfector" in October 1941

15. Dr. Franz Lucas: SS first lieutenant and camp doctor in spring and summer 1944

16. Dr. Willi Frank: SS captain and head of the dental station from spring through fall 1944

17. Dr. Willi Schatz: SS second lieutenant and dentist from spring through fall 1944

18. Dr. Victor Capesius: SS captain from the end of 1943 to Christmas 1944, and SS major and head of the pharmacy in Auschwitz-Birkenau from September 11, 1944, to December 1944

19. Josef Klehr: SS staff sergeant, medical orderly, and head of the so-called gassing commando from 1941 to 1944

20. Herbert Scherpe: SS staff sergeant and medical orderly from 1942 to 43

21. Hans Nierzwicki: SS corporal and medical orderly from 1942 to 1944

22. Emil Hantl: SS private/corporal and medical orderly in the prisoner hospital from 1943 to 1944

23. Gerhard Neubert: SS staff sergeant and medical orderly from 1943 to 1944

24. Emil Bednarek: prisoner functionary—namely, block elder in the Auschwitz main camp between 1940 and 1945, and from winter 1942–1943 block elder in the penal division at Birkenau[57]

The charges against the defendants varied widely. Baer, Mulka, and Höcker faced no specific individual charges of murder, but were charged only with one offense that could be considered part of an ideological mentality and would therefore go to "base motives." For each of these three defendants the prosecution alleged that the accused had taken part

The defendants' bench: Viktor Capesius (in dark glasses), Oswald Kaduk (to his right), and Wilhelm Boger (to Capesius's left), April 3, 1964. Boger and Kaduk were among the "excess perpetrators" whose sadism came to dominate the trial and the press coverage. Capesius was the main camp pharmacist, responsible for dispensing poison as well as medication. SOURCE: DPA/LANDOV. PHOTO BY HEINZ-JÜRGEN GÖTTERT.

in the realization of the National Socialist extermination program (establishment, activity, securing of the gassing facilities, provision of the Zyklon B necessary for gassing, organization, processing, and securing of the selection of incoming transports of civilians through the watch guards, participation in the sorting process on the platform, transport of selected people for gassing to the gas chambers on trucks, supervision of selections in the camp for the commander), as adjutant/commander, who according to camp procedure was responsible for the quickest and most precise execution of his orders, in the knowledge of the illegality of these orders, in the measures created for killing these people.[58]

None of the other defendants had this charge against them; it applied only to the highest officials of the camp. It accused these men not only of conducting measures at the camp designed to exterminate people, but also consciously following orders that were illegal. Presumably, a murder conviction could be have been secured on such a charge, because "base motives" would have applied to anyone who killed Jews out of antisemitic beliefs; however, in the end none of these three defendants was convicted of murder. According to both Alfred Bongard and Ingo Müller, these motives could rarely be shown for the defendants who functioned in the camps but applied more to the policy makers like Hitler and Himmler. Defendants Mulka and Höcker could insist that they had not understood the illegality of the measures they enforced and that they themselves possessed no inner disposition toward racial hatred, and no one could find evidence to dispute this claim. It is noteworthy, though, that the prosecution made an attempt to convict these defendants of murder for their part in implementing the extermination policy.

In fact, much of the prosecutions' case against Baer rested on witnesses' testimony that he had instituted new measures in the camp that were "even more radical than Höss's."[59] Baer succeeded Arthur Liebehenschel as the camp commander, and many witnesses stated that Liebehenschel was a more benevolent camp leader. Some of the torture and abuses in the camp were limited during his time. However, once Baer appeared on the scene, the abuses resumed.[60] Baer was held responsible for making the camp the most efficient killing center it had ever been, and the prosecution cited as proof that Baer had stepped up the extermination program at Auschwitz the rapidity with which the Jews transported from Hungary were gassed. Because the prosecution counted on "participation in the development of the extermination program" to qualify under charge of the base motives, it was hoped that proof of Baer's ruthless escalation of the process would lead to a murder conviction.

Of course, most defendants, especially those in command positions, denied their understanding of or involvement in the Final Solution. All three of the camp superiors (Commander Baer and Adjutants Mulka and Höcker) insisted that they had never been on the platform or carried out selections. Although the indictment did not include their testimony, it did include statements by former SS witnesses and other defendants that refuted this contention. Former SS officer and witness Karl Heinrich Hykes testified: "When I am informed that the accused Baer, as the last commander, and the accused Mulka and Höcker, as adjutants to the commanders, say that they had nothing to do with the operation on the platform, I would call this representation ridiculous. In fact, I'd like to say this even more bluntly. Not only did all of these people participate; they personally made sure that the operation was working. I am certain that the above-mentioned were all on the ramp at Birkenau. I maintain this with a good conscience."[61]

Defendant Oswald Kaduk, accused of some of the most gruesome crimes at Auschwitz, implicated his fellow defendants: "I know for certain that Mulka was on the platform. These gentlemen should really not lie today, but as real men they should stand by what actually happened . . . The gentlemen came out [to the platform] in the jeep. I saw Baer, I saw Höss, and I saw Mulka. They went past the selection process and observed how it went on. They practically led the supervision of it." Defendant Franz Hofmann also insisted that every single guard at Auschwitz had to take part in selection in the platform, and when the commanders contended that they were never there for the arrival of a transport, he said, "I can only laugh at this."[62] There was very little doubt, for the prosecution or anyone who had been at Auschwitz, that the camp leaders had taken part in the killing operations.

In retrospect, the prosecution had an extremely difficult time convicting any defendant of murder on an "unspecified" charge. Schobert, Breitwieser, and Schatz were all charged with participation in various unspecified crimes. Schobert had three charges leveled against him: participation in a shooting action (no time or date, an "uncertain number of cases," in an unspecified place), selections of prisoners (in summer 1944, at least once), and gassing (at least once he supervised such an action).[63] The enormous amount of witness testimony placing the accused at these events (carefully examined by the prosecution before the charges were leveled) was still not specific enough. Breitwieser was charged with one count of participation in a selection, and Schatz with one charge of participation in an execution at the Black Wall. All three defendants were acquitted for lack of evidence.

Defendants Lucas, Schatz, and Frank were all charged only with one crime, and each received a different sentence. The charge (which was leveled against other defendants too, but in conjunction with other charges) was that the defendants took part "in supervising or carrying out selections, in an unspecified number of cases, after the arrival of Jewish prisoner transports at the platform of Auschwitz-Birkenau, whereby an unspecified number of prisoners were selected and ultimately transported for gassing to the gas chambers; there [they] supervised the dispensing of Zyklon B by the medical orderlies."[64]

For such defendants as Wilhelm Boger and Oswald Kaduk, the abundance of evidence and the sheer volume of specific charges of sadistic behavior and cruelty made the outcome appear certain before the trial began. The charges against these two changed little between the motion and the indictment. Some were removed and others added, depending on which witnesses agreed to appear on the stand and which crimes had been witnessed by numerous survivors. In the case of Boger, the women who worked in the Political Department provided the most detailed and consistent testimony on Boger's activities. The indictment quoted witness Helen Mehler on the subject of the Boger swing. Her testimony demonstrated his personal initiative and the requisite incriminating motives behind it. The prosecution paraphrased her testimony in the following way: "The witness can remember the accused Boger very well, who came to the Political Department a few months after her arrival at Auschwitz. This memory was lasting, because right after his appearance he determined that the interrogation methods were much too humane. The witness indicates that after a short time Boger introduced the so-called swing and used finger screws in his interrogations. In his interrogations, he often abused the prisoners until they were unrecognizable."[65]

Lilly Majerczik, Mehler's sister and also a secretary in the Political Department, made a similar report. Her testimony was even more graphic and left little doubt of Boger's brutality as a result of his quest for personal power. Her testimony as quoted in the indictment stated:

> Although all the SS people in the camp abused the prisoners, Boger was by far the cruelest. He noticeably wanted to be "number one" *(Primus)*. The office helpers were obliged, among other things, to stay at their machines when the SS people interrogated prisoners, women as well as men, and write down their statements. These interrogations took place in the offices themselves. I myself often had to put these interrogations by Boger onto paper. The prisoner had to sit on a chair, so that he was very close to me. Each prisoner who was interrogated by Boger, was immediately, in my presence, beaten with his [Boger's] riding crop and further on the floor

worked over on every body part with the heels of his shoes, so that the unlucky one was already lying there like a wreck before he could be properly interrogated.[66]

Majerczik's statement, though, is also unclear about Boger's activities, and this problem would become especially glaring during the trial itself. Whereas the pretrial testimony was given freely and without interruption and the witnesses could speak with authority, in the courtroom they would be questioned and badgered and their assertions would be dissected, so that all the activities they were certain had taken place suddenly came under suspicion. It is quite possible that the prosecutors had become so convinced of Boger's guilt by the multitude of statements and evidence that they did not imagine there could be any doubt. The continuation of her statement, however, foreshadows the problems to come. For example, she stated:

> Often, the prisoners didn't want to say everything in the interrogation. These prisoners would be brought by the SS people to the "swing" in a room that bordered on the office, so that the office helpers couldn't see what was happening. Although I was never in that room, and therefore didn't see the "swing," I learned from the prisoners that the victims were tied by their wrists to a stick on this apparatus and then worked over with a whip. Although the office helpers couldn't see this, they could of course hear the piercing wails of the victims. While being force to testify loudly, the prisoners would then have their nails ripped out and have to undergo other tortures . . . Countless times I personally saw victims of the "swing" who were brought back into the office, and who were unrecognizable from the blood and whose clothes were clinging in shreds to their bodies. Staff Sergeant Boger was one of the most zealous for tortures on the "swing," as I personally established.[67]

The fact that Majerczik did not actually see Boger using the "swing" would prove to be problematic. Further, her assertion that these interrogations almost always led to the death of the prisoner was vulnerable to the contention that this was conjecture. However, the prosecution included this testimony, and similar statements from countless other witnesses, to demonstrate the widespread knowledge that Boger was engaging in sadistic acts with fatal consequences.

Some witnesses testified to having actually seen the swing and having had occasion to be in the room when a prisoner was beaten senseless. Many of the charges against Boger did specify the date and place of a particular incident, and the names of the prisoners actually killed (the murder of Lilly Tofler, described in the previous chapter, appears as charge 7). Also, Boger was charged with ordering the execution of a Polish resistance group in the fall of 1943. Witness Henryk Bartoszewicz, prisoner #9,406, listed the names of at least ten men interrogated and tortured by Boger before he ultimately gave the order to shoot them. Very little doubt remained about Boger's guilt as an excess perpetrator. Interestingly, though, Boger's incensed response to the charges does appear in the indictment. He denied ever taking part in the executions at the Black Wall or in selections on the platform. He did admit to conducting intensified interrogations using the swing, but he claimed to have done so only on the orders of the head of the Political Department, Maximilian Grabner, and stated that the interrogations had never led to death. Boger insisted that none of his actions were taken on his personal initiative. As for murder, Boger made a similar declaration: "On the accusation of murder, I must especially point out that Auschwitz was the execution place for all death sentences that the courts-martial in the so-called General Gouvernment had handed down . . . I would like to point out that the General Gouverneur at the time, Dr. Frank, was responsible for the confirmation of every single court-martial judgment."[68]

According to Boger and many of the "small men" who appeared on the stand at the Auschwitz Trial and other German trials, the responsibility for all the murders that took place in the concentration camps lay solely on the shoulders of the higher SS officials and policy makers. Camp guards and members of police battalions used this defense time and again: they were incredulous that they should be held responsible for following orders and murdering millions of defenseless victims.

No defendant appeared more unsophisticated and brutish than Oswald Kaduk. Described as a primitive, uneducated man who could barely speak German, he was, as the testimony against him showed, fond of drowning, beating, whipping, shooting, running over, strangling, gassing, hanging, or in any other way killing prisoners. He was clearly prone to temper tantrums and had a drinking problem. He was famous for a certain kind of torture, described by numerous witnesses, in which he put a cane over a prisoner's neck and stood on it until the prisoner died. He would often shoot randomly into a group of prisoners, thus killing whoever was in the way. He was almost always drunk on such occasions, and the prisoners knew to be fearful of him when he appeared in their blocks obviously inebriated. The charges against Kaduk span almost fifty pages and are virtually entirely made up of individual instances of brutality and terror. In Kaduk's case, his response was noted after each charge, and each response was a denial of having taken part in any type of torture or murder. The prosecution made its skepticism known with such remarks as "the accused claims to have used his pistol only once or twice," and then only to shoot into the air.[69] Kaduk would be more easily convicted, for he fit perfectly into the West German penal code's definition of murder. He exemplified sadism, desire to kill, and even sexual drive (some of his crimes were directed at women's genitalia). Kaduk was a brute and a murderer, and his individual crimes overshadowed his larger crime, that of being a guard in Auschwitz for one purpose: to participate in the mass murder of European Jewry. The individual actions of these men upstaged the true crime that landed these them on the stand in 1963: Auschwitz and the Final Solution.

A few of the defendants, Baretski, Stark, and Bednarek included, behaved in such a depraved manner that, it is clear from the charges, sadistic individual initiative was provable. For the other defendants, varying degrees of motivation were obvious throughout the

Defendants Emil Hantl (left) and Oswald Kaduk (right), April 3, 1964. Kaduk was one of the most sadistic guards at Auschwitz; witnesses considered Hantl, by contrast, to have been more "decent" in his treatment of prisoners. SOURCE: DPA/LANDOV. PHOTO BY HEINZ-JÜRGEN GÖTTERT.

indictment. It should not be forgotten that the murder charge and the distinction between perpetrator and accomplice included more than one element; apart from sadism, base motives, treachery, and cruelty also qualified as inner dispositions motivating a person to commit murder. However, the trial and the judgment will show that these other charges were not commonly brought, as the emphasis fell more concretely on sheer violence and sensationalism. The more gruesome the crime, the stiffer the sentence. Only personal initiative and clear evidence that a defendant had not followed orders would result in a murder conviction. Nowhere does this become more obvious than in the testimony of Dr. Konrad Morgen, a former SS judge whose appearance on the stand forever altered the atmosphere in the courtroom. The indictment still had all the elements Fritz Bauer had originally intended, with the goal of bringing to trial Auschwitz in its entirety. But already at this early phase, the confines of the law were making themselves felt. They hampered the prosecution in its pursuit of the objectives: heightening public awareness and indicting the camp system as a whole. A distorted picture of Auschwitz and its criminals was emerging, in which many volunteer SS officers who had killed hundreds of people were beginning to look innocent, and a few vicious sadists were becoming the sole legal focus. The press picked up on this development. Invaluable information about the Nazi past was becoming public for the first time, but much of it was distorted because of the exigencies of the West German penal code.

CHAPTER 4

The Trial

THE TRIAL BEGAN on December 20, 1963, with the interrogations of defendants Mulka, Höcker, Boger, Stark, Dylewski, and Broad.[1] In the courtroom, the Holocaust faded almost entirely into the background, as excessive, unauthorized brutality was emphasized by the judges and the prosecution (in an attempt to convict the defendants of murder within the confines of the West German penal code), the defense (in order to exonerate their clients) the witnesses (because cross-examination limited them to specific descriptions of individual crimes), and the press (to sell newspapers).[2] The testimony of survivors and former SS judges and press coverage are useful focal points to demonstrate the increasing concentration at the trial on individual initiative.

Survivors on the Stand

Early scholarship on the Holocaust had a tendency to discount the value of survivors' narratives about their experiences. Documents and textual evidence took precedence over the victims' recollections and sometimes questionable memories. There is still debate today about the usefulness of such testimony. Peter Novick, in his book *The Holocaust in American Life*, states, "It is held that survivors' memories are an indispensable historical source that must be preserved, and elaborate projects are underway to collect them. In fact, those memories are not a very useful historical source . . . [That] is not to say that they haven't been, or won't continue to be, important in evoking the Holocaust experience."[3] Novick calls on the writings of Primo Levi, the foremost philosopher of the Holocaust, to solidify his argument that survivors' memories are problematic and blurry at best. Scholars see testimony as a valuable commentary on lived emotional experience that evokes the astounding pain and cruelty of Nazi persecution but sometimes consider that it lacks a substantial historical context and obscures evidence rather than illuminating it. I contend that survivor testimony is an essential historical source that has shaped the narrative of the Holocaust and provided historians with much of the basis for our knowledge of the Final Solution. This contribution is most obvious in the abundance of historical information, especially about the concentration camps and death camps, that has come from survivor testimony; the value of survivors' testimony far exceeds mere evocation of a visceral reaction. Such testimony in fact forms the foundation for our understanding of life at Auschwitz.

Survivor-witnesses made an essential contribution to the prosecution at the Auschwitz Trial by recounting the horrors of Auschwitz and reconstructing the actions of the accused at the camp with painstaking accuracy some twenty years after the fact. Necessarily, the state gathered evidence from survivors who had played important roles at the camp and worked under SS officers and observed them closely. The survivors could provide the court with extraordinary details of the activities of the camp guards. Most of the survivors who testified were Polish or Ukrainian political prisoners or German criminal prisoners, for Jews did not work closely with the SS guards and therefore did not supply much eyewitness evidence. As a conse-

View of the judges and jurors, April 3, 1964. There were three judges and six jurors at the Auschwitz Trial. SOURCE: DPA/LANDOV. PHOTO BY HEINZ-JÜRGEN GÖTTERT.

quence, the Jewish voice was muted at the trial. A few important Jewish witnesses did, however, try to bring their particular plight into the testimony. One of these was the first witness to take the stand at the trial.

On day 19, after the interrogations of all the defendants and the testimony of the expert historians, a soft-spoken Austrian Jewish doctor named Otto Wolken took the stand. He had arrived at Auschwitz on July 9, 1943, and been tattooed with prisoner number 128,828. He was initially taken to Auschwitz I, but very soon thereafter he was transferred along with eight hundred other prisoners to Auschwitz II. Also known as Birkenau, this second part of Auschwitz had been constructed in 1941. It had barracks for prisoners, mostly Jews, and after 1942 came to house the women's sector, the Theresienstadt camp, the Gypsy camp, and the medical-experimentation barracks. Birkenau's function mainly as a death camp, with four permanent

and two provisional gas chambers.[4] Wolken escaped the frequent selections for death in the gas chambers, thanks to his profession
and his acquaintance with the senior block prisoner (*Blockälteste*),
who had connections with the Political Department and persuaded
the administrators that Wolken could be useful at the hospital. He
worked in various sections of Birkenau until the liberation of Auschwitz in January 1945.[5]

After approximately two months in the work camp at Birkenau,
where he witnessed the incoming transport and the execution of
Greek Jews from Salonika and survived a selection in which four
thousand Jews were gassed overnight at the end of August, Wolken
was transferred to the emergency block in the men's quarantine section of Birkenau to work as a doctor. It was in this section that
Wolken witnessed the worst crimes of the various doctors on duty
there and the generally horrendous conditions at the camp. From
this position he witnessed defendant Baretski performing his favorite
ritual, a "rabbit hunt," in which prisoners at the roll call were ordered to take their hats off, and those who reacted too slowly were
beaten and murdered on the electrical fence. Wolken's testimony on
such matters was particularly valuable to the court because of his
meticulous recording of these events directly after they occurred. He
had begun to write a report or chronicle while still at Auschwitz after
its liberation in February 1945, for the use of the Polish courts and
the international tribunal at Nuremberg. Jan Sehn, the investigative
judge for the Commission for Investigating German Crimes in Poland, first used this testimony for the Polish tribunals on Nazi crimes
in Kraków in June 1945. Wolken later sent this report to the IAC and
Langbein, who passed it on to Frankfurt. Wolken's written chronicle of his experiences at Auschwitz and his oral testimony at the
trial were among the groundbreaking initial accounts of daily life
at Auschwitz. For this reason he spoke for almost two hours before
being interrupted and questioned by the judge at his first court appearance.

Wolken spoke not only as a witness to specific crimes but also as
an expert witness of sorts, whose recollections form the basis of

much of our current knowledge of the atrocities perpetrated at Birkenau. Wolken could state with certainty, for example, that one such action took place on April 10, 1943, when SS-men Baretski, Weiss, Kurpanik, and Dargelis slaughtered prisoners on a transport from Lemberg (now Lwów).[6] Despite the fact that twenty years had passed, Wolken could turn to his written reports and state with accuracy what he had seen. The courts gave Wolken extra time and ample leeway to describe events, circumstances, and impressions that went far beyond the necessary testimony required to convict specific defendants of specific crimes. The defense attorneys, particularly Hans Laternser, were openly irritated by Wolken's vast store of knowledge and in persistent interruptions attempted to establish how much of his testimony had been "influenced" by Hermann Langbein, who had communicated with many of the witnesses (including Wolken) at the pretrial phase. Wolken was clever in his responses, insisting that he was simply reading from his chronicle, written nineteen years before, and none of it had been influenced by anyone.[7] His usefulness to the Auschwitz Trial was twofold, then: not only did he give accurate testimony about defendant Baretski and help through his testimony at the pretrial interrogation to convict him of murder, but Wolken provided testimony on the nature of the everyday crimes at the camp. His role at the trial was unique. It offers one instance where Bauer's goal of trying the whole Auschwitz system came to fruition.

Another witness who made a vital contribution to the case in Frankfurt and to our historical information about the Auschwitz concentration camp was Hermann Langbein. Langbein, an Austrian Communist political prisoner, was sent from Dachau to Auschwitz on August 17, 1942. There he became the secretary of garrison doctor Dr. Eduard Wirths. Many witnesses, including Langbein himself, described Wirths as much less brutal than his predecessor, Dr. Kurt Uhlenbroock. Wirths ended some of the experimentation and decreased the number of fatal injections of phenol, carried out in large part by defendant Josef Klehr, that were performed daily. Langbein was in a position to witness almost everything that happened at the hospital or HKB of the camp; he also wrote the reports and sometimes secret memos that Wirths sent out to various SS administrators, including Dr. Enno Lolling, the chief medical administrator of the concentration camps.

On the stand, Langbein was given the opportunity to speak freely about what he had experienced at Auschwitz. This testimony did not necessarily relate to the defendants themselves and therefore would have been considered irrelevant at a normal murder trial. However, the courts allowed the most important witnesses to speak at length about the structure of the SS hierarchy at Auschwitz, the daily activities, and their impressions in general. This information helped create a more complete picture of the surroundings at the camp. For example, Langbein talked about the system of prisoner identification, and the badges that each type of prisoner wore. He made the important contribution of describing the terrifying conditions in the HKB, which all prisoners dreaded as a place of certain death. Sick prisoners would avoid being sent there at all costs, for they were generally pronounced unfit for work and then either gassed or sent to Block 20 for an "injection."[8]

Langbein's office overlooked the entrance room to the old crematorium, also called Crematorium 1, in the main camp. From this vantage point he could see prisoners being brought into the gas chambers alive and carried out dead by the Sonderkommando. On one night he saw that hundreds of sick prisoners were killed in the gas chambers as part of a "typhus action" (Fleckfieberaktion) designed to curb a terrible outbreak of the disease. According to Langbein, the camp authorities dealt with it by "gassing the lice along with the people."[9] Langbein's job included the registering of deaths, and the next day he added a huge list to the death books. According to his testimony, Dr. Wirths was forever battling the typhus epidemic at the camp and had signs posted everywhere announcing, "One louse, your death." Dr. Wirths promised that only prisoners who were deathly ill would be killed by injection, but Langbein and the rest of the inmates knew that this assurance was false—though Langbein said that Wirths really believed it and did not know that

Dr. Friedrich Entress, who was in charge of the injections, was carrying them out behind his back, along with defendant Klehr. Langbein sought the help of Ludwig Wörl, the camp elder *(Lagerälteste)* and senior block leader at the HKB, and the two started to document the injections performed on healthy prisoners. Wörl also testified at the trial. He and Langbein had arrived on the same transport and been involved together in the resistance movement. When they came upon a German prisoner who had been murdered, and whose medical records were complete because as a German national he was treated more humanely, they managed to convince Wirths, who reprimanded Entress. The injections tapered off and eventually stopped in the spring of 1943.

Langbein stated that prisoners were most fearful of defendant Klehr, because he was known to undertake injections on his own initiative, as mentioned in discussion of the pretrial testimony by witness Paczuła and others. When the injections stopped, Klehr was promoted from corporal to staff sergeant and put in charge of throwing the gas pellets into the gas chambers—which Langbein could see from his room. Such details not only helped to convict Klehr of murder, but painted a vivid picture of the camp itself. Langbein did his best to describe the conditions at the camp, although for the most part he continued to say that they were "unimaginable." Yet his depictions silenced the courtroom and astounded the public. His most horrific testimony came in his description of the HKB in the Gypsy camp. The Gypsy camp was a cruel experiment in which families were allowed to live and function and continue to suppose that they would survive, until they were all gassed in one night in 1944. Before this, the hospital in the Gypsy camp allowed women to give birth. The babies were immediately tattooed and then taken to the corpse closet; according to Langbein, it contained a "mountain of children's corpses . . . among which were the rats."[10]

Langbein provided insight into the ability of an individual to change the atmosphere, and in fact the fate of many people, within the camp. Such a change came in November 1943, when Arthur Liebehenschel replaced Commander Höss. From then on, a calmer atmosphere began to prevail at the camp, as Liebehenschel made many improvements: he had the standing cells ripped up, he brought in prisoner Wörl, a gentle, respected man, as senior block leader of the entire Auschwitz I camp, and the selections within the camp stopped. "In general," said Langbein, "one could establish that even those SS members who were very bloodthirsty before became a bit more reserved because they realized that their fanaticism would not necessarily be tolerated anymore."[11] It was important for Langbein, and for the prosecutors, to demonstrate that despite orders from Berlin that made certain executions inevitable, individual guards could make a difference and save lives if they were so inclined. The implication, of course, was that they could also commit murder on their own initiative (as Langbein described), and that was exactly what the prosecutors were trying to prove.

A fellow prisoner from the hospital blocks, Dr. Ella Lingens, provided corroboration on the witness stand. When Judge Hofmeyer asked her, "Do you wish to say that everyone could decide for himself to be either good or evil in Auschwitz?" Lingens replied, "That is exactly what I wish to say. It was pure free will. Everyone could do as he wished and never know the consequences—one could kill thousands, and nothing would happen, or kill one person and be in trouble."[12] Langbein also made it clear that the guards knew that they were doing something evil, particularly during the spring of 1944 when the Hungarian transports came in. They became nervous, and began to acknowledge their possible guilt by telling prisoners, "We're going to get it, but you're coming with us."[13] In the summer of 1944, Liebehenschel, accused of being "too soft," was replaced by Richard Baer, whom Langbein described as much more like Höss, albeit lazier and less fanatical. The improvements immediately began to disappear, and with the new commander came a new camp elder who terrorized the inmates once again.

Langbein's account of camp life was in some ways less helpful to the prosecution's case than it has become to the general understanding of life in Auschwitz. He supplied very few specific details about any of the defendants, except Josef Klehr. He was better at giving his impressions of the defendants' characters, but often these worked against him; For example, in describing defendants Neubert and Hantl, Langbein characterized both as reluctant to kill and "decent" in their relationships with prisoners. He qualified these remarks, though, by interjecting: "Please remember that this was relative." The defense lawyers instantly cross-examined him on this point, asking him point blank: "No, no, tell us in the absolute; was he brutal?" Langbein had to answer in the negative.[14] The shades of complicity and the overall circumstances of which Langbein was trying to remind the court—that these were volunteer SS officers at a concentration camp—were irrelevant to the law. It mattered only if Hantl or Neubert had been brutal or sadistic in their actions.

Still, Langbein's testimony was invaluable for the image of Auschwitz that was being reconstructed before the eyes of the public in West Germany in 1964. History was being made, for a real sense of it did not yet exist at that time. The trial itself made history when the trial participants visited Auschwitz in December 1964, after civil plaintiff Christian Raabe suggested it and the Supreme Court ruled that the visit was important to the case. The court took most of the lawyers and some of the defendants with them to the site of the camp. The court's unusual visit to Auschwitz reaffirmed much of what Langbein had described geographically. The court received visual confirmation of his depiction of the location of his room, the hospital blocks, the crematoriums, and the view he had had, and his testimony gained even more credibility. The court took these details very seriously because they helped establish proof of the actions of the defendants. The information also forms the basis for a great deal of the evidence we have today about Auschwitz.

The difficulties with survivor testimony and the limitations of the law become obvious in the testimony of Walter Petzold. Petzold was a political prisoner brought to the camp in 1941. Much of his testimony was directed against defendant Arthur Breitwieser. According to Petzold, he saw Breitwieser shaking gas pellets into the gas chamber for the first gassing action at the camp, in the fall of 1941. The judge asked Petzold for very specific details about this particular incident, which took place at night, at a distance of sixty meters from the witness. Nevertheless, Petzold insisted he was right. The questioning continued, becoming more specific, until it became clear that from where Petzold had been standing, he could not have seen the actual hole into which the gas was shaken, only the defendant standing over some part of the gas chamber and shaking the canister. To make matters worse, Petzold's pretrial testimony was read aloud and contradictions were found between his earlier statements and his trial testimony; for example, whereas he reported in his first interrogation that he had overheard a conversation between Breitwieser and Grabner, at the trial itself he could no longer remember what they had been discussing. The details of the conversation were unimportant to the court; however, the inconsistency in this story made him appear an unreliable witness. The court's visit to Auschwitz in December 1964 gave the final blow to Petzold's credibility, for it was determined there that it would have been impossible for him to have seen the gassing from the spot he had described. His account of Breitwieser's activities was not enough for a conviction, and Breitwieser was subsequently acquitted.[15]

Often the prosecutors were frustrated, in their attempts to get exact, eyewitness details of the defendants' actions, by the very nature of Auschwitz and the Nazi regime. Survivors of course did not expect to become survivors. After what they had witnessed at Auschwitz, particularly those on the stand in Frankfurt who had seen so much murder and had been aware that they "knew too much" to be allowed to live, they had had little hope that they might come out alive. They certainly had had little inkling of any possibility that the SS guards would come to trial twenty years later. Therefore, very few prisoners actually wrote accounts or made concerted attempts to observe the actions of the SS officers. In fact, they often did everything to avoid doing so. This was the case with Dr. Tadeusz Paczuła, whose pretrial testimony on Josef Klehr I discuss in Chapter 2. At the trial Paczuła was questioned once again about the incident on Christmas Eve in 1942, when Klehr undertook his own selection and began injecting prisoners. According to Paczuła, the prisoners were taken from the camp to Block 28, and Klehr selected forty of them for injections. These forty prisoners were then taken to Block 20, where prisoner Głowa took their cards and wrote their notices of death, while they were still alive and standing naked in the corridor. Paczuła then recorded the death notices. Judge Hofmeyer then asked Paczuła: "Did you see Klehr performing the injections with your own eyes?" Paczuła replied: "I could see, [but] I didn't want to see."[16] In fact, Paczuła went on, when he had to communicate with Klehr, to give him a message, for example, he would walk into Block 20, ask the corpse bearer if someone was being killed, and if so, he would wait outside until it was over. He could see Klehr with his jacket off, his sleeves rolled up, wearing a rubber jacket and rubber gloves with a needle approximately twenty centimeters in length in his hand. In the case of Klehr, so much damning evidence and so much corroboration by other witnesses existed that he was convicted of murder; however, Paczuła's testimony on its own would not have been enough to convict him. Paczuła's natural instinct to shield himself from the sight of killing frustrated the prosecution and the judge.[17] The same problem occurred with the witness Dr. Władysław Fejkiel, who worked as a nurse at the hospital from January 1941 until January 1945. Fejkiel could describe the rooms where the injections had taken place; he knew that approximately thirty thousand people had been killed, and that the victims were initially sick Jews, then sick Aryans, then healthy prisoners. He also knew that Dr. Entress, then Klehr, then Scherpe, and then Hantl had performed the injections. When Judge Hofmeyer asked him if he had actually seen the injections, however, Fejkiel responded, "I was never in the room; we didn't want to see—it wasn't something interesting to us." Hofmeyer replied in exasperation: "Maybe for you, but for us it would be most interesting to know how Klehr participated in this." Hofmeyer then collected himself and, after watching the witness scramble to remember, straining for the memories, told him, "I won't be angry with you if you don't know."[18]

In the defense cross-examination, defendant Hantl's lawyer, Herbert Naumann, attempted to call Paczuła as an exonerating witness for his client. Naumann referred to Paczuła's pretrial investigation, in which he had said that Hantl very often tried to help people. Hantl also spoke at this point, presenting a long list of actions he had taken to save people's lives, including taking a friend's father off the selection list. Paczuła had spoken of Hantl's character, and he reiterated that he was kinder than the rest; however, said Paczuła, "Hantl was a disappointment to me. I saw him acting only well and kindly to prisoners, but I found out later, in the camp in 1944, that he took part in the injections . . . He didn't do good things, but he didn't do bad things either. He treated us politely."[19] Paczuła, like Langbein, attempted to establish some balance in the courtroom, to underscore the circumstances into which people like Hantl had put themselves. Paczuła did not want to portray Hantl as a "good guy," despite the fact that he was nicer than many others. Even so, Hantl's lack of individual initiative, sadism, or (provable) base motives got him a conviction of aiding and abetting murder, with a sentence of three and a half years in prison.

One of the greatest difficulties the courts faced was the discrepancy between the pretrial and trial interrogations. An excellent example is the contradictory testimony of the survivor Leon Czekalski, one of the prosecution's most important witnesses. His testimony before the trial described a massacre of ninety-four men and eight women by defendant Boger and SS officer Palitsch, which he claimed to have seen from an attic window. At the trial itself, he changed his story and reported that from the first floor he saw the prisoners being led into the crematorium, and then he ran upstairs (to the attic) and he saw two people come out into the yard between Blocks 10 and 11, where they were shot. He claimed in the courtroom that the women were already dead, and that Palitsch was not there. Much of what he knew had come from a conversation with Rottenführer Barre and not from eyewitness experience.[20] Czekalski had a difficult time distinguishing his own experiences from hearsay. In the pretrial testimony, no one questioned Czekalski on the accuracy of these details, and he could therefore freely describe as fact what he may not actually have witnessed with his own eyes. At the trial, though, his testimony was less credible; for example, charges from the indictment that Boger had led a group of Hungarian Jews into the crematorium in 1944 had to be dropped when Czekalski admitted on the stand that he had seen Boger leading a group of prisoners but had not seen them go directly into the crematorium (he had heard this later on). There was evidently no doubt in Czekalski's mind that Boger had undertaken such tasks, and the chances are good that he was right; however, official charges that stemmed from pretrial testimony like Czekalski's did not always hold up in court.

The survivors were not immune to disputation among themselves. This was particularly evident in the relationship between Polish and Ukrainian witnesses. The testimony of Jósef Kral provides an interesting glimpse into this conflict and demonstrates yet another difficulty the court faced in the attempt to find out the exact truth about each defendant. Kral's testimony was by far the most gruesome and devastating of any from witnesses at the trial. Shaken and frightened on the stand, he broke down more than once during his testimony. He had been a prisoner of the Political Department and therefore knew defendants Boger and Stark very well. He had spent six weeks in a standing cell, during which time he was fed three meals and was "interrogated" every day for three to four hours, sometimes by Boger on the infamous swing. His sufferings were unimaginable. He had been forced to lick moisture from the walls of the standing cell; he had watched his friend next to him die after eating his own shoes; he was force-fed plates of salty herring after six weeks with no food and was then forced to ingest what he had vomited back onto the plate; he was hung by his arms, which were strapped behind his back, until they broke *(Pfahlhängen)*. Judge Hofmeyer, who showed great sensitivity toward Kral, interrupted defense attorney Laternser any time he tried to cross-examine Kral. Kral's testimony prompted Judge Hofmeyer to change the charge against Hans Stark from aiding and abetting murder to perpetrating murder, after Kral reported that he had stood four meters from Stark and watched him kill two of his friends from Katowice with a shovel. Despite the defense's protests that this was new evidence and could not be admitted in court, Stark was put into investigative detention the same day.[21]

Once Kral finished testifying, however, the defense brought in two witnesses, both Ukrainian, who testified that Kral was a brutal "Oberkapo" and that he was responsible for beating to death the two Bandera brothers, famous Ukrainian resistance fighters who died at Auschwitz. Both these witnesses were active Communists who had worked together with the Bandera brothers, and neither could provide very specific details about Kral's activities. They had clearly been brought in to discredit the witness. Kral was then exonerated by Dr. Stanisław Kłodziński, who testified on the stand that despite the animosity between Polish and Ukrainian prisoners, they had a great deal of contact with each other and Kłodziński had never heard before that Kral was supposedly guilty of this murder. In fact, Kłodziński portrayed Kral as a hero for enduring his torture and speaking about it afterward.[22] The witness Fejkiel further exonerated Kral, stating that the Bandera group had been "privileged prisoners" (Ehrenhäftlinge) who often worked together with the SS, and one was a spy for the Political Department. It was difficult for the court to determine how much of this testimony was accurate and how much was the result of political and national divisions among the prisoners within the camp. In the end, the court did not accept all Kral's testimony because of the questions surrounding his credibility; however, the general information about life in Auschwitz that he provided remains part of the greater body of historical knowledge about the camp.

One of the best ways for the court to determine how much of the testimony was accurate, and how much was impaired by prisoners' loss of memory or by political and national divisions among the prisoners at the camp, was through corroboration. The judges and the prosecution established the validity of the testimony by asking multiple witnesses for exact information on seemingly irrelevant details; for example, Paczuła, Kłodziński, Kral, and Fejkiel were all asked to describe how the blocks were built, how extensive the foundations were, how much groundwater existed, how big the cells were, how many people were in them, and other, similar questions. If the witnesses could supply these details, which could be verified by other witnesses and by the on-site visit to the camp, their testimony could be accepted, despite some inevitable lapses of memory.

Kral's testimony was corroborated by the next witness, Kazimierz Smolen, a survivor of Auschwitz and the director of the Auschwitz museum at the time of the trial. According to Smolen, when he was organizing the exhibitions and archives for the museum in 1959, no proper description of the Boger swing was yet available. He turned to Hermann Langbein, who gave him Kral's name. Kral provided the first real information about the swing and a representation of it to the museum. It also appeared in the pretrial files for the Auschwitz case.[23]

In the courtroom, truth is established through the testimony of witnesses about what they have seen. The accumulation of evidence leads to a verdict in which it is decided whether something did or did not happen. The law of every democratic nation puts its trust in witness testimony as the ultimate source of fact, of truth, and of the history of what has happened. There are, of course, flaws in this system, as it relies on human memory and is bound by the law. The frustrating results of these flaws were most obvious in the difficulties survivors sometimes had giving specific information about the defendants twenty years after the end of the Holocaust. In their eyes, the people at Auschwitz who killed people were all guilty of murder. The prosecution hoped to show this too. But failing memories and the narrow definition of murder made the achievement of this goal impossible in many cases. In *Admitting the Holocaust*, Lawrence Langer argues that witnesses were incapable of presenting a coherent, accurate depiction of life in Auschwitz because the defense could tear apart their every statement, and the nature of cross-interrogation made testimony disjointed and confusing. Langer writes: "Readers of the proceedings of the so-called Auschwitz Trial . . . will discover not a narrative leading to insight and understanding, but a futile dispute between accusers and accused . . . Little in this bizarre courtroom drama leads to a unified vision of the place we call

Defendant William Boger enters the court room. Boger, who was known as the Devil of Birkenau, became the most famous defendant because he had invented a torture machine called the Boger swing.
SOURCE: DPA/LANDOV. PHOTO BY HEINZ-JÜRGEN GÖTTERT.

Auschwitz. Scenes remain episodic and anecdotal; scenarios never coalesce; characters stay vague, as protagonists dissolve into helpless victims . . . while antagonists collapse into mistaken identities or innocent puppets moved from afar."[24]

Langer's depiction of the trial as a "futile courtroom dispute" misassigns the reasons for the deficiencies of the trial.[25] The distorted consequences of the trial both legally and in its public representation derived not from the inadequacies of eyewitness testimony but rather from the requirements of the German penal code and the kind of testimony that was needed to secure convictions. By design, the trial did not accurately portray the role of all guards at Auschwitz. This was not its purpose. Still, a new historical understanding of Auschwitz emerged from the testimony of witnesses who were given the opportunity to speak about their experiences. Through rigorous interrogation, cross-examination, and legal inquiry, a clearer picture of past events emerged than had existed before. At the Auschwitz Trial, the history of the camp was reconstructed for the first time before a mass public audience.

According to Martin Walser, who spent time in the courtroom, those moments that though not necessarily historically exact were emotionally evocative made Auschwitz more present and comprehensible than the "hell on earth" that was otherwise inconceivable. Walser wrote, "When a former 'prisoner' cannot go on speaking in the courtroom, when he has the courage to even look at his former torturer, in order to identify him . . . , when for a few minutes the memory gives forth its horrible contents, simple and unabridged, then a little bit of Auschwitz becomes real."[26] Walser was most interested in the representation of the survivors in the public eye, and most especially in the press. Although I return to the subject of the press later in this chapter, I will note here that press reports are a good indication of the importance of survivor testimony to the trial and to public awareness of Auschwitz and the SS camp system. Most of what appeared in the newspapers was based on the courtroom testimony of the survivors. So although the public could have no access to the files and tapes for the trials for thirty years after the trial, the descriptions of everyday life at Auschwitz became part of the public understanding about the camp and provided invaluable factual information for historical reconstruction of the crimes of the Holocaust.

Survivors supplied the specific details needed to convict the defendants, and the general information to create a clear image of the camp. Some had roles at the camp that provided them with a great deal of insider information. Others were determined to document accurately what they experienced, either for purposes of resistance and as part of the effort to smuggle out the information, or because they wanted to be sure that the crimes did not go unnoticed. Much of what historians know about Auschwitz-Birkenau came from this testimony. Its historical value should not be overlooked.

The Morgen Commission

Former SS officers also testified at the trial, both for the prosecution and for the defense. Neither the prosecution nor the defense called many former SS members, largely because they were reluctant and fearful about being implicated themselves, or because their testimony was often unusable, riddled with lies and omissions.[27] Many former SS officers were not sworn in on the stand (swearing in, in the German criminal courts, is a process that takes place after the witness has testified). One group of former SS witnesses, though, proved terribly important to the prosecution's case.

At the end of 1943, Reichsführer SS Himmler sent judges Konrad Morgen, Gerhard Wiebeck, and Wilhelm Reimers, as part of the Special Commission and Police Court in Kraków, to Auschwitz to investigate alleged corrupt practices by SS guards. This included the theft of valuables from new transports (stored in the Canada bunker of the camp) and excessive cruelty and murder not ordered by the officials of the RSHA or the WVHA in Berlin.[28] The former SS judges personify the paradoxical situation that the prosecutors and judge at Frankfurt faced. The cross-examination of these SS witnesses signified a turning point at the trial, in that it brought the constraints of the law most glaringly and publicly to the fore.

The defendants and their attorneys could not use the testimony of these witnesses to demonstrate the superior-orders *(Befehlsnotstand)* defense used by many guards who insisted that they were only following orders. Instead, the prosecution used the former SS judges to show that the actions of the defendants on the stand had been undertaken on individual initiative and in knowledge of the illegality of the act, and could therefore be tried and punished as perpetration of murder. Thus the ironic situation arose in which the standard of the Nazi state was adopted in the courtroom in Frankfurt in order to try the very crimes committed under that state. Judge Hofmeyer repeatedly had to ask witnesses which actions had been ordered by Berlin and which by the camp commanders, knowing full well that this lent an air of legality to the command to murder millions at Auschwitz. This line of questioning reached its most extreme form with the testimony of Dr. Morgen.

Georg Konrad Morgen was already familiar with war crimes proceedings. He had been a witness in August 1946 at the Nuremberg trial, where he testified for the defense on the question of the criminality of the SS as an organization.[29] Morgen was first interviewed for the Auschwitz investigation on March 8, 1962. Dr. Heinz Düx, the court's investigative judge, interrogated him in the "interim trial phase." By that time, the prosecution had submitted its case to the district court of Frankfurt and the court had taken over the investigation and proceeded with its own inquiry to determine the validity of the prosecution's case. This was not the first time Morgen had appeared in the files. His testimony from another case—against two Buchenwald guards at the district court in Cologne in January 1961 —appeared in the pretrial files of the Auschwitz Trial at the same time. In that interrogation, Morgen described his educational history and his entrance into the Nazi party and then the SS. According to Morgen, in June 1943 he became an official in the Reich's criminal police department (Reichskriminalpolizeiamt), which was part of Office 5 of the RSHA. He worked on cases involving capital crimes, and his first job was as part of an investigation into corruption at Buchenwald.[30] Morgen's testimony on his duties at Buchenwald set the parameters for what was to be considered questionable guard behavior, both for the Nazis and for the court at Frankfurt. He reported:

> During my investigations at individual camps, I pursued numerous criminal offenses that were made known to me and which were, in my opinion, pursuable. It was not possible for me to press charges against people who had carried out the orders of my own court superiors *[Gerichtsherren]*, for example the executions that had been ordered by Reichsführer Himmler, or the carrying out of euthanasia, which after all went back to an order by Hitler. *Gerichtsherr* is an institution of the war crimes investigation law, which gave the military commanders [Hitler and Himmler] jurisdiction in the widest sense, including over the opening of investigations, the issuing of arrest warrants, indictments, appeals, confirmation or dismissal of a sentence, its execution, and the power to pardon. However, insofar as I was informed of crimes against life or limb that occurred on the private initiative of an SS member, I began investigations against them.[31]

In his interrogation for the Auschwitz Trial, Morgen was more specific about the circumstances at the camp. He stated that he had gone to Auschwitz on his own accord after his investigations at Buchenwald led him to suspect that similar corrupt activities must also be going on at the much larger camp. After seeing that the SS in the Canada bunker at Auschwitz were a "bunch of demoralized and brutalized parasites" and finding heaps of stolen gold and jewelry in their coats, he requested that a *Sonderkommission* be created to investigate corruption. He immediately arrested the guards who had been stealing, and Boger was among them. His activities continued when he decided to widen the investigation to include offenses of excessive brutality after discovering that Commander Höss had carried out a relationship with a female prisoner named Hodys. When he found out that she was pregnant, Höss had her put into a standing cell and left her to die of starvation. Luckily, Morgen "came just in time to save this woman and had her transferred to a clinic in Munich." Höss was then transferred from Auschwitz. Still, Morgen defended Höss: "I don't mean to imply that Höss was in principle a bad person . . . The overall circumstances in Auschwitz . . . at that time demoralized him as well. No person can bear to rule boundlessly over life and death, to turn a person into ashes from one minute to the next."[32]

Morgen's pretrial testimony was a carefully crafted narrative in which he gave away few specific details about the defendants, meanwhile attempting to present himself as a tireless and courageous pursuer of justice. He did not remember Franz Hofmann, although he had guided Morgen through the camp, and remembered only having possibly investigated Boger for corruption and murder offenses. He could no longer remember the trial in Weimar in 1944 of Maximilian Grabner, the head of the Political Department at Auschwitz who was notorious for excessive cruelty. This forgetfulness was implausible, given that Grabner's arrest had been a central part of the SS investigative commission's activities; indeed, at one point Morgen insisted that he had arrested Grabner himself. Yet he presented himself as an instigator of reform. He had seen the gassings, and although he could not say for sure, he thought it possible that "because of my report in 1944, the gassings were discontinued."[33] At the very least, he imagined that he was responsible for ending the secrecy surrounding the gassings and making them public knowledge. He could not do more than this, however, because in the end, the final authority was Hitler's.

Morgen referred to the overriding authority of Hitler and Himmler once again at the trial. He did so with such eloquence and force that his testimony commanded authority. When Judge Hofmeyer asked him about the atrocities taking place in the camp and inquired why he had not taken everyone with any power and responsibility and arrested them, Morgen insisted that he had not had the authority to arrest people. In a normal legal atmosphere, he would have sent a proposal to the public prosecutors of a district, and it would have gone through all the channels of justice that were part of the bureaucratic chain. However, during the Nazi period, under military jurisdiction (*Kriegsgerichtbarkeit*), all judges were responsible to Hitler and Himmler. Therefore, he would have had to ask Hitler and Himmler to open an investigation against themselves; Hitler would have been the judge, the prosecutor, and the law enforcer. According to Morgen, Hitler was the "chancellor of the Reich, the president, the chief commanding officer of the Wehrmacht, the lawmaker, and the highest officer of the law [*Oberstgerichtgeber*]."[34]

Morgen insisted both in the pretrial interrogations and at the trial that he had absolutely no power beyond his duty to investigate acts of private initiative such as theft, brutality, and unauthorized murder. The blame for everything else lay squarely on Hitler's shoulders and was subject to the complex laws of military jurisdiction. In a remarkable performance, Morgen expressed his disgust at the slaughter going on at Auschwitz and his regret that it had been impossible for him to do anything to stop it. Instead, then, he used his small role to investigate and prosecute wayward crimes, hoping that he would at least take some of the killers out of the system.[35] In this way, in Morgen's version, he began investigating corruption at Auschwitz.

Morgen testified that to his surprise (because, he maintained, he had no prior knowledge of what Auschwitz was and how many millions of people were being murdered), his office had intercepted a box filled with three pieces of gold that had been sent by a medical orderly at Auschwitz to his wife. Morgen discovered that this was high-carat tooth gold, melted together into the size of fists. Morgen realized that "twenty, fifty, one hundred thousand corpses must have made up this one package." This was a chilling thought; but for Morgen's purposes, "what was even more unbelievable was that the perpetrator [had] managed to keep a quantity without being noticed."[36] Morgen attempted to convert his appearance on the stand into the story of his ignorance about this camp called Auschwitz. He said, "From this point, I comprehended for the first time that Auschwitz, unknown at that time . . . must have been one of the largest places of human destruction that the world had ever seen."[37]

Morgen insisted that he would have liked to investigate and try everyone involved in the killing at Auschwitz. But because his investigation had been ordered by the very men committing the crimes, he could investigate only corruption in the implementation of the orders.[38] He claimed to know, for example, that Oswald Pohl, head of the WVHA, was stealing from the gold as well; he and his closest co-workers had set up a system whereby some of the gold sent to Degussa in Frankfurt—a gold- and silver-melting company—was redirected into an account there from which Pohl could siphon off hundreds of thousands of marks. Obviously, Pohl was Morgen's superior in rank and therefore above investigation, and so Morgen started with the smaller men.

During his time at Auschwitz, Morgen became aware of the horrifying activities in the Political Department, especially the "Stalin swing" (presumably his mistaken name for the Boger swing). According to Morgen, defendant Wilhelm Boger and Maximilian Grabner had been among the most brutal guards at Auschwitz and had taken part in executions "of their own accord; they were not ordered to do so, and they did not give any notices of death to their bosses."[39] Morgen decided to try these intensified interrogations as murder, and he had Grabner arrested. He was then ordered to see Lieutenant General Heinrich Müller, chief of police at the RSHA in Berlin. According to historian Gerhard Reitlinger, Himmler's decision to send Morgen to Auschwitz was a strange one, for "he must have known that he would come up against Kaltenbrunner, Nebe, and Müller" (that is, Ernst Kaltenbrunner, Arthur Nebe, and Heinrich Müller).[40] In fact, at his pretrial interrogation in March 1962, Morgen addressed the question of opposition to his work there: "As far as I know, the sharpest resistance came from General Pohl, the chief of the Gestapo, Lieutenant General Müller, and the head of the RSHA, General Dr. Kaltenbrunner. They tried every conceivable means of stopping me, gently at first and then with offers of a fabulous career in another section of the SS, then through typical military measures, through complaints to the Reichsführer SS and the Reich criminal police, through massive threats, and finally through an attack on my investigative commission, in which our entire office barracks and files were destroyed through arson."[41] Reit-linger seems to believe Morgen's contention that he genuinely wanted to punish the atrocities of Auschwitz: "He believed that if he brought a charge against some of the individual murderers in the camp, the official system of mass murder at the crematoria would have to come to light, too."[42] In his study of the Wehrmacht War Crimes Bureau, historian Alfred-Maurice de Zayas also presents Morgen as an honest judge who did his best to stop the extermina-tion process when he finally learned about it in his first investi-gations of corruption at the Buchenwald concentration camp. De Zayas also comments on Morgen's efforts at Auschwitz, and particu-larly his attempt to put Grabner behind bars and to have Adolf Eichmann investigated.[43] Despite these seemingly noble pursuits, I contend that Morgen presented himself in a much more positive light after the fact, to avoid investigations into his own activities. His reluctance to state anything specific about the defendants on the stand in Frankfurt (despite his having investigated Boger and the in-jections) demonstrates that he was not willing to provide specific, pertinent information to the court.

In Müller's office, Morgen was severely reprimanded for his activ-ities at Auschwitz, particularly the arrest of the head of the Political Department. Müller told Morgen that he "had no understanding of his duties as part of the state police." Morgen, in what must have been a moment of immense moral courage, pleaded with Müller: "After all, we still live in a constitutional state, and there are limits that even the Gestapo has to hold themselves to." Müller turned "as white as calcium" and threw Morgen out of his office. In yet another courageous act, Morgen went back "into the lion's den" and tried a new approach with Müller. Asking for advice, in a deferential tone, Morgen again entered into conversation with him, which according to Morgen went as follows:

> MORGEN: Herr Müller, isn't it the Führer, and you, the chief
>   of the Gestapo, who have the ultimate decision on every
>   sentence?
> MÜLLER: Yes.

MORGEN: Well, how would you judge it, if someone went far
   beyond your orders, and without informing you,
   through his own decision, killed a hard-working prisoner?

MÜLLER: That's impossible, that just doesn't happen!

MORGEN: You see, Lieutenant General, Sir, that is how people are ignoring your authority in the camps, that is
   what Grabner did, and that is why I arrested him.

MÜLLER: Well, this is very different, this I understand.
   (Müller then recalled some of Grabner's disobedience
   himself.)[44]

Grabner was indicted for murder in at least two thousand cases.
Morgen was able to open investigations against Rudolf Höss, camp
commander, Hans Aumeier, camp leader, and others, including
Boger. The trial against Grabner, however, was dismissed midway
through the proceedings, and he was transferred to Berlin.[45]

At the Auschwitz Trial, Morgen created the impression that he
was a good man trying to do something about the injustices, resisting
in his own ingenious way. His impassioned performance and informed description of what was one of the only channels for punishing the crimes of the Holocaust at the time that it was occurring was
so convincing that it helped reinforce and legitimize the Nazi rules
of behavior at Auschwitz. Morgen argued that the Nazi laws of procedure were so ruthlessly enforced that it was impossible for him
to investigate anyone but the guards who took the law into their
own hands and undermined the authority of people like Müller.
Whether or not his claim was accurate, it lent credibility to Nazi
laws and diminished the legal responsibility of subordinates who carried out the orders of their superiors, in that it focused attention on
those who went beyond these orders.

The question-and-answer exchange between Judge Hofmeyer and
Dr. Morgen once again demonstrated the problems with the law.
During his appearance on the stand, Morgen suddenly found himself unable to remember any specific details about any of the defendants; for example, he knew only vaguely about the Boger swing or

the fact that it was illegal, because not one protocol was taken during any of the interrogations—although the procedure was required in the camp regulations that appeared in the indictment. When the judge broached the subject of the injection of prisoners with phenol, Morgen was also reticent. When reminded that defendant Josef Klehr was a medical orderly involved in the injections, Morgen remembered that Klehr had taken part in secret injections and had used fake death certificates. He knew that Klehr was doing something illegal. Morgen said that those who had had orders "did not have to fear the light of day"; but that people like Klehr, who had "tried to throw sand in the eyes" of the commanders and had conducted the injections in such secrecy, knew that it was forbidden. The interrogation continued:

> HOFMEYER: Were all the injections unlawful?
> MORGEN: In some of the euthanasia cases, they were done
> legally, if they were incurably ill. "14F13"—the heading
> for death cases—was also a euphemism for the euthanasia program.
> HOFMEYER: Was it ordered?
> MORGEN: Yes, it went out from the Reich head doctor, von
> Grabitz.[46]

Hofmeyer moved on to the subject of intensified interrogations. He asked Morgen "what was allowed, when was it allowed, and who allowed it," to the noticeable irritation of the audience in the courtroom. Morgen answered by reciting almost verbatim the camp regulations for interrogation that appear in Chapter 3. The prosecution's greatest stride forward with Morgen came in the form of an answer to Hofmeyer's question about the Boger swing:

> HOFMEYER: Was the swing officially or unofficially allowed
> in the framework of the intensified interrogations?
> MORGEN: As far as I know, it was not allowed. After
> Grabner's arrest, Müller did not say it was allowed.

HOFMEYER: So you arrested Grabner for murder, but also for
    using the swing?
MORGEN: Yes.
HOFMEYER: So what about Boger . . . ?
MORGEN: I can't remember any details.[47]

Hofmeyer's voice registered annoyance that Morgen could not give any specific details about Boger. Morgen appealed to Hofmeyer as a colleague, saying that after twenty years it was difficult to remember. "You, as fellow judges, would understand this." Still, Hofmeyer was relentless. On the subject of the Black Wall, an execution site at Auschwitz between Blocks 10 and 11, Hofmeyer pressed Morgen on his pretrial testimony about Boger's participation in executions there along with another guard. Morgen insisted on the stand that his memory was not "reliable anymore."[48]

In retrospect, Hofmeyer's questioning seems preposterous. His queries about what was allowed and when it was allowed deflected the blame, and shifted the focus to the crimes *not* allowed by the Nazis. Another example occurred in Hofmeyer's questions about the Political Department. According to Morgen, every member of the Political Department had a piece of paper in his pocket that said, "Only the Führer decides the fate of enemies of the state." Hofmeyer then asked him: "Let's say if here in this trial we had to establish that this or that defendant killed prisoners without this specific order from Lieutenant General Müller, would it be allowed or not?" Morgen insisted that what Müller didn't allow was considered illegal.[49]

Hofmeyer was clearly exasperated with these distinctions. He began to talk freely to Morgen, complaining about the unbelievable contradictions at Auschwitz: the difference between official and unofficial activity, the desire for healthy people who could work, and at the same time the experiments in which people were injected with measles, brought to the point of death, and then brought back to life, only to be shot at the Black Wall. Morgen acknowledged that Auschwitz was a place of "grotesque contradiction" where "backwards rule" prevailed and "everything was possible." These conditions were a result of the huge changes in prisoner numbers that occurred monthly—first they badly needed people to work; then they suddenly had thousands too many. Morgen seemed genuinely disgusted with the hypocrisy of the laws at Auschwitz, as did Judge Hofmeyer and the prosecution; however, these same laws were constantly being reiterated and legitimized in the Frankfurt courtroom. Public prosecutor Kügler asked about the suspension of the case against Grabner, and wanted to know if it had been dismissed because either the defendant or the witnesses asked, "What do you want, anyway? Why would you go after us for a few shootings when thousands are killed every day in Auschwitz? Wouldn't that mean we didn't do anything wrong?" Morgen responded: "But no—the subtle but essential distinction is this: with the ordered executions or gassing, any initiative disappears; it was simply the carrying out of orders. But for the other shootings, the defendants couldn't use an order as their defense and they . . . did it out of personal motivation."[50] This was the exact distinction between perpetration of murder and aiding and abetting murder as defined in the West German penal code.

The defense and the prosecution battled over these differences. Defense lawyers tried to argue that the rules for intensified interrogations had changed in 1943, when a relaxing of procedure made more torture permissible. Morgen conceded this possibility. The defense also tried to establish that there might have been special camp laws for each camp, in which commanders could in certain situations order executions themselves. Morgen said that such a situation was only possible in the case of open resistance or an attack against an SS-man. He insisted that it was always clear to him which guards were acting on their own initiative, as they created a whole "theater" around their actions—they destroyed proof, they behaved secretively, and most especially, they falsified death certificates.

The question of falsified death certificates brought the courtroom to a new level of absurdity. The defense and prosecution not only disputed which deaths had been ordered, but which false explanations of these deaths had been ordered. Defense attorney Naumann asked Morgen to clarify what the death certificates were: some covered up murder that had been ordered (injections); and some covered up illegal murder (on the swing). If Morgen had used the false death certificates for his investigations, how could he differentiate between the two? And wasn't it possible that if the orders to create false death sentences came from above, as we saw in the indictment, then the orders to kill did as well? Morgen insisted that some falsifications had indeed been ordered, but for Grabner's activities, for example, neither the mode of killing nor the recording of a false cause of death had been ordered.

Finally, Morgen was questioned on SS duties in general. Hofmeyer hoped to bring to the fore the relationship between morality and murder. He asked Morgen about the military penal code and particularly paragraph 47, which stated that an order that constituted a crime should not be followed. Morgen confirmed that this law was in place throughout the Nazi period (despite Himmler's infamous 1943 *Posener Rede*, which could be interpreted as issuing a formal exemption from the law), but it was very difficult to determine what a crime meant in this "situation," particularly during war. A soldier could not criticize a political decision, for this would mean that everyone who had committed murder on the Russian front, if this was defined as a crime, was guilty of murder. Hofmeyer was outraged at the comparison. In reference to earlier testimony about an SS guard who had killed children without an order, he had the following exchange with Morgen:

> HOFMEYER: There can be discussion about that; but there
> can be no discussion about whether or not a soldier
> should follow an order to throw innocent little children
> into burning fires. It must be clear to a soldier that this is
> a crime.
> MORGEN: You are absolutely right about that, Director
> Hofmeyer . . . But I cannot imagine, and I hope I'm
> right, that that kind of thing happened, because it contradicts the entire direction [of the Nazi regime].[51]

We know now, from witness testimony at the trial and from countless survivor accounts, that such things happened all the time. Morgen steadfastly defended the laws of the SS, arguing that individual and sadistic murder "was beneath a true German; and despite everything that everyone says about them, despite everything that happened, the SS never ordered or demanded such cruelties. On the contrary."[52] The restrictions of the law reinforced his contention in Frankfurt, even though Morgen was certainly mistaken in his assertion that the SS legal officials investigated or punished all acts of excessive cruelty.

The pretrial testimonies of Gerhard Wiebeck and Wilhelm Reimers, also judges on the SS commission, echoed much of what Morgen had reported. Wiebeck had gone to work for Morgen in February 1944, when the Auschwitz investigation was already under way. He had interrogated Boger for the Grabner investigation and could remember Boger proclaiming: "We killed far too few. Everything should be done for the Führer and the Reich."[53] Reimers had also worked on the investigation of the "illegal killing of prisoners" in the Political Department, but he insisted that this investigation had had nothing to do with the *Judenaktionen* (mass murder of the Jews). His role was simply to look into the "illegal theft" of Jewish belongings. He claimed that he was constantly attempting to maintain secrecy about his role there, so that he would not arouse suspicion. The SS guards soon learned what he was doing, however, and they hated him. They attempted to bribe him into dismissing certain investigations, but he stoically refused. In this capacity he witnessed shooting executions of men, women, and children in a large room attached to the small crematorium. He insisted that he "couldn't clamp down on these shootings—that is to say prevent these actions, however, because my power of authority did not go that far. My job was only to establish what was going on at Auschwitz and then to report it."[54] Reimers testified more readily about the arrival of transports at Auschwitz and the subsequent gassings, and he gave relatively specific details about such actions that he witnessed. He reported them matter-of-factly, his interrogation betraying no hint of

remorse or disgust with what he saw. In fact, the way he saw it, prisoners who had been gassed looked very peaceful and had normal ex-
pressions on their faces, "as though they had died a natural death."[55]
At the end of his interrogation Reimers discussed the "spiritual burden" of being at Auschwitz, where people had lost all regard for human life. However, he maintained his subservience to the state and
asked no questions beyond this. After all, that was precisely the kind
of behavior that he was investigating.

Reimers did not appear on the stand at the trial, but Gerhard
Wiebeck did. Judge Hofmeyer asked him what constituted an action
worth investigating, whether "the 'general line' *(Generallinie)* ended
at unauthorized killing." Wiebeck responded: "You could say that.
The investigation of general killing was not authorized. I heard that
the extermination of the Jews had been verbally ordered by Hitler."
The commission, then, did not investigate such activities as gassings.
When prosecutor Kügler asked why, Wiebeck replied, "That didn't
interest us at that time. Those were 'supreme acts beyond justice'
(justizfreie Hoheitsakte)."[56] Paradoxically, gassings became 'supreme
acts beyond justice' at the Auschwitz Trial as well.

The claims of all of the SS judges to have done their best to bring
about some form of justice were reiterated on the stand by Dr.
Werner Hansen, the former SS judge who had presided over the
trial against Grabner in Weimar. Hansen, who reported that Morgen
had told him about the mass murder at Auschwitz, assumed that
"obviously orders from the highest levels were involved." Hansen
continued, contending that "these actions lay outside of the realm of
power of justice. An investigation of this mass murder was therefore
absolutely out of the question . . . The best that could be done was to
indict Grabner."[57] Grabner stood trial for two thousand unauthorized murders and two thousand falsified causes of death.

Heavy emphasis was therefore placed in the courtroom on a
handful of SS judges who investigated and proceeded against a
handful of SS guards accused of theft or murder at Auschwitz.
Morgen had been working on a commission that was investigating
and punishing people who were stealing goods that had already

been stolen from millions of Jews and who were torturing and killing people who had already been selected for torture and death. The
purpose of the *Sonderkommission* seemed ridiculous at the trial.
Nonetheless, Morgen served a very important role for the prosecution and judges in Frankfurt: as a member of the court (he was at the
time a lawyer in Frankfurt) he gave specific details about the activities that showed individual initiative and murderous intention, and
made their cases against Boger, Klehr, and the other unrepentant sadists stronger. These judges who testified appeared dignified on the
stand and commanded authority, as they retained legal positions after the war. They were colleagues of the presiding judges during and
after the Nazi period. Their testimony carried immeasurable weight
and significance, in legitimating the Nazi laws and Nazi justice on
the one hand and exonerating themselves on the other. It seemed
derisory that such detail about an "unauthorized" shooting had to be
pursued so vigorously and meticulously despite its seeming irrele-
vance. How could it be that only those murders undertaken without
an official order were emphasized at the Auschwitz Trial? Was not
the entire camp a place of murder? Why were these defendants on
the stand: for murdering millions of innocent men, women, and
children, or for disobeying the commands of the Nazi rulers? Increasingly, the focus of the trial was shifting to a select few defendants. The sadists became the main targets of scrutiny, just as they
had been in 1943 at Auschwitz itself. The larger evil of the Final Solution became submerged, for, as one observer notes, "the murder
machinery would have functioned, probably even better, without
the 'excess perpetrators.' "[58] The courtroom applied standards that resembled those of the Nazi state. This resemblance is most evident in
the fact that only those who had disobeyed Nazi orders were convicted of murder at the Frankfurt Auschwitz Trial.

Press Coverage in the West

The Auschwitz Trial was a very public process. It ran for one hundred and eighty days over a two-year period, and all the major news-

papers in West Germany covered it. The *Frankfurter Rundschau*, *Frankfurter Allgemeine Zeitung*, *Frankfurter Neue Presse*, and *Süddeutsche Zeitung* were some of the major newspapers that sent reporters to the courtroom each day. The *Frankfurter Allgemeine Zeitung* reporter, Bernd Naumann, later turned his daily reports into an important book chronicling the trial that provides the only other documentary source after Hermann Langbein's work. The press reports were so extensive and varied in content that in themselves they merit an independent inquiry; however, I will focus on a sample of reports from the *Frankfurter Allgemeine Zeitung* and the *Frankfurter Rundschau*, which were two of the most important newspapers to provide extensive coverage of the trial.

Their daily coverage demonstrates two things. First, the public was exposed to the trial on a constant basis and from these reports

Spectators at the trial of twenty men from the Auschwitz concentration camp, April 3, 1964. More than twenty thousand people came to watch the trial over its two-year duration. SOURCE: DPA/LANDOV. PHOTO BY HEINZ-JÜRGEN GÖTTERT.

could get a very strong sense of the atmosphere in the courtroom, the daily proceedings, and most important, the crimes that had taken place at Auschwitz. Second, the news coverage they received largely emphasized the grotesque, "incomprehensible" brutality of the most sadistic events described at the trial. It was almost a pornography of the Holocaust, that both sold papers and distanced the general public from the monsters on the stand whose actions were reported in graphic detail. Hence, historian Devin O. Pendas has stated that the Auschwitz Trial attracted "considerable attention from the mass media while remaining a matter of indifference, if not open hostility, for much of the German public." Pendas argues convincingly that the limitations of the law and the attempt to prosecute extraordinary crimes under ordinary law created a kind of press reporting that was very much shaped by the courts' focus on excessive brutality. The press mirrored this focus and created an enormous dichotomy between "published" and "public" reaction. The public felt a lack of interest in the trial and its possible lessons because the press presented the perpetrators as monsters and sadists. According to Pendas, "the press replicated the legal narrative of individual culpability . . . The press reports shared . . . the legal emphasis on perpetrator motivation . . . [and] perhaps unintentionally displaced attention from the Holocaust as a historical process with continued historical implications for German society onto Auschwitz as an infernal, largely incomprehensible netherworld."[59] The reports in the daily papers as well as some longer, more analytical articles written during the trial as both newspaper commentaries and journal articles show the roots of this indifference. Both the limitations of the law and the exacerbation of these limitations in the media coverage of the trial shaped public perception.

In an important article entitled "Our Auschwitz" (1965), Martin Walser presented his critical view of the press coverage of the Auschwitz Trial. Walser blamed the press for creating a schism between the German public and the defendants on the stand:

> For over a year we have read headlines of this sort: "Women Thrown Alive into the Fire," "Soup and Mud Stuffed into

Their Mouths," "Deathly Ill Gnawed on by Rats," "Chicken and Vanilla Ice Cream for the Executioners," "The Death Shot during Breakfast Break," "In the Gas Chambers the Victims Cry for at Least Fifteen Minutes," "Alcohol Flowed Freely at Auschwitz," "Shots to the Neck at the Black Wall," "The Torture Swing of Auschwitz," "The Devil Sits on the Defendants' Bench," "Just like Beasts of Prey . . ." The newspapers like best to describe Kaduk and Boger . . . The more horrible the particulars, the more minutely they will be shared with us. The more incomprehensible the detail, the more emphatically it will be described to us . . . And the more horrible the Auschwitz quotations, the more pronounced our distance from Auschwitz becomes. We have nothing to do with these events, with these atrocities; we know this for certain. The similarities [with the defendants] aren't shared here. This trial is not about us.[60]

Walser would argue that this was the only way for Germans to feel comfortable with themselves and to move beyond the Holocaust; they got some satisfaction out of addressing it judicially and condemning the crimes of the SS guards, while distancing themselves and considering the subject closed. Others have made similar arguments about the choice of defendants being represented in the press; Heinrich Hannover called them "scapegoats upon whom the society can unload its collective guilt."[61] Two other factors contributed, however, to this type of press coverage. First, it sold newspapers. It was sensationalist and titillating, and it satisfied people's darkest curiosity about torture and "hell on earth." Second, the law had created the emphasis on the brutality of the excess perpetrators, and the press reflected that perspective in its coverage of the trial.

Daily in the courtroom, the judges asked questions—variations on "Did the defendant have orders from Berlin?"—in an attempt to uncover the responsibility of each of the accused. The answers that proved most shocking and most likely to elicit a murder conviction were those printed in the press. And the witnesses on the stand described no shortage of overwhelmingly gruesome torture. Defendants like Boger, Kaduk, Baretski, and Bednarek had committed endless acts of brutality. Witnesses referred to them as devils, animals, and executioners. These accusations provided excellent fodder for the press, whose tone of disgust was clear in the newspaper coverage. However, the emphasis on extreme sadism detracted attention from the majority of defendants and in fact the majority of guards at Auschwitz, who had gone about their murderous tasks in an orderly, mechanical, and sometimes even reluctant manner.

A sampling of the coverage in the *Frankfurter Rundschau* illustrates the point. On June 9, 1964, the headline on the trial read: "Auschwitz Witness: Human Flesh in the Experimentation Lab. Every Week Two Large Pots . . . 'Small Children Almost Always Sent to the Gas Chambers.' "[62] Without giving any context for the testimony or explaining why it would be described that way, especially in legal terms, the article began: "In an agricultural experimental laboratory of the Auschwitz concentration camp, human flesh was used to discover new forms of nourishment for plants."[63] The article then gave some information about the witness providing this testimony, and what he had to say about the defendants on the stand (he accused Victor Capesius of having taken part in the gassings). These two pieces of information had nothing to do with one another, and the first, grotesque testimony that also appeared in the headline was neither connected with any of the defendants nor used as a charge in the indictment. It provided the newspaper, however, with an attention-grabbing headline. A positive reading of this report might be that it gave the public a "larger understanding" of Auschwitz, by showing the horror at the camp in its totality; however, the report presented Auschwitz as a place so bizarre that no ordinary person could in fact possibly understand what the bigger picture at Auschwitz really was: a place created by a popular German regime that had slowly and publicly alienated, persecuted, and expelled, and murdered its Jews. Instead, the press coverage degenerated into a theater of the grotesque and voyeuristic. The article continued:

> The representations of cruel details that have so far been
> given in the Frankfurt courtroom were outdone on Monday

by the testimony of thirty-nine-year-old dentist Imrich Gönczi from Teplitz-Schönau. This witness, who was deported to Auschwitz at age seventeen, worked there in an agricultural experimental laboratory, and his duty was along with other prisoners to make bouillon out of meat in test tubes, to be used as plant food. The witness said, "At first, the SS brought us beef and pork for that, each time about fifteen kilos. The remaining cooked meat was garbage, but we prisoners ate it, it helped us a lot. One day an SS man brought another fifteen-liter pot with pieces of meat. It seemed strange to me. There were two pieces of liver in there. I had the suspicion that it wasn't beef but human flesh . . . I took the meat and put it in the test tube. I found a piece of skin in there too . . . Then I found two large pots with human flesh."[64]

This testimony, irrelevant to the case, was followed in the article by another witness's less sensational description of a gassing he saw, in which defendant Klehr allegedly took part. The article ended with yet another horrific description of the murder of infants in the gas chambers, "as long as they hadn't already been kicked to death by the SS guards."

Why did the press include such details? The reporters were, after all, only reporting what was taking place in the courtroom. Witnesses were telling these stories on the stand, and in some ways they represented the degeneration of the trial itself into a macabre morality tale. The press did not make it clear to its readers, however, that this testimony would not be admissible and would not be used against the defendants. The newspapers were selective about their fidelity to the trial itself, depending on what was most beneficial to them. In other words, the press capitalized on the legal emphasis on excessive cruelty and individual sadistic behavior. They also pursued this line of reporting even when it had nothing to do with the law. Walser describes this kind of reporting as negligent, catering to the lowest instincts, to a "fascination with cruelty," and promoting the image of Auschwitz as Hell, specifically "Dante's Inferno," a phrase used repeatedly in the press.[65] Walser sees an even more sinister implication in this kind of reporting: a justification of Auschwitz, for Dante's Inferno was a place in which the sins of the guilty were atoned for. According to Walser, the comparison of Auschwitz with Hell allowed readers to forget that the result of the torture endured by prisoners in Auschwitz was not atonement, but extermination. He drove this point home by reminding his readers, "Auschwitz was not Hell, but a German concentration camp."[66] At the very least, the reporting style of the German press demonstrated the unwillingness of the reporters and the public to see Auschwitz as a real place, a product of a German government. Heinz Abosch shared Walser's objection to this distanced view of the Hell of Auschwitz. In a 1964 critique of the lopsided press coverage, Abosch, Ursula Rütt, and Arthur Miller wrote: "Auschwitz was the last stop of an antihumanism that placed 'Germanness' above everything else and viewed 'foreigners' as inferior. Auschwitz began in 1933 with the outlawing of Jews and the burning of books."[67]

The continuing coverage by the *Frankfurter Rundschau* illustrates yet another problem with the press coverage, mentioned earlier: the relativization of "lesser" crimes at the camp, particularly those not undertaken on the individual initiative of the staff. The next day in court (June 11, 1964), the *Frankfurter Rundschau* reported on the testimony of witness Stanisław Głowa. Głowa was called as a witness against defendant Klehr. Although Klehr was indicted and later convicted for killing thousands of prisoners with phenol injections, the report mentioned this fact only in passing. Its emphasis was somewhat different: "The witness . . . described the former orderly Josef Klehr as a man who often became a beast within seconds while torturing prisoners. Klehr, who is alleged to have killed thousands of prisoners through his own initiative with a shot of phenol in the heart muscle, burned newborn infants in the central heating system of the camp at least two or three times."[68]

Klehr's voluntary torture and slaughter of infants was juxtaposed in the report with the witness's description of the other orderlies on the stand, Emil Hantl and Herbert Scherpe. Here the reporter chose not to interject his own analysis but reported Głowa's statement verbatim:

At this time, I want to indicate the following, in the name of justice: if I have to create a scale of responsibility for the actions of the three defendants (who were all medical orderlies in Auschwitz), Scherpe and Hantl would seem like angels in comparison with Klehr. They were polite and friendly, and this is the important thing: when they came early into the camp, they said good morning, and when they left, they said good-bye. For us, who were so degraded, these were signs of humanity. Notwithstanding, both also took part in the injections.[69]

This last remark went unexamined by the reporter. Both defendants were presented to the public as kind, decent people, people more like the readers, who did not fit the mold of sadists and devils and therefore could not be seen as murderers. This distorted representation of SS officers who had taken part in the murders at the camp was to some degree a product of the limitations of the murder law and the definition of perpetration. But it was also the result of the press corps's fascination with the extreme and the brutal. People like Hantl and Scherpe seemed innocent and good by comparison with Klehr and Boger and Kaduk. This kind of coverage extended to non-German papers, as well; on January 5, 1964, at the very beginning of the trial, an article in the British paper the *Observer* attempted to describe what kinds of defendants were on trial in Frankfurt. Novelist Sybille Bedford chose only two out of twenty defendants for her character study: Wilhelm Boger and Oswald Kaduk. She stated: "Thugs often find their way into prisons, if not as inmates then as guards . . . It is always the same combination of low human material and the uses that society puts it, or allows it to be put, to. Some of the accused men were very likely scum material from an early start. The point is that the Nazi regime deliberately cultivated, trained, and licensed this potential scum."[70]

The early reports about the trial, just before and directly at its opening, did make an attempt to give some background into the history of Auschwitz, and of the defendants themselves. However, in these first articles the tone was set for the incredulity that would be expressed on a daily basis about the participants in the killing at Auschwitz. On December 13, 1963, the *Frankfurter Neue Presse* included a lengthy article entitled "The Machinery of Murder at Auschwitz."[71] This article (and similar ones in the *Frankfurter Allgemeine Zeitung* and the *Frankfurter Rundschau* at this time) spoke less about the trial and more about the circumstances of life and death at Auschwitz. Providing the German public with graphic and expansive detail about the SS system and the camps, all articles had in common a tone of revulsion and shock at the horrors of the Holocaust, and at the fact that the perpetrators of mass murder had been living among the German public for so long. Using an important book compiled by H. G. Adler, Hermann Langbein, and Ella Lingens-Reiner (the last two names being familiar from the trial) entitled *Auschwitz: Zeugnisse und Berichte* (Auschwitz: Testimony and Reports), the article in the *Frankfurter Neue Presse* reconstructed, in five pages, a disjointed, inflammatory picture of Auschwitz.[72] The first paragraph of the article introduced the subject of the Holocaust in this way:

> It strains the understanding and the emotions to believe what happened between 1940 and 1945 in a German concentration camp not far from the Polish town of Oświęcim (Auschwitz). But it is true: more than two million men, women, and children from twenty-three countries had to die here, merely because they were Jews or because they stood in the way of the megalomaniacal elite at the top of Germany's hierarchy. Auschwitz—this was Hell on earth, the biggest extermination project of the inhuman Brown executioners, a death factory cleverly created by diabolical minds, in which murder was carried out in a rational and machinelike way.[73]

Peppered with quotations about the functionings of the gas chambers from Rudolf Höss's infamous diary and graphic witness depictions of experiments and torture, the article attempted to reconstruct the violence and slaughter that had taken place at the camp.[74] It described the camp as a "combine" in which whole ethnic groups were exterminated by a well-oiled machine—a slave labor camp that doubled as a death factory. Using language that combined the cold, efficient bureaucracy of Auschwitz as both conveyor belt industry and gruesome kingdom of torture, the article insistently portrayed the "Brown executioners" at the camp and in Berlin as beasts and devils, set apart in their lust for murder and desire for expansion from all decent Germans.

Four days later, *Frankfurter Allgemeine Zeitung* journalist Kurt Ernenputsch wrote a more sophisticated, contemplative article depicting the defendants who would be on the stand in Frankfurt. Ernenputsch expressed indignation at the historical amnesia about the accused, about their ability to slip through the cracks and back into German society. He wrote: "How could the defendants, now located, have remained unrecognized for so long, although only one of them was an unknown name until now? How was it possible that even after their arrest by the Americans, the English and the Russians, so many of them could not be identified as SS-men from Auschwitz, and if some of them actually were put in an internment camp or went through denazification trials, they were classified as collaborators or minor offenders?"[75]

Ernenputsch bemoaned the fact that defendant Höcker, the adjutant to the commander, was so low on the government's priority list that he had had to apply for his own denazification. His description of each defendant's relatively safe position after the war (with the exception of Hofmann, who had been sentenced to life in an earlier trial), revealed his naivety about the hundreds of thousands of former Nazis with suspicious pasts who lived freely throughout Europe after 1945. Either ignorance about the fate of the many perpetrators really was widespread and the journalist was expressing genuine distress about these former Nazis, or a collective amnesia had settled over Germany and this was the first public questioning about where all of the participants in mass murder had actually gone.[76] Such psychological reactions to the Holocaust are complex and have been examined at length elsewhere.[77] I am concerned here with the style and content of the press coverage, which functioned not only as a mirror of the law and of the public reaction, but as a shaper of public consciousness as well.

Some of the most critical examinations of the trial, the law, and the Nazi past appeared in letters to the editors of the major newspapers. On December 21, 1963, the first day of the trial, the *Frankfurter Rundschau* printed at least four letters concerning the defendants from Auschwitz. One skeptical reader noted: "The dark years of the dictatorship left mountains of guilt behind. An earthly court cannot contain such an expanse."[78] Still, the reader urged, the guilty must be held accountable, and the trial must function as some sort of memorial to those who died at Auschwitz. Another reader, recognizing that the responsibility for Auschwitz extended far beyond the defendants, addressed the issue of extensive complicity. The reader wondered:

> Could they have functioned without the informed, without employers, without politicians, who incited and terrorized the masses? Without judges and district attorneys, without administrative and police agents . . . let's also just say without the hundreds of thousands, the millions who "knew something" or "guessed" but couldn't summon the courage to ask: What is happening to our neighbors? Only if we dare to answer these questions openly and honestly, and understand the consequences, can we determine whether we have really overcome this terrible past.[79]

Although it is difficult to determine what public perception and reaction were to the trial—which people learned about only through the press, as no television or film coverage was allowed—such snippets of public opinion help indicate that some measure of critical analysis was going on outside the trial and the press. Such questioning of the trial and the entire nation was rare, however. As is stated in the write-up of a survey conducted by Lothar Vetter of the *Frankfurter Rundschau* inside and outside the courtroom, "You hear from every other person: 'Let's finally leave the past in peace! Who still wants to hold an accounting today?'" About twenty thousand people, especially large groups on school field trips, visited the courtroom. Vetter reported that many onlookers were skeptical about the trial in general. They felt that it had no meaning, that the truth could not be established—or worse, according to one teacher, that such a trial should not take place at all, as it "wasn't all that bad back then." The popular sentiments were voiced by men in a café outside the courthouse, who asked Vetter, "Should we still be conducting such trials in fifty years?" One proclaimed, "I won't go in there—on purpose! That was too long ago. I feel sorry for the women who were affected, who often didn't even know what their husbands were up to." Vetter's own analysis was more judicious than that of many reporters, who chose to focus on the grotesque and the extreme. He attempted to make the public confront the bigger issues, and in this context, he condemned people's greater concern for the fate of the families of the perpetrators than for the victims themselves. His examination of public reaction ended with a call for introspection and perspective. He wrote: "In the end the question remains: Are we Germans willing to see this trial as a trial against ourselves? Are we capable of guarding ourselves against two extremes, both of which suit the situation equally poorly: an all-too-exaggerated self-accusation on the one hand; an all-too-comfortable self-exoneration on the other. It is about exactly this—to quote the words of a Norwegian state official: 'We are ready to forget, if the Germans are ready not to forget.' Are we?"[80]

In any examination of public reaction, a danger of overgeneralization always exists. This holds true for the press as well. Some thought-provoking, sophisticated editorials and lengthy articles addressed the subject of Auschwitz, the trial, and the Nazi past with critical distance; however, the majority of press coverage did exactly what Martin Walser urged Germans not to do: it took refuge in a "flight into fantasy," giving a description of Auschwitz that was "half *Bildzeitung* [Germany's equivalent of the *National Enquirer*] and half Dante."[81] This, according to Walser, was exactly what survivors recalling their experiences would not have wanted, for it distorted the reality of the camp. He further explained:

> One has to imagine the death factory without the properties and peculiarities of which the defendants are now accused: without Kaduk's walking cane; without Boger's swing; without Broad's wish to shoot the most beautiful women first; without Hofmann's "doing sports "; without Baretski's deadly "special blow" with the side of the hand . . . ; without Klehr's longing to play the doctor; without Bednarek's desire to beat people to death with chairs . . . Auschwitz without these "colors" is the real Auschwitz. Selections on the platform, transport into the gas chambers, Zyklon B, crematoriums.[82]

Walser's insights into the deficiencies of the press representation of the trial reflect the limitations of the law. Still, it must not be forgotten that it is not the purpose of a trial, despite Fritz Bauer's best intentions, to provide insight into the definition of fascism, to create a greater political awareness about the dangers of a nationalistic and antisemitic worldview, or to teach lessons of history. Walser is correct in his assumption that one can learn nothing about Auschwitz through a "collection of subjective brutalities," and that if that were so, the reality of Auschwitz and the trial would soon be forgotten. But the media's concentration on the grotesque was the product of the legal focus: the subjective inner motivation of each defendant. The prosecutors were working with limited means, and the judge was especially insistent that the trial function as a criminal court attempting to establish perpetration or aiding and abetting murder, according to the letter of the law as set out in the West German penal code.

The "incomprehensibility" of the perpetrators' actions was the main theme of virtually all the reports during the trial. Daily coverage invariably emphasized the inhumanity of every defendant, his utter foreignness in the eyes of decent people. On April 25, 1964, the *Frankfurter Rundschau* headline read, "Death Came Twenty Thousand Times." The article described the "sadist and people-hater" Josef Klehr, who killed at least that many people with his own hands, through injections. The witness Czesław Głowacki estimated that at least ten thousand of these had been undertaken without any orders. Following an extremely graphic description of the technique used for the injections and the reaction of the victims, the report went on to give Klehr's inhuman and sarcastic response to the charges: "There were only sixteen thousand prisoners in the main camp. If I had injected sixteen thousand of them, then only the musical orchestra would have remained."[83] The judge's reprimand for this flippant "joke" reinforced the image of Klehr as demonic, and incomprehensible.

Occasionally a tone of realism was adopted in the press, and this generally occurred in editorial form. Bastian, a regular contributor to the *Frankfurter Rundschau*, wrote a short piece about Dounia Wasserstrom's testimony on Boger's murder of the small boy with the apple. He commented on the effect that this testimony had in the courtroom, stating that it functioned as "a blow of a club, worse than the reports about the murder in the gas chambers. Suddenly one can imagine something [as being real] again."[84] I have commented earlier on the change in the judge's tone of voice, the sensitivity that he showed toward the witness, and the intense questioning that occurred afterward in an attempt to corroborate this story. It was one of the few moments in which the brutality of a defendant evoked personal identification with the victim and the witness in the listeners: everyone in the courtroom could understand the crime as a violation of parental protection.

Lost in the press coverage was the fact that the majority of guards at Auschwitz who participated in murder were not unrepentant sadists with a penchant for brutality. In an article entitled "Beyond Imagination," key witness Hermann Langbein's open discussion in a suburban school was reported. Langbein attempted to shed some light on the reality of Auschwitz, as it was becoming so distorted in everyday press coverage. Foreshadowing Christopher Browning's conclusions on perpetrators some forty years later, Langbein told the audience that the majority of the defendants at the Auschwitz Trial did not possess inherently criminal personalities, but were completely "ordinary men" who had sunk to extraordinary lows after being corrupted by a totalitarian system that turned them into mere "receivers of orders."[85] Langbein hoped in his lecture to convince the public that the trial also brought the routine mass murder, the daily genocide, to the fore. And it was certainly possible to see that side of Auschwitz in the courtroom, for countless witnesses described the machinery of murder and the hundreds of thousands who were killed in the gas chambers. But Langbein was aware that the law and the press coverage were highlighting only the exceptional cases of personal brutality. He hoped to reverse some of this distorted emphasis.

What made this representation of Nazi crime all the more disturbing was that it came on the heels of the Eichmann trial, and after the shocking revelations of the "banality of evil" that Hannah Arendt made so famous. Her book centered on the idea of the indifferent, bureaucratic killer, unmotivated by ideology or brutality but driven by ambition and careerist self-interest. Had this representation of the Nazi perpetrator not penetrated into Germany? I would argue that it had, but had been neatly pigeonholed to describe only a small percentage of perpetrators: the upper echelons of bureaucratic killers who wrote out the orders on their desktops and left the grisly deeds to be carried out by the unfortunate "small men" who were now on trial. In fact, in the courtroom the constant refrain was now heard among defendants about the unfairness of these trials, that they were not responsible but were being scapegoated so that the real perpetrators, the architects of genocide, could go free. One gains no sense from the trial or the press coverage that the majority of murderers in Auschwitz were quite ordinary, motivated by mundane selfish ambitions. Instead, these people were not deemed to have been murderous at all, and their crimes were minimized in favor of placing the emphasis on the Bogers and the Kaduks.

Readers of the daily newspapers were faced with a contradictory picture. Most reports informed them that "Christmas Eve Was Celebrated with Mass Murder" or "Death Injections Were Rewarded with Cigarettes." Alongside these daily reports were editorials that asked deeper questions of the trial and the public. Occasionally, witnesses—like Hermann Langbein and Kasimierz Smolen—who were concerned about the larger issues surrounding the trial gave public lectures and talked to reporters about the "lessons of the Auschwitz Trial." The newspapers also reported on other complex issues that arose at the trial: the defense strategy to discredit any witnesses from the East as Communists working for government agencies, and therefore fabricating much of their testimony; the battles between defense attorney Hans Laternser, a right-wing Nazi sympathizer, and Karl Friedrich Kaul, the lawyer representing survivors in East Germany; the treatment of and attitude toward survivors from Poland; the court's visit to Auschwitz in December 1964; the transfer of the trial in April 1964 from the Römer courthouse to the new Gallus Haus facility, which resembled a theater more than a courtroom. Wading through the thousands of newspaper reports on the trial (not to mention those covering the closing arguments and the judgment) reinforces the paradoxical nature of the trial that I have posited throughout this book. The law, now buttressed by press coverage and a relatively indifferent public reaction, limited the focus of the trial to those who had defied the chain of command and disobeyed Nazi orders. Even the Nazi investigators could see them as sadists. This obscured the real criminality of the camp system as a whole. But glimpses of historical perspective were to be found in the lengthy overview of the SS system in the indictment, in the testimony of witnesses who were allowed to expound upon their experiences of the camp, and in editorials by critical analysts. Despite the inefficiency of the German criminal code, some sense of history was being articulated and recorded for the future. It becomes clear that from all perspectives, the trial had a contradictory result. On the one hand, the goals of the prosecution were met, because Auschwitz and the SS came to public attention for the first time since the end of the war. Thanks to incipient historical research on the subject, vast amounts of testimony by eyewitnesses, and the often sensational closing arguments of the lawyers, the trial created an audience the Holocaust had not had before. On the other hand, the kind of information disseminated was distorted through the law. Emphasis on the barbaric actions of a few sadists detracted from an examination of the criminal nature of National Socialism as a whole. The West German penal code was not equipped to "teach lessons" about how to prevent or punish genocide, especially since the genocide charge was not applicable to these proceedings. In fact, in the exclusive legal pursuit of defendants who had exceeded their orders and taken individual initiative, Nazism and its crimes found a kind of legitimation.

This outcome was not what the prosecution had had in mind when it had initiated the case against the Auschwitz perpetrators, although the prosecutors were aware that they had to work within the confines of the law. The distortion is obvious already in the indictment, where Nazi regulations were cited to buttress the individual charges against defendants who had allegedly perpetrated murder. The difficulty was further exacerbated by the testimony of survivors on the sadism or "decency" of different defendants, and then most obviously by the testimony of Dr. Konrad Morgen and the other former SS judges. In many ways, the press coverage simply reflected the legal strategy, especially since it satisfied the need for sensational headlines and lurid details. The prosecution did, however, try to bring the Holocaust back into the picture in its summations. How effective were they? What was the end result of the trial, in the court's judgment, in light of the prosecution's goals? Could the prosecution send a message about the participation of an entire country in a corrupt regime and help prevent further atrocities? A look at the closing statements, the judgment, and the reaction to the judgment in the press will shed light on these questions.

CHAPTER 5

The Summations and the Judgment

T HE CLOSING ARGUMENTS at the Auschwitz Trial began on May 7, 1965. Although technically these summations were part of the trial, they clarified the positions of both the prosecution and the defense at the end of the trial, and they preceded the deliberations and judgment of the court. No doubt the closing arguments also had a great deal of influence on the final decision-making process, which was in the hands of the three judges and six jurors. The closing arguments by the prosecutors show that they were not willing to abandon their goal of putting the entire Auschwitz complex on trial, even after the proceedings demonstrated that it would be virtually impossible to do so. The summations reflect the unique nature of the trial itself, and that is particularly true of the general statements made by prosecutors Großmann and Vogel before the prosecution addressed the defendants' cases individually. The closing arguments by the defense attorneys are illustrative of the strategies they had used throughout the trial in an attempt to exonerate their clients. The innovative and often intelligent arguments of the defense merit consideration. Their focus on the law itself and their insistence on the narrowest possible definition of murder under the West German penal code—in contrast with the prosecution's choice to see the defendants' actions in the larger context of the criminality of mass murder—greatly strengthened the arguments for the defense. In many ways, the law was on their side, and if they could cast some doubt on the defendant's individual initiative and awareness of the illegality of his actions, they hoped to avoid a murder conviction.

Closing Arguments

The judgment itself is an extremely complex document, which was made public ten days after the trial. How did the convictions compare with the charges in the indictment, and in the prosecutors' closing arguments (which were often amended after the proceedings)? What justification was given for the sentences imposed, and particularly for the acquittals? How did the judges address the Final Solution, and its relevance to the trial? Did they judge the defendants solely by their individual activities? Which charges were dismissed, and why? I argue that the court was determined to maintain the "integrity" of judicial process as defined by West German penal code, and to conduct the Auschwitz Trial as an ordinary criminal trial. At the same time, the judges sometimes yielded under the pressure of the extraordinary circumstances of this trial and allowed the backdrop of the National Socialist regime, Nazi ideology, and the extermination program to influence their decisions. This contradiction inevitably gave rise to inconsistencies and mixed results. On the one hand, the prosecution's determination to keep the mass murder of the Jews in focus was successful and is perceptible in the verdict; on the other hand, the court's leniency toward defendants supposedly manipulated and corrupted by Nazi propaganda was disappointing to victims of the Nazi regime. The sentences finally meted out were very mild, considering the nature and magnitude of the crimes of all the defendants. It was virtually impossible for the court to contain the proceedings within the narrow confines of the law. Still, the trial engaged the public in a new dialogue on the crimes of the Third Reich and opened the door to discourse about the Nazi past.

The Prosecution

Dr. Hans Großmann, head public prosecutor at the trial, gave the first summation. He addressed two main issues: the superior-orders defense cited by the accused and their lawyers, and the Final Solution and its resonance at the trial. He therefore made it his duty to "reintroduce" the backdrop of genocide at Auschwitz into the trial. The Holocaust had, as I have argued, been neglected during most of the proceedings, as the focus was predominantly on the specific actions of the defendants and the ways in which they met the qualifications for murder in the legal discourse of the day. Following Großmann, prosecutor Georg Friedrich Vogel also made a general statement, before launching into arguments regarding defendant Hans Stark. The prosecution gave closing arguments on the various defendants until May 17, after which the civil plaintiffs *(Nebenkläger)*—Dr. Karl Friedrich Kaul, Christian Raabe, and Henry Ormond—made their case for the conviction of all the defendants. Thereafter, the defense lawyers spoke to their defendants' cases individually. The arguments took three months, ending on August 6, 1965. Thirteen days later the oral judgment was given.

Großmann's argument was entirely devoted to contextualizing the actions of the defendants in the Holocaust. His intention was not to minimize their alleged crimes, but to demonstrate their illegality on all counts. He wanted to argue that not just actions undertaken on individual initiative, but any participation in this system was murder. Großmann began his summation by quoting West German president Heinrich Lübke at the Bergen-Belsen memorial on the twentieth anniversary of the liberation of the camp: "Nobody does us a favor in trying to persuade our people that there should finally be a end to this conjuring-up of shadows out of the days of a terrible past. We don't conjure up the shadows, but they conjure us up, and it is not within our power to withdraw from their spell."[1]

Lübke's words were meant to epitomize Großmann's main argument. The past would not be "softened" by the judgment, whatever that might be. It could be only partly dealt with at the Auschwitz Trial, as part of a larger working-through of the Nazi era that had to continue on a consistent basis.

The prosecution could address only a few of the enormous issues raised by this past, and Großmann felt that certain misconceptions about the "small men" on the stand at Frankfurt had to be permanently laid to rest. He argued that first and foremost, although these men kept referring to themselves as "cogs in the wheel," and the defense lawyers reiterated this line, they had in fact been vital members of the system that made mass murder possible. He felt that neither the argument that at Auschwitz they were part of the war effort overall nor the argument that they were simply following orders could hold up to legal examination, and that therefore these men should be held accountable for participation in wholesale mass murder. Großmann put it this way: "He who 'liquidates' [he used the word ironically] hundreds of thousands of civilians in the framework of his occupation is not shielded by the norms of war; rather, he commits a legally relevant crime: namely, murder."[2]

Großmann's remarks were meant to answer two important and opposing questions that would be asked by the public: "Why only now?" and "Why still today?" In order to answer the first, Großmann argued that many factors had delayed the beginning of this large trial. The collapse of Germany and the concentration on reconstruction had allowed the pursuit of past crimes to fall into the background; the Allied trials had made it seem as though justice had been adequately pursued; and, as mentioned in Chapter 2, states could not initially determine the jurisdiction for the trial before the ruling of the West German Supreme Court made it possible for German prosecutors to arrest suspects who had been born in that jurisdiction or who had at some time lived there. In answer to the second, more contentious question (Why still today?), Großmann cited two important reasons. First, public prosecutors had the duty to pursue crimes that came to their attention, so this was in some ways a simple case of pursuing charges of alleged criminal activity. Second, he felt it was also the duty of the prosecutors to attack the "inner resistance" of so many Germans, particularly among the older generation, and make them think about what they had or had not done. This was not to say that all Germans were murderers, or that there was some sort of "criminal collective guilt." Rather, Großmann wished to express it the way that the Evangelical Church had on March 13, 1963, in a discussion of Nazi trials: "It was the mistaken ways of our entire people and the omissions of us Christians that made this crime possible. We cannot beautify this and should refuse all attempts at self-justification."[3]

In his closing statement at the trial, Großmann echoed Fritz Bauer's goals. Arguing that "deathly silence creates incomprehension, not peace with past committed crimes," and reiterating the need to "clean out the nest," Großmann also acknowledged that "it is not the job of this court to clean the entire nation with this trial." Once again citing the words of the church, however, he argued, "It is your holy duty to reestablish the adherence to the law that our people had and that was destroyed in the past [during the Nazi period], in order to facilitate an essential contribution toward inner recovery in our people."[4]

Großmann's goals were lofty, and in many ways impossible. His desire to address the Nazi past judicially became most obvious in his explanation that he hoped the trial would be seen in the context of the worldwide human rights movement that had begun with the creation of the United Nations and had been solidified with the human rights convention. The very mention of the United Nations, which had also drafted the genocide convention in 1948 and permanently introduced the four international charges on war crimes into its charter, showed the prosecution's inclination to see this as much more than a criminal trial conducted under the West German penal code. The prosecutors clearly retained some hope that although crimes against humanity were not being legally addressed in the Frankfurt courtroom, the judges would bear them in mind when deliberating on the fate of defendants. This was not to be.

Großmann was of course arguing about a most extraordinary set of defendants, whose actions had taken place within the context of the largest genocide in history. Somehow he wanted this context to be recognized as the "crime complex" *(Tatkomplex)* within which the defendants had acted. The court showed considerable flexibility in this matter by allowing, for example, expert testimony on the Third Reich from the historians at the Institute for Contemporary History in Munich. Legally, the history of Nazism had little relevance to the individual actions of the defendants. In fact, its relevance lay only in showing that a crime complex had existed and had been ordered by the state, and therefore that only those actions which exceeded orders demonstrated individual initiative and therefore murderous behavior. Making this point, though, was not Großmann's intention in explaining the relevance of the Nazi Final Solution to the crimes of the defendants. The prosecutor meant instead to show the criminality and murderousness of the entire plan. Even though none of these defendants might have committed their alleged crimes without the connection to National Socialism, Großmann explained, this was no indication that they were not guilty; rather, their personalities could not be separated from National Socialism and from the SS. Therefore, their actions had to be viewed against the charge of base motives, which for Nazi trials, as we have seen, included antisemitic or racial hatred.

Großmann addressed the issue of the superior-orders defense directly, by quoting the relevant paragraphs from the West German penal code. In this way he could show that the defendants could not legally use this defense. The paragraphs in question state:

> *Paragraph 52:* A punishable act does not exist if the perpetrator was forced to commit the act through overpowering violence or through the threat of immediately present danger to life and limb to himself or his subordinates, a threat that could not be avoided in some other way.
> *Paragraph 54:* A punishable act does not exist if that act occurs outside a state of emergency, in an innocent way that was not avoidable, in order to save oneself or one's subordinates from immediately present danger to life and limb.[5]

These definitions clearly show that all other avenues of action had to be pursued before a defendant could plead superior orders. There was a difference, Großmann said, between avoiding a life-threatening situation and deciding to take the easiest way out. Here the head prosecutor was echoing the words of the expert witnesses, Hans-Günther Seraphim and Hans Buchheim, both of whom argued that SS guards had generally been under no threat, and that had any risk existed, it was that of being sent to the front—a prospect that could not be classified as a threat. Großmann argued: "The weightier the demands of a new legal system, the more one has to require that common knowledge prove [the perpetrator's] actions—in this case the participation in the mass murder of people—to have been the *only* way out of danger."[6] In his eyes, none of the defendants, with the exception of Dr. Lucas, had even made an effort to show that he would have been in extreme danger if he had not committed the alleged crimes. Instead, most insisted that they simply had not taken part in any of the actions of which they were accused, particularly selections on the platform.[7] This defense also proved faulty, because under repeated questioning some defendants did finally admit that they had actually been there (although never as participants in selections), an admission that discredited all of their previous statements.

Großmann realized that he was directing most of his closing arguments toward the defendants whose sadistic intent could not be adequately demonstrated. The problem of superior orders, he freely admitted, was irrelevant to the excess perpetrators. Their guilt was much easier to prove, and the plethora of witnesses who attested to their brutality had established it with a fair degree of certainty, particularly in the cases of Boger, Kaduk, Klehr, Stark, Baretski, and Bednarek. These defendants were sadistic murderers whom even the Nazis had investigated, and in the general summations little time had to be spent explaining why their actions constituted murder. The others, though, who had allegedly either participated in selections (virtually all) or provided phenol to Klehr (Capesius) or thrown gas pellets into the gas chambers (Breitwieser and Stark) or served as second in command in the camps' overall operation (Mulka and Höcker), were more challenging cases. The prosecution was determined to show that their participation in the implementation of mass murder constituted at least aiding and abetting murder, if not perpetration of murder.

For the remainder of his summation, Großmann then turned his attention to the Final Solution. His chosen emphasis on the persecution of the Jews and the chronological unfolding of the extermination policy indicates three things. First, the prosecution hoped to show that this was a program of systematic annihilation of a whole group of people. Because the fate of the Jews was not the central focus of the trial, they were brought back into the picture at the end. Second, Großmann's presentation of the progression of the Final Solution was strictly intentionalist, showing the development of Nazi policy from 1933 on, beginning with boycotts and the Nuremberg Laws, progressing to Kristallnacht and the invasion of Poland, which was seen as part of the plan to rid Europe of its Jews, coming to a head with the Wannsee Conference and the switch from motor gas vans to Zyklon B and gas chambers, and culminating in the construction of the concentration camps and death camps.[8] Third and most important, this was the best public opportunity to teach a lesson about the past and the role the defendants had played in the extermination of the Jews. The indictment had not been public, the judgment would be largely a written one and therefore ignored by all but the most curious of spectators, and the trial itself was so long and complex that few could get a real picture of what Germany had wrought in 1933. The closing arguments would be closely monitored by the press and could provide the main dramatic interest for the largest public audience so far. Großmann used this opportunity to bring his point home:

Hitler, Himmler, Höss, and the others—*but also in their own roles the defendants in this room*—all equally met the hidden goal to a terrifying and startling extent; true to Himmler's diabolical conclusions in his notorious Posen speech to the district leaders (*Gauleiter*) of the NSDAP on October 6, 1943: "I ask you truly only to listen to, and not to discuss, what I tell you in this circle. The question came to us: What happens to the women and the children?—I have decided to find a very clear solution for this as well. Namely, I did not consider myself authorized to exterminate the men—meaning: to kill them or have them killed—and allow the avengers, in the form of their children and grandchildren, to grow up. The difficult decision had to be made, to let this entire people disappear from the earth." This is exactly what occurred, in a decisive measure, in the gas chambers and crematoriums, in the barracks and on the streets of Auschwitz.[9]

Großmann ended his summation by pointing to the presence of the Holocaust as the crime structure behind the defendants' actions, as much as the law obscured it and the defense attempted to deny it. This trial, he posited, could by its very nature not be seen as a regular criminal trial. To ignore the backdrop of the Final Solution would therefore be to lack perspective. For this reason, Großmann urged the judges, the jury, and the public to use the newly reconstructed justice system to speak out against the murderers of yesterday, when millions of innocent victims had no chance to defend themselves before a court.[10]

Großmann's colleague Georg Friedrich Vogel expanded on the attempt to inform the public about the important place of these defendants within an enormous, corrupt crime complex. Mainly addressing the witnesses' testimony and the persistent efforts of the defense to discredit most of it, Vogel argued that witnesses could not possibly have falsified their stories in the face of so much cross-examination, careful explanation, and corroboration from the hundreds of other witnesses called to the stand. Further, and running completely contrary to the norms of legal discourse and courtroom evidence gathering, Vogel stated that "there are no exaggerations about Auschwitz: the truth is the toughest indictment." Vogel argued that although the trial was not meant to help Germany overcome its past at the expense of a few defendants, it was at least to be a new beginning for an open discussion in Germany. The defendants should be judged only on the basis of their "personal guilt" and what could be proved at the trial as evidence of aiding and abetting or perpetrating murder, as the law dictates. However, Vogel cleverly insinuated that this was not possible without in some way understanding the backdrop of the Holocaust. This caveat applied particularly to those defendants like Scherpe and Hantl, whom witnesses had described as "decent" or kind, hesitant to take part in the murder, by comparison with others. Vogel cautioned that decency did not rule out participation in murder, for "often criminal trials have shown that criminals can also have good emotions; that is what makes them criminals, that they are capable of anything!"[11] Vogel was clearly aware that paragraph 211 required that "sadism, lust for killing, sexual drive, cruelty, treachery, or other base motives" be present in order to obtain a conviction for murder. Both individual initiative and knowledge of the illegality of the act also had to be present to secure a conviction for perpetration. According to these legal standards, it would be difficult to find either Scherpe or Hantl guilty. Neither of these defendants revealed any of the motives needed to uphold the charge. Vogel pleaded with the judges and jury to realize that "decency" was no defense in a case where the defendant had clearly murdered innocent men, women, and children, however reluctantly he had done so.

The prosecution lawyers then addressed the case of each defendant. After reexamining the evidence given in the court, they amended some of the charges and asked for life sentences for perpetration of murder for sixteen of the twenty defendants.[12] For defendants Scherpe and Hantl the prosecution proposed sentences of twelve years' imprisonment for a conviction of aiding and abetting murder. Presumably, this was because witnesses had testified that these two men had generally treated them with respect and humanity, meaning that they showed neither individual initiative nor specific subjective intent to murder. The prosecution proposed acquittal for defendants Schobert and Breitwieser. The prosecutors argued that Schobert "should not be portrayed as any worse than the hundreds of other SS members whose investigations had been dropped."

The case of Breitwieser is also perplexing, given that during his cross examination the defendant admitted to taking part in one of the gassings, which would at least have counted as aiding and abetting (as in the case of Scherpe and Hantl), no matter how much he might have disliked the activity or regretted it later.[13] However, Breitwieser insisted that he had taken part only in the disinfection of clothing with the gas, not the extermination of people. This contention, along with the faulty testimony of witness Walter Petzold, presumably left the prosecution with the realization that it would be impossible to find irrefutable proof of Breitwieser's guilt.

The closing statements of the civil plaintiffs were even more polemical than those of the prosecution. The civil plaintiffs were the lawyers representing survivors who wished to press their own charges, independently from the prosecution. Dr. Kaul represented witnesses from East Germany; Ormond and Raabe, witnesses from France.[14] Although they were generally in agreement about defendant Hantl, and in fact recommended a lesser sentence than the prosecution had for both Hantl and Lucas, they demanded much harsher sentences than the prosecution for defendants Höcker and Mulka. Raabe called these two men "the most vital cogs in the extermination machinery"—playing on their own defense that they were only "cogs"—and asked that Höcker be given four hundred thousand life sentences for participating in the murder of the Hungarian Jews at Auschwitz in the spring and summer of 1944. Raabe recommended more than thirty thousand life sentences for Mulka. These requests seem almost ridiculous in the context of a murder trial, but in many ways the civil plaintiffs were not exorbitant in their demand that each defendant be sentenced for each person murdered. Kaul's closing arguments were directed at the capitalistic nature of the entire endeavor of the Final Solution and pointed the finger at industry—particularly IG Farben—which had set itself up at Auschwitz to exploit slave labor.[15]

Henry Ormond, in the last of the prosecution and civil plaintiff summations before the defense made its closing arguments, chose to address some of the "functional and structural problems" that had come to light during the trial, particularly the "fairy tales, legends, fables, and myths" adduced by the defendants in an attempt to protect themselves.[16] He also examined the larger structure of the camp itself, the role of the defendants as functionaries of the camp and of the SS system, and the kinds of witnesses that had appeared on the stand. Ormond's comprehensive closing summary was meant to pull together all the other statements and show the mendacity of the defendants throughout the trial. Ormond wanted to remind the court that the expert witnesses had proved that Auschwitz had been designed, constructed, and ruled by the SS, and these same men had participated in the murder that took place there. None of these elements could be separated out when it came time to determine each defendant's particular crimes.

Ormond made an interesting argument regarding the "myth of the iron discipline of the SS." From the testimony heard at the trial about the motley group of defendants on the stand, it was arguable that SS guards were more prone to drunkenness, excessive brutality, and theft than to carefully following orders. Ormond quoted the testimony of Dr. Hans Münch, former head of the Hygienic Institute at Auschwitz, who had been the only defendant acquitted at the Polish Auschwitz Trial in 1947 and who had subsequently been a witness in Frankfurt. Münch said that "there was a big difference between what was ordered and what actually happened."[17] Ormond argued that defendant Kaduk, who had been notoriously drunk on many occasions, drank not so that he could bear the orders he was obliged to carry out, as he insisted, but so that he could be even more "uninhibited" in his brutality. This claim was important because, as we have seen from the indictment and the trial, the prosecution relied heavily on camp regulations and the testimony of the former SS judges about corruption to show that defendants had acted on their individual initiative. Ormond attempted to show that the guards in fact rarely followed the camp regulations and that excessively brutal behavior, sadism, and chaos were everyday occurrences at Auschwitz. Therefore, neither the superior-orders defense nor the claim that they had been reluctant to carry out their tasks had much validity.

What did Ormond's contention mean for the prosecution's argument that one could determine individual initiative by examining documents and testimony explaining what criminal activity had been ordered in the Nazi period? If the official camp regulations on intensified interrogations or executions at the Black Wall were rarely enforced and existed merely as formalities, could the West German prosecutors use them to determine individual initiative? The camp regulations were almost irrelevant to the reality of the camp. Therefore, all acts of killing should have been considered murderous and Nazi standards should be thrown out entirely. However, whether regulations had been followed by the SS guards or enforced by Nazi authorities was not important for the prosecution at Frankfurt. The camp rules existed as written documentation of what was considered activity conformable to higher orders, and any action surpassing these regulations and laws, since it could be considered intentional, demonstrated individual initiative. In effect, the prosecution was not concerned, as Ormond was, with the reality of the camp standards and whether or not the SS leaders had strictly enforced these limitations (as on occasion they actually did, as we have seen with regard to the investigative commission headed by Konrad Morgen). The existence of regulations of camp conduct meant that some defendants had had their own personal motives that helped substantiate perpetration of murder.

In his final general remarks before his consideration of the individual cases of defendants Broad and Capesius, Ormond reflected on "the bad conscience of the defendants." He argued that their bad conscience should be understood in legal terms as synonymous with "knowledge of the illegality of the act." The lies, the cover-ups, and the overall unwillingness of the defendants to admit to any of the charges until they were pressed demonstrated to Ormond that these men did indeed have bad consciences. Their complete silence about their time in Auschwitz—the defendants had spent more than a year there on average, as Großmann reported—bespoke an unwillingness to admit to their crimes. This silence, according to Ormond, in contrast with the mountains of testimony by witnesses, did not amount to "statement versus statement," but "lies versus the truth."[18]

All the statements by the prosecution and civil plaintiffs in some way spoke to the importance of these trials for the German public, however reluctant most people were to think about the Nazi past some twenty years after the fact. The pursuit of justice at this trial did not affect only individual murderers to be tried and sentenced according to their crimes but rather should also address the mass murder of Jews, political prisoners, "asocials," and Gypsies through a systematic state-ordered genocide. The horrifying context could not be ignored, no matter how limiting the law. The summations allowed the prosecutors to reiterate and drive this point home in a succinct and public way. According to Ormond, the presence of Nazism could be perceived in the behavior of the defendants, who "when they open their mouths, bring me back into the years of the Third Reich, in the years when nationalist phrases clouded the brain, in which there was no gentlemanliness or fairness to the opposition."[19] For the prosecution, as long as this "ghostly disposition" still existed in the Germany of the 1960s, such trials of former Nazis had to continue. There could be no doubt that the prosecution in its summations appealed to the judges to keep the big picture in mind, to recognize defendants who had perhaps not acted out of sadistic impulses as having nevertheless acted on base motives of antisemitism and racial hatred, which had led them to go voluntarily to Auschwitz, and to participate voluntarily in the murder of millions.

The Defense

The defense lawyers, in many ways, had an easier task than the prosecution, especially in representing those defendants who had taken part in platform selections or ordered executions, seemingly without demonstrating any individual initiative. The defense could refer to the law itself; defense lawyers were in fact participants in the interpretive process, and they did everything in their power to reinforce the prevailing subjective definition of perpetration. One after another, that is exactly what each did. On May 31, 1965, Rainer Eggert, defense attorney for defendants Mulka, Höcker, and Bednarek, cited the backdrop of the Nazi state in his summation to show that it actually obscured rather than enhanced the case against these men: "In this trial the scope of the crimes threatens to overwhelm the question of individual guilt."[20] There was no need for the defense to deny that Auschwitz was a horrible place where terrible mass murder occurred daily, as the prosecution constantly reminded the courts. Most defense attorneys did not reject the testimony of hundreds of survivors that genocide had taken place at the camp. Rather, the defense used the victims' experiences against them. Defense attorney Dr. Hermann Stolting proclaimed, "Every witness who was himself a prisoner had to experience such humiliation, suffering, and torture there, and was daily in fear of death; he could no longer be objective, even if he wanted to be, and even if he is subjectively convinced that he is objective."[21] The mass murder at Auschwitz was used to obscure the individual charges against the defendants. This was an absurd extrapolation, and yet legally acceptable because of the current interpretation of the penal code. This defense strategy was also the ultimate example of the ways in which the law hindered the pursuit of justice on a grand scale for the entire Auschwitz complex.

More often, defense attorneys referred only to the intricacies of the law, and hence to the specific testimony of each witness on claims with respect to individual defendants. Mulka and Höcker, therefore, were relatively easy to defend, as no one had really established that Höcker was the all-important "iron fist" as adjutant to the commander, or that either defendant had selected prisoners on the platform or supplied the camp with gas. Those documents with Mulka's signature on them showing his receipt of shipments of gas were photocopies, argued Eggert, and therefore their authenticity was not beyond doubt. Eggert pleaded with the judges, jury, and public to use the same standard of judgment and fairness that would be accorded any defendant in a murder trial. He found it lamentable that at this particular trial, because of its inflammatory political nature, the defendants' denials were all categorically disbelieved, but "everyone sat up, almost audibly so, if one defendant incriminated another."[22] This was not a consistent standard, and equal consideration had to be given to every statement uttered by the defendants and the witnesses.

The defense attorneys' favorite tactic was the discrediting of witness testimony. Dr. Hermann Stolting II, co-defense lawyer with Eggert for the same three defendants, accused the witnesses of engaging in a trial of revenge, not justice, in which only vague testimony was given and survivor statements "projected" the screams of tortured people onto the defendants without showing any real personal guilt. Stolting blamed the prosecution, the press, radio, and television for influencing the proceedings and presenting the defendants' explanations as ridiculous, while at the same time taking the witness testimony at face value, or according to the whims of each party. The worst of the offenders, according to Stolting, was Fritz Bauer himself, who had participated in public discussions about Auschwitz while the trial was in session, and in fact helped organize an exhibit on Auschwitz at St. Paul's church in Frankfurt, steps away from the courthouse. Included in this exhibit were pictures of the defendants. The prosecuting attorneys gave lectures at the university, witness Hermann Langbein spoke publicly and to the press, and the prosecution had much too close a relationship with the IAC and other international organizations representing victims of the Nazis. The defense accused the civil plaintiffs of having "far-reaching international connections"—in Kaul's case with the East German government but also with various communist agencies such as "Soviet-Russian and Polish headquarters and the rulers of the East-zone" (Hans Laternser would refer to this group constantly during the trial and again in his summation), Ormond to Israel and various other Jewish organizations throughout the world.[23] Stolting argued that this was all highly irregular for a criminal trial, even though it was hardly illegal for historians to write books about National Socialism, the SS, and the concentration camps. Bauer was also completely free to mount exhibitions about Auschwitz, as was Langbein to discuss his experiences at the camp. Stolting was calling for complete public silence about the Holocaust, for the sake of the integrity of the trial. This was an impossibility, considering the magnitude of this historical event, and yet in many ways public discussion of the crimes at Auschwitz did run counter to normal standards of confidentiality and defendants' rights in a criminal trial held under the West German penal code.

The individual statements about each of the defendants reveal a repeated emphasis on the general unfairness of the prosecution for choosing to try the "small men," while bureaucratic murderers, or even officials with more authority at the camp, went unpunished. Hans Schallock and Dr. Rudolf Aschenauer, attorneys for Wilhelm Boger, both bemoaned the fact that the officials at the major conferences planning the Final Solution, particularly the Wannsee Conference, were above the law. Schallock made the press responsible for the terrible image of Boger, which, although certainly a reality of the press coverage, was largely only a reflection of the hundreds of brutal acts described by numerous witnesses. Asking that Boger be sentenced only to fifteen years for aiding and abetting murder, Aschenauer argued that base motives—that is to say racial hatred and antisemitism—were not present in Boger's case, especially considering his relatively good treatment of the Jewish women who worked in the Political Department.[24] In addition, the burden of proof rested upon the prosecution's shoulders, and Aschenauer felt that it had not adequately searched for documentation of orders from the General Gouvernement regarding executions at the Black Wall. This defense seemed rather unconvincing, for that particular task was obviously one the defense should have undertaken, in order to exonerate its client. Boger's lawyers clearly had a much more difficult task than those for such defendants as Lucas, Hantl, and even Mulka, for whom virtually no evidence of sadistic individual behavior was produced. Ostensibly, however, the excess perpetrators too enjoyed the benefit of reasonable doubt.

Hans Laternser, perhaps the most right-wing of the defense lawyers, closed with representations of defendants Capesius, Broad, Frank, Schatz, and Dylewski. Described by Bernd Naumann of the *Frankfurter Allgemeine Zeitung* as "ironic, insulting, but very logical and smart," Laternser focused on the reliability of testimony summoned from memories of events that had supposedly unfolded twenty years before. He argued that "a trial of this scope cannot be carried out with the precision demanded by the serious accusations. It transcends human capabilities."[25] Such sweeping statements about the nature of human memory had of course some basis in truth. Survivors had often spent many years trying to forget; many did have difficulty with exact details and did confuse dates and times. But Laternser hoped to discredit all witness testimony, even that which had been written down meticulously during or shortly after the events (for example, Otto Wolken's chronicle, Erich Kulka's book *The Death Factory*, and Rudolf Vrba's report, written in 1943 for the British government, about his escape from Auschwitz), and dismiss it as colored either by desire for revenge or by underhanded political motivations.

Some of Laternser's more far-fetched strategies included attempting to prove that defendants who had selected prisoners at the platform were actually saving lives: they therefore could not have been susceptible to base motives, nor could they have been aware of the illegality of their actions. He argued that the selections diminished the number of deaths in the gas chambers, for if the defendants had not selected able-bodied workers for slave labor, all would surely have been sent to the gas chambers.[26] Although in hindsight this argument seems weak at best, it was made to a public that was receptive to the possibility that most camp officials at Auschwitz were just doing their duty, as "decent men" who truly did believe that they were selecting for life rather than death.

Laternser's partner, Fritz Steinacker, argued that this was a purely political show trial and therefore served no real judicial purpose. The attempt to prevent such crimes from reoccurring had to take place in the political arena, he insisted, where the totalitarian, corrupt nature of the state could be indicted, rather than simply the underlings who had been forced to carry out the orders of that state. In an attempt to reinterpret paragraphs 2 (on retroactivity) and 211 (on murder), Steinacker hoped to challenge the general consensus that both paragraphs had been in force throughout the Nazi period. Bernd Naumann paraphrased Steinacker's argument as follows: "Granted, present legal thinking holds that Hitler's basic order did not have the force of law. This nonlegality has been proclaimed by the federal court by referring to natural law. However, that is not a firm legal foundation. Article 211 of the penal code says that one must not kill. But the state power and the creators of the Third Reich not only had abolished this commandment but had in fact said 'Thou shalt kill, because this is in line with national needs, the historic mission, and the duty of the individual towards the German people.' "[27]

Steinacker was on thin legal ice with this argument, for paragraph 211 had in fact not been rescinded during the Nazi period. Combining legal and religious metaphors, Steinacker contended that the Nazi Final Solution had in fact been legally ordered. This argument, and those explained earlier, were intended to bring the judge and jury to view the defendants as ordinary citizens doing their duty toward state and country, even if that duty was daily murder at Auschwitz. Laternser drove the point home in his summation regarding defendant Capesius. Returning to the familiar refrain and reminding the court that this was a purely criminal proceeding, Laternser insisted on the limited nature of the trial: "Your task here is not to make history or to master the past. Your task here—and it is a considerable one—is to mete out justice to the men accused here and to judge their deeds, if these can be proved after twenty years to the full satisfaction of the law."[28] Laternser certainly had a point. As the judge agreed, and as he reiterated in the verdict, this courtroom could not be the place in which to judge history.

The Judgment

On August 19–20, 1965, after a weeklong deliberation, the court reached its verdict.[29] Even though the court had a six-member jury, the judgment was mainly the product of the three judges' deliberations. The judges estimated the numbers of murders that each defendant was convicted of having taken part in. In each case, the phrase "at least" appeared in the conviction. The judges clearly had a difficult time determining specifically how many people each defendant had helped to kill or had killed, because the numbers were so overwhelming. One could argue that the demand for specific information about the actions of each defendant and each murder was in the end irrelevant to the actual judgment, because nobody was convicted of exactly the number of murders he had committed or helped commit. The charges in the indictment, and to some extent the written explanation of the individual convictions, included the names of many victims of the defendants. The Nazis, although they kept fairly meticulous records of the numbers of victims brought in on transports and then divided up for work in the camp or extermination in the gas chambers, tallied exact numbers only for prisoners who had been admitted into the camp and tattooed. In the end, the mass executions and gassings of those who had never been officially admitted left the court no choice but to abandon any attempt at numerical precision in its verdict.

The Opinion of the Court

The reading of the verdict was followed by the Opinion of the Court. This condensed version of the written judgment that Judge Hofmeyer read aloud to the defendants, the public, and the press would become the subject of much critical discourse both in the press and among scholars. Despite the prosecution's requests that the court take into account the importance of the Nazi backdrop and the involvement of the defendants in the program of mass murder, Hofmeyer took a much more conservative approach to the proceedings and placed the trial in the context of the German criminal code and within its boundaries. Although he made extensive reference to historical information on the SS and Auschwitz in both the indictment and the judgment, Hofmeyer rejected the argument that the trial should teach lessons. He began:

> It was only to be expected that attempts would be made to have this trial serve as a basis for a broad, comprehensive presentation of events leading up to Auschwitz, to unravel the background leading up to this catastrophe, to depict and try to understand the political developments after World War I that led up to Auschwitz. However, the court did not give in to the temptation and did not permit itself to be led astray from the

path staked out for it by law and venture into regions closed to it. It is the task of every criminal procedure to examine the validity of the indictments submitted by the prosecution and to examine those circumstances which must be clarified in passing judgment on a defendant. The court does not have the right to pursue any other goal . . . At the beginning of its summation the prosecution raised the questions of why an Auschwitz Trial at all and why an Auschwitz Trial still today. These questions must have been of concern to the prosecution when it had to decide whether to initiate these proceedings. The court does not have to deal with questions of this nature. Although the trial has attracted attention beyond the borders of this country and been given the name "Auschwitz Trial," as far as the court is concerned, it is the proceedings against Mulka and others. That is to say, as far as the court is concerned, the only consideration was the guilt of the accused men. The court was not convened to master the past; it also did not have to decide whether this trial served a purpose or not.[30]

Hofmeyer's judgment adhered to a conservative elucidation of the law, and the verdict reflected this slant. His assertion that the court had to turn a blind eye to the historical background of the crimes of these defendants came in for a good deal of criticism among scholars. Many argued that stating what the court "did not have to do" or was not obliged to decide or deal with was simply an easy way to hide behind the law rather than to make bold, precedent-setting decisions that would resound and affect future trials of Nazi perpetrators.

Hofmeyer went on to address the most important issues that had arisen during the trial and in the closing arguments of the prosecution and defense. He criticized the insistence of the defense that this had been merely a "show trial," by pointing out that it had actually been anything but. The adherence to the law, the rigorous search for exact details, the dismissal of testimony that was uncorroborated or in no way specific, and in the end the convictions themselves, lent credence to his argument and in fact supports the contention that the trial was so hamstrung by the law that it could not judicially address the "bigger picture" of Nazism and the Holocaust. As to the charge by the defense that this was a trial of the "small men," the scapegoats for the big players and "desktop murderers," Hofmeyer pointed out that all the leading figures of National Socialism were dead or had already been tried, and the superiors at Auschwitz—Grabner representing the Political Department, Entress as head of injections, Baer and Höss as commanders of the camp—had all been executed or had committed suicide. In addition, "it would be a mistake to say that the 'little people' are not guilty because they did not initiate things. They were just as vital to the execution of the extermination plan as those who drew up the plans at their desks."[31] Here it would seem that Hofmeyer strayed from his argument that the court would deal only with the individual actions of each defendant outside the context of the machinery of murder. However, he was referring to the crimes that led to a conviction of aiding and abetting murder rather than perpetration of murder. The aiding and abetting conviction was applicable to defendants who had not shown individual initiative but had been involved in the murdering process, literally as accomplices. For this charge, participation in the extermination of the Jews was a valid element of the crime.

Still, Hofmeyer firmly dismissed any attempts by the prosecution to address moral and political issues, and any claims by the defense that the trial was either covertly or overtly addressing them. He argued that, "in considering the problem of guilt, the court could consider only criminal guilt—that is, guilt in the sense of the penal code." He acknowledged the valid attempts by the defense to cast doubt on this guilt too but warned against defense arguments which insisted either that the court was not within its rights in punishing actions from another phase in history or that "the German Reich in the era of National Socialism was another state, which had developed its own public morality and own laws, and therefore could not today be held responsible before the courts of the Federal Republic."

In addition, Hofmeyer pointed out that the defense's contention was an "erroneous argument because of the existence of the 1871 penal code throughout the Nazi period," and although "National Socialism did exercise all-embracing power in Germany, that did not give it the right to turn wrong into right . . . National Socialism was also subject to the rule of law."[32]

The Question of Guilt

Hofmeyer made an interesting argument in response to criticism that had already been leveled against such trials and would inevitably follow the verdict—the argument that anyone who had worked at Auschwitz should be considered guilty. Earlier in this book I quoted Fritz Bauer's sentiment that the guards at Auschwitz were "all accomplices."[33] In strong opposition to this standpoint, Hofmeyer stated:

> How about the individual guilt of these defendants? If this were a court like the summary court of Auschwitz, the question would have been answered within hours, for all the defendants were at Auschwitz, where incomprehensible crimes were committed, and they were members of the SS . . . This circumstance would have been enough for any summary court to find the defendants guilty. But therein lies the difference between the rule of law in a state of laws and the so-called rule of law as practiced at one time in Auschwitz.[34]

Hofmeyer was arguing that to convict the defendants on the basis of their membership in the SS and their presence at Auschwitz was to imitate the system of "justice" used by the Nazis with their victims. In this way he cast the courtroom in Frankfurt as just and democratic by its very opposition to the kind of punishment meted out at Auschwitz. Ironically, Hofmeyer missed (or deliberately ignored) the more apt comparison to the Nazi legal system of punishment *not* of innocent victims but of Auschwitz guards suspected of individual murder and corruption. Had he compared the federal German criminal proceeding against the twenty Auschwitz perpetrators with the proceedings conducted by Konrad Morgen at the camp in 1943, he would have had to acknowledge that the Auschwitz Trial had applied similar measures of justice.

Having heard the testimony of more than 250 witnesses, Hofmeyer drew distinctions between the disadvantages and advantages of survivor testimony.[35] Because the documents available to the court were "scattered and not very informative," because he felt that the defendants had been unhelpful in giving "any clues in the search for the truth," and because no documents at all existed regarding the individual murders allegedly committed by the defendants, the court was almost entirely dependent on witness testimony. He realized that it was "asking a great deal of the witnesses to expect them to recall details," especially about a place where no watches or calendars were allowed. He also worried that witnesses could not make absolute declarations about the truth because twenty years had elapsed, because witnesses had experienced the events under conditions of "unbelievable unhappiness and suffering," and because witnesses run "the danger of projecting things [they] experienced onto others and things others described vividly in that setting as [their] own experiences."[36] Although Hofmeyer was slightly out of his element in his psychological evaluations, he was certainly speaking from experience. He argued that unlike in a regular criminal trial, the court had no access to forensic evidence, postmortem reports, murder weapons, fingerprints, or evidence from the scene of the crime that would in any way aid the court in coming to a decision. Because of this, witnesses had to be questioned meticulously on exact details. Hofmeyer supposed that "for this reason, witnesses repeatedly voiced surprise over being asked for precise accounts of those past events." Hofmeyer did not consider that witnesses' surprise might have been more the result of questions that included the seemingly irrelevant and trivial queries "Was this murder ordered by officials in Berlin," or "Did the defendant execute people at the Black Wall with a valid death sentence." For survivors, Auschwitz was a place where innocent men, women, and children were massacred daily, and the limitations of the West German penal code were not justification enough for validating Nazi orders.

Despite all these problems, and despite Hofmeyer's recognition that the court was working with limited means of gathering evidence, he insisted, "this was an ordinary criminal trial, regardless of its background. The court could reach a verdict only on the basis of the laws which it has sworn to uphold, and these laws demand that subjectively and objectively the concrete guilt of a defendant be established." At the end of his statement he reminded those in the courtroom that "the court had to base its verdict on the deed for which the concrete proof has been established, because the penal code does not deal with the concept of mass crimes." These two statements seemed to contradict each other, as his acknowledgment of the lack of real physical evidence eradicated the possibility that this would be considered an "ordinary criminal trial." The court was dealing with mass murder, whether the law ignored it or not. The situation was extraordinary, notwithstanding the ordinariness of the law. Hofmeyer was attempting to minimize these enormous contradictions and chose therefore to interpret the law narrowly and strictly. Hofmeyer was aware that the general atmosphere compromised the integrity of the judicial process and the possibility of meting out adequate punishment for the crimes. He alluded to this difficulty in his final comment on the sentences: "It cannot be assessed arithmetically how high the penalty for a single crime should be. Even the life sentences, considering the number of victims, could not be considered an even approximately just expiation. For that, human life is much too short."[37]

The Written Judgment

The judgment in the files of the Auschwitz case is more than nine hundred pages long. It includes specific reasoning and evidence for the verdict issued in the case of each defendant. Hofmeyer's oral judgment appears in different sections throughout the written document. Like the indictment, the judgment includes a section on the history of Auschwitz within the National Socialist state, and the camp as a place of extermination. This approximately eighty-page section is a condensed version of the much longer history that appeared in the indictment, gathered from the expert witnesses, the testimony of survivors, and the memoir by Rudolf Höss.

A variety of factors often led to the dismissal of certain charges: the reliability of the witness, the amount of corroboration, and the facts accumulated both about the defendant's time in the camp and the camp itself through the on-site visit by members of the court. Sometimes the most infamous accusations of brutality were surprisingly dismissed. Nevertheless, they remained important parts of the public and historical consciousness about the camp and have gone down in history as "truths," even if they were discounted judicially. This legacy further demonstrates my argument that the trial had a paradoxical outcome, which was legally unsatisfactory but publicly enlightening.

Pages 90–744 of the judgment examined each defendant's actions closely and provided lengthy justifications for the convictions. For each defendant, the judgment included the following: his personal history (*Lebenslauf*), the established facts and list of convictions (*tatsächliche Feststellungen*), the defendant's response (*Einlassung des Angeklagten*), the evidence and the assessment of the evidence (*Beweismittel und Beweiswürdigung*), the judicial evaluation (*rechtliche Würdigung*), and the assignment of punishment (*Strafzumessung*). The three defendants who were acquitted—Schobert, Schatz, and Breitwieser—were not included in this section but were examined according to the accusations against them that could not be proved. After these rulings, 140 pages were dedicated to other charges that could not be proved against the defendants who had been convicted of various crimes. This section merits closer attention, for it demonstrates how carefully the court deliberated over each individual charge and how meticulously the judges attempted to use every piece of information gathered, primarily from the witnesses. The judgment ended with a brief section on the obstacles faced by the court—specifically, Kaduk's previous sentencing by a Soviet court in East Germany, and the statute of limitations on murder and aiding and abetting murder—and related decisions by the court. I will divide my analysis of the written judgment into four sections: first, the charges against the group of defendants accused of only one overarching crime, participation in the extermination of the Jews; second, the convictions against the excess perpetrators, whose crimes were much more easily proved than those of the other defendants, as the defendants themselves had generally initiated them; third, the charges against defendants whose crimes fell somewhere in between these two categories, and who were convicted of aiding and abetting murder in varying degrees; and finally, the charges that could not be proved, against either the acquitted defendants or the others.

The rulings on defendants Mulka and Höcker both address their sole conviction, "participation in the mass murder of Jews at Auschwitz."[38] This conviction also applied to defendants Boger, Dylewski, Broad, Hofmann, Baretski, Lucas, Frank, and Capesius. For defendants Lucas, Frank, and Capesius it was also the only conviction, despite the number of other charges against them. For the other defendants, this conviction always appeared as the first offense under "Established Facts," but was followed by a list of other convictions. It is unclear why other defendants, particularly Kaduk or Klehr, were not convicted of this charge. Presumably, they occupied lower ranks and positions at the camp and therefore were not seen as decision makers or superiors who were aware that they were participating in the "mass murder of the Jews."

This conviction is interesting, in that its wording differs slightly from the actual charge brought solely against defendants Mulka, Höcker, and Baer in the indictment. Whereas they were initially charged with participating "in the realization of the National Socialist extermination program," without specific reference to the Jews, the conviction called it a program of mass murder of the Jewish people. For each defendant convicted of this crime, the judgment gave a specific, lengthy explanation of the ways in which the defendants had participated. For example, the court determined that defendant Mulka had signed at least one document on October 2, 1942, which the court had in its possession, requesting that the WVHA send a five-ton truck containing Zyklon B to Auschwitz for the gassing of so-called RSHA Jews in the gas chambers at Auschwitz. He had also signed an order requesting doors and windows for four newly built crematoriums. The judgment went on to state that

> through the above-described actions, the defendant Mulka participated in the killing of at least 750 people from four different RSHA transports that came to Auschwitz at different times. The defendant Mulka knew that the Jewish people who came in the so-called RSHA transports would be killed in the gas chambers, if they were not selected for labor and brought into the camp. He also knew that they were being killed only because they were Jewish. He was also informed that the deportation of Jews to Auschwitz was under the strictest code of secrecy and was to be concealed, and that the Jews were deceived about their fate up until the very end and were therefore oblivious when they went into the gas chambers. He also knew about the fear, the terror, and the torture that the victims experienced when they realized their fate, and that they would die a torturous death when the gas was shaken into the chambers.[39]

Important in this explanation were the elements of "knowledge" of the cruel fate of these people, knowledge that they had been deceived about their fate, and knowledge that they were being killed for their race, which fell under the charge of base motives. In addition, the fact that these crimes had been conducted under strict secrecy implied that Mulka could deduce that the mass murder was not legal.

The court used the information provided to it by the historians and the witnesses to determine the number of victims in Mulka's aiding and abetting conviction. Whatever its scientific limitations, the method the court used was the only possibility. The evidence on Mulka's case was gathered in the following manner:

> In 1942 and at the beginning of 1943, the size of the RSHA transports fluctuated between one thousand and two thou-

sand people. This is shown in the statements of the defendant and from the statements of witnesses Filip Müller, Kagan, Wasserstrom, Laks, and Vrba. In the smallest transports, then, at least one thousand people were deported to Auschwitz . . . [Defendant Mulka] told us the number of Jews who were pulled off the transport for work and brought into the camp. It was between 10 and 15 percent and in some cases more, but never more than 25 percent . . . The court, in order to be totally certain, decided from the start in defendant Mulka's favor, that 25 percent of the people on the four RSHA transports in whose extermination he took part—that is to say 250 people—had been brought into the camp for work. Therefore, it has been established that he took part in the killing of 750 people from each transport.[40]

Such were the decisions the court had to make when dealing with defendants against whom no specific eyewitness testimony was available, or no charges of individual cruelty and murder. The method used to decide his sentence makes clear the likelihood that Mulka participated in the deaths of many more people. Establishing these numbers for certain was impossible, and he was therefore convicted on a minimum number of deaths.

Mulka was convicted of aiding and abetting murder—that is, he was an accomplice. To establish that he was, the court, in its section on "judicial evaluation," first had to ascertain for whom Mulka was the accomplice. In the case of the RSHA transports, who was the principal perpetrator? The court named Hitler as the main instigator and perpetrator of the crime of murder. In its justification, the judgment pointed to the base motives of Hitler (antisemitism and racial hatred), the treachery of the act (the Jews in these transports were deceived about their fate), and the cruelty of the way in which they were killed. All these justifications were elements of paragraph 211 of the StGB. The judgment went on to demonstrate that Hitler, like any other German citizen, was not above the law, and that he had acted illegally. Just because he had ordered the mass murder of Jews in his capacity as head of state did not mean the order was legal. First, because the order was top secret and never publicly declared, it could not be considered valid. Second, even if it had been a legitimate order, "right could never be made out of wrong. The freedom of a state to decide what it right and what is wrong is not unlimited. There is a core area of justice in the consciousness of all civilized peoples, despite all differences that individual nations have in their systems of law. This core, determined by a general sense of justice, cannot be injured by any law or government measures."[41]

The court therefore established that Hitler was not above the law. In the case of the extermination of the Jews and mass murder in the gas chambers, he was the principal perpetrator. Because, however, mass murder was not a valid charge, the court chose to judge each individual act of extermination—determined to be murder because of base motives—separately. Mulka could not be convicted of participating in the entire Final Solution, because this would be a mass murder charge, and because (in the court's opinion) each act of extermination was different. Mass shootings by the *Einsatzgruppen*, for example, had to be considered separately, depending on where they had occurred, who had ordered them, who the victims were, and how many people had been killed each time. While this might appear to be a political statement about the nature of the Nazi program of extermination, it was in fact the court's way of dealing with the exigencies of the criminal code and the lack of a mass murder charge.[42]

Mulka, then, was guilty as an accomplice to his immediate superiors and to Hitler, for these murders could not have been undertaken alone, and he had participated in killing at least three thousand people. As a member of the SS, Mulka was also bound by the Military Criminal Code, and particularly paragraph 47, which stated that a person was not to obey the order of his superior if he knew that the order constituted a universal or military crime. According to the judgment, "defendant Mulka knew that the order to kill innocent Jewish people was criminal, and that the killing, despite Hitler's order, was a universal crime. He himself does not contend that he believed in the legality of the killing. In his statement he called the killing an 'injustice that screams to heaven' and a 'crime.' "[43] There was little patience in the courtroom or in the judgment for the argument that the defendants did not know that the orders were illegal. In a complete and final dismissal of this defense, the court ruled:

> In general, the killing of innocent people, especially small children, just because of their origin, is a blatant violation of every human being's right to life, of which even the most primitive people are conscious. And it is a blatant violation as well of the authority conceded to the state only in the most exceptional cases, namely the authority to require the death of a human being if he has seriously violated the order of the law. Therefore, no one could doubt the illegality of the ordered annihilation of the Jews. It is the belief of this court that the accused did not harbor any such doubts either.[44]

Finally, the court had to determine Mulka's inner attitude and motivation in deciding whether he was to be convicted as a co-perpetrator (*Mittäter*—paragraph 47), guilty of joint murder and therefore eligible for a life sentence, or as an accomplice (*Gehilfe*—paragraph 49). He was determined by the court not to be a perpetrator of murder because he had not issued the orders. He had, however, willingly and knowingly participated in the murders and had therefore shown enough understanding of his actions and free will in his job that he could be considered guilty of aiding and abetting the deaths of the three thousand transport victims. If he had been in a situation where he was forced to participate in murder, the court argued, "it would be incomprehensible that he did not try everything to avoid the final step of being called up as adjutant or try to be relieved of his duties as adjutant."[45] This explanation, supported by the evidence that SS officers could decline their duties without repercussions, sufficed to reject any defendant's claims that he had not wanted to take part in mass murder. Mulka was convicted of aiding and abetting the murder of 750 people on at least four separate occasions.

A similar ruling was made in the case of defendant Höcker, who, like Mulka, was described as a "willing receiver of orders" *(willige Befehlsempfänger)* whose loyal compliance to the program of extermination—that he knew to be illegal—made him guilty of aiding and abetting the murder on at least three separate occasions of at least one thousand people.[46] Mulka was sentenced to fourteen years in prison, Höcker to seven years. The lengthy written rulings against both men establish their guilt in the mass murder of the Jews. Interestingly, the judgment denounced them for being receivers of orders and for not refusing to perform their duties. These written statements acted as the decisive counterargument to the superior-orders defense through which the defense attorneys had attempted to exonerate the defendants. The court made it clear that both these defendants knew they were following orders that were illegal or at least immoral, and both should therefore have done everything possible to avoid obeying them. The tone of the judgment indicates that these defendants were finally being severely punished for their actions as participants in the extermination of the Jews. The sentences themselves though, seemed mild in view of the magnitude of the crimes.

Why was there such a contrast between the statement of the court on each defendant's participation in the extermination of the Jews and the actual verdict against him? Why did defendant Mulka receive twice as much prison time as defendant Höcker for fewer murders? The judgment addressed these problems in the section called "Allocation of Punishment" that followed the verdict of each defendant. As Mulka was defendant number 1, the court included within his ruling "general considerations on the allocation of punishment for aiding and abetting murder."[47] In this section, the court reminded the public and the prosecutors that its duty was only to punish the specific crimes that could be proved. The judges also addressed the length of imprisonment for each convicted defendant and the reasons these sentences were not higher than the fourteen years Mulka received, even though the court was free to sentence anyone who had been convicted of aiding and abetting murder to anywhere between three years and life in prison.

The judges stated their role in determining punishment as such:

> In assigning punishment to each defendant convicted of aid-
> ing and abetting murder, the court could not concern itself
> with atonement for the entire body of crimes committed at
> Auschwitz. Considering the countless victims of a criminal
> regime and the unspeakable suffering endured not only by
> the victims themselves but by countless others, especially the
> entire Jewish people and German people, through the histori-
> cally unprecedented, systematically carried out, diabolically
> devised extermination of hundreds of thousands of families, it
> seems barely possible that earthly punishment can atone for
> crimes of such extent and weight as those which were com-
> mitted at Auschwitz.[48]

Because of the impossibility of atoning for these crimes, the judgment continued, it might be argued that justice would have been
better served if the defendants, who had all contributed to Hitler's
program of extermination, had received the most severe punishment
that the court could legally assign. The judges, however, considered
this approach faulty, and in fact just as unfair as any other option.
Why? Once again, "the court could not allow itself to be misled into
uniformly burdening the defendants with the entire success of the
planned-out actions of a criminal regime that had access to organizational and technical materials. Its task and duty was to allocate
fair punishment to each defendant according to the crimes he was
proved to have carried out personally and his personal, proven, punishable guilt."[49]

In determining the length of sentence each defendant would receive, the court carefully examined each case of aiding and abetting.
It then decided that none of the defendants had acted in such a
manner as would incur a punishment of more than fifteen years.
The justification for this conclusion comprised ideological and psychological considerations. The court stated:

> In general, it can be said that for all the defendants convicted
> of aiding and abetting murder, the instigation for the crimes
> came from the highest levels of state leadership and occurred

in a time, under the rule of National Socialism, when unprecedented spiritual confusion prevailed. Through years of propaganda and clever intellectual influence, the NS leaders understood how to call into question normal values and to blur the boundaries between right and wrong. In the SS, these defendants were especially intensely affected by this propaganda and influence. The defendants were abused by the criminal regime to which they had sworn unwavering obedience.[50]

The court cited, as proof of their corruption by the regime, that before the Nazi period the defendants had lived their lives without being lawbreakers, and that after the Nazi period they had gone back to orderly, employed lives: "Under normal circumstances . . . they would never have committed murder or aided and abetted murder, despite their occasional weakness of character." Because of the corrupting nature of Nazism, instigated by the leaders of the regime, and because of the impossibility after two weeks at Auschwitz of any "normal reactions," according to former head of the hygienic institute at the camp, Dr. Hans Münch, people began to follow the negative example of their superiors and throw their values overboard. In this way they collaborated in crime; and although the justifications did not excuse their crimes, their guilt appeared in a "milder light" by comparison with that of the principal perpetrators, especially in view of the corrosive atmosphere prevailing at Auschwitz.[51]

In many ways, these statements regarding the corrupting nature of Nazism and the influence of propaganda and ideological training strayed from the purely legal framework to which the judges otherwise repeatedly referred as their only guiding force. They expressed in this section their opinion that the main source of Nazism's destructiveness was the leaders who created the program of extermination. The receivers of orders, although guilty of aiding in the mass murder, were in some ways also victims of the state, "abused" by its corrupting and confusing atmosphere. The judgment made a clear distinction between the instigators and the followers, thereby demonstrating a belief on the judges' part that a sharp division existed between the creators of the state and the collaborators who brought it to power and helped in its program of mass murder. This political predisposition seems out of place in the judgment of the trial, not because the trial really was an ordinary criminal trial, but because the judges insisted that it was. Nonetheless, one could argue that an examination of the role of the defendants within the larger framework of Nazism was necessary in order to determine their personal motivation. Although this interpretation had already been present in the convictions, it was also important for the sentences; and significantly, this political position justified the subjective interpretation of the law.

Finally, in examining the assignment of sentences, it is important to understand the court's justification for the different lengths of sentences. This is most obvious in the cases of Mulka and Höcker, who, as mentioned earlier, received very different sentences—both were convicted of aiding and abetting in the murder of at least three thousand people, but Mulka's sentence was double Höcker's in length. In the assessment of Höcker's sentence, the court explained:

> Although defendant Höcker had the same function as defendant Mulka, namely as adjutant to the camp commander . . . and participated in the mass extermination of the Jewish people, in determining his sentence the court has decided that his guilt cannot be judged in the same way as defendant Mulka's. When defendant Höcker came to Auschwitz, a well-coordinated organization for killing Jewish people already existed . . . The defendant Höcker was not—in contrast to defendant Mulka—on the selection platform, or at least this could not be proved. It could not be established—unlike with defendant Mulka—that he participated in the supervision of the selection of the RSHA transports on the platform or that he was personally involved in any other way in the extermination of Jewish people. He therefore was not as close to the events as defendant Mulka.[52]

Each defendant was sentenced not only for the number of murders he participated in, but also according to the way in which he participated. The judges' assessment of Höcker went on to describe him as a "desktop participant," who was never proved to have acted in a personally brutal manner toward any particular prisoner. This explanation of his actions was not meant to exonerate him, but rather to establish that he was less of a participant than defendant Mulka, who had been at the selection ramp and had been a more "hands-on" murderer. Finally, the discrepancy in the terms of imprisonment was influenced by the number of victims on the three occasions on which Höcker was convicted of aiding and abetting murder (one thousand people on each occasion), and by the fact that Höcker had never been convicted of a crime before, and after the war had gone back to a productive and "orderly middle-class life."[53] In fact, in 1952 he had gone to the public prosecutor's office in Bielefeld and filed charges against himself in order to initiate a denazification proceeding. The court weighed these factors to determine the length of his prison sentence. Such reasoning was used for each of the defendants, and helps explain the different sentences given to the excess perpetrators as well. Defendants Hofmann, Kaduk, and Bednarek, for example, received sentences of life imprisonment, whereas defendant Boger received life plus five years, defendant Baretski life plus eight years, and defendant Klehr life plus fifteen years. Often, the number of murders each defendant had been involved in was not the principal determining factor, but rather the ways in which the murders had been committed, the personal motivation of the defendant, his rank in the camp hierarchy, and his understanding of the actions he was undertaking.

The verdicts against the defendants who were considered excess perpetrators constituted the opposite extreme to those of Mulka and Höcker, who had been charged with only one crime. The excess perpetrators had hundreds, if not thousands of charges against them, most of which included crimes characterized by individual initiative and sadism. The convictions of these defendants reflected the mountain of evidence against them, as for example in the case of Klehr, who was convicted as the instigator and sole perpetrator in the murder of 475 people. The verdicts against the excess perpetrators were much more straightforward in terms of the law, because these defendants could be found guilty on individual charges of murder, rather than through such a process of elimination and deduction as in Mulka's case. All of these excess perpetrators—Boger, Hofmann, Kaduk, Klehr, Baretski, and Bednarek—were found to be principal perpetrators and sentenced to life in prison. Stark would have also belonged in this group, but having been under twenty-one when he committed his crimes, he was sentenced under the juvenile act. Even Bednarek, who had been a prisoner at Auschwitz and therefore presumably under a threat to his life that had not existed for the other defendants, was a relatively clear-cut case.

Defendant Boger was found guilty of murder as an accomplice to murder, a principal perpetrator of joint murder, and a principal perpetrator of at least 114 murders. "Joint murder" alluded to his participation in selections on the platform, particularly from the RSHA transports of Jews who were brought there solely as members of an "inferior race," and to his participation in the mass shooting executions at the Black Wall, in addition to his commission of individual murders witnessed by multiple survivors. His actions on the platform were considered particularly cruel, because he made sure that incoming prisoners did not speak to the prisoner commandos working on the platform, he allowed no one who was not fit for work to slip into the line for slave labor (that is to say, he was very strict about sending the elderly, the young, and the ill to the gas chambers, thereby demonstrating his cruel nature), and he watched closely over other SS personnel to make sure that they too were fulfilling their platform duties.[54] Boger did all of this with the knowledge that "he was an important part of the extermination machinery and that through his duties on the selection platform the extermination process was advanced."[55] The enthusiasm with which Boger undertook these actions, which he knew to be illegal and aimed against innocent victims (as established earlier in the judgment) determined the severity of his convictions and sentence. What was deemed to be his inner motivation was crucial to the judgment against him.

The convictions against Boger included very specific details about each of the crimes he had committed or participated in. For

example, the court described at length the process of "bunker evacuation," which was carried out under the supervision of the Political
Department and especially its head, Maximilian Grabner. The Political Department was constantly arresting and interrogating prisoners
within the camp, and then putting them into arrest cells in Block 11.
Because these cells were always overcrowded, the prisoners were
"cleaned out"—that is to say murdered—on a regular basis. Defendant Boger had arrested a large number of these prisoners and was
therefore implicated in their deaths. During the evacuations, prisoners were randomly taken from the cell and quickly given a mock trial
in which their fate was determined and immediately carried out.
This usually meant execution at the Black Wall. The judgment described the preparations for the shootings, during which SS officers
were laughing and joking as they retrieved their small-caliber guns
and silencers.[56] Prisoners were brought out to the wall two by two
and shot in the neck while other SS officers looked on. If there were
many prisoners to execute, they were brought out in groups of four,
and two SS officers committed the executions. The officers often
traded places with those who were looking on. There was a drainage
ditch along the wall of Block 10 for the blood of the murdered prisoners. After the executions, a list of the murdered prisoners was
brought into the HKB, so that the report takers could enter the prisoner numbers into a registry that listed them as ill patients. In this
way their deaths could be registered as normal deaths of sick prisoners. The deceit involved in this activity constituted treachery, an
offense defined in paragraph 211. In fact, these bunker evacuations
were the impetus for the investigation of Grabner undertaken by
Konrad Morgen that had led to Grabner's unfinished trial in
Weimar.

What did this four-page description have to do with defendant
Boger? The court concluded:

> Boger was one of the most zealous of the SS men in the
> bunker evacuations. He hated Poles, and they constituted
> the majority of the arrested prisoners. With fanatical zeal, he

searched throughout the camp for secret Polish resistance
and underground organizations . . . He spread fear and terror
in the camp. He was therefore one of the most feared SS men.
He was known to the prisoners by the names Beast of Auschwitz, Black Death, Terror of Auschwitz, Advancing Death,
and Devil of Auschwitz . . . Boger was proud of these names.
It filled him with a deep sense of satisfaction that he produced
fear and terror in his prisoners.[57]

Boger's sweeps through the camp were followed by rigorous intensified interrogations on the Boger swing. Often these interrogations
culminated in the prisoner's being beaten to death. Otherwise, the
prisoner was often one of the victims at the Black Wall. Even if the
fate of the prisoners was in the hands of Grabner or Aumeier, Boger
exercised a great deal of influence over them and often suggested
that the prisoners be murdered. Defendant Boger was willingly and
fanatically involved in the killing process from beginning to end.
This evidence came from numerous, corroborated witness statements; for example, that of witness Stefan Boratynski, quoted in the
judgment. He was a prisoner in the arrest cells and witnessed a
bunker evacuation on March 3, 1943. He was selected along with fellow prisoner Gestwinski for execution and taken into the washing
room inside Block 10, as was usual with all prisoners who were to be
shot at the Black Wall. He was ordered to strip naked, and his number was written on his chest, and after all numbers had been reported, the SS officers came into the room, joking jovially with each
other. Boger was among them. A capo named Bunker Jacob then
led the prisoners in groups of two out to the courtyard to be shot.
Witness Boratynski managed to escape death with the help of witness Jan Pilecki, who was in charge of recording the prisoners.
Pilecki threw him a uniform, and the SS men mistook him for a
corpse bearer. It was then his duty to remove the bodies of the shot
prisoners from the courtyard. In this way he saw defendant Boger
shoot at least six prisoners, among them his cell mate Gestwinski.[58]
   The list of convictions against Boger continued for more than

twenty pages. Included were the individual murder of prisoners through intensified interrogations, and the murder of at least one hundred prisoners after the 1944 uprising of the Jewish crematoriums' *Sonderkommando*. Witness Filip Müller, as one of the only surviving members of the unit assigned to clean out the gas chambers and take bodies into the crematoriums, testified about this. He also appeared in the film *Shoah* and wrote a memoir describing his experiences in his book *Auschwitz Inferno: The Testimony of a Sonderkommando*. Boger was not convicted of the murder of Lilly Tofler, an episode described in Chapter 2 that became one of the most famous Auschwitz stories. In response to all these charges, Boger admitted to taking part in platform duty and in the bunker evacuations. He insisted, though, that the shootings at the Black Wall had been ordered by the RSHA or the WVHA, and that although sometimes a prisoner was shot without such an order, that occurred usually as the product of a misunderstanding and under the supervision of Grabner or Aumeier. Until March 23, 1965, Boger insisted that he had never shot a prisoner himself. Then he suddenly changed his story and admitted to having shot two prisoners, on Grabner's orders. Boger was charged with aiding and abetting joint murder (paragraphs 47, 49), co-perpetration of murder (paragraph 49), and murder (paragraph 211). The latter charge applied to his initiation and implementation of intensified interrogations, in which prisoners died an agonizing death, and which "were illegal, also according to the perception of that time."[59] His service on the selection platform, because it was undertaken to aid the principal perpetrator, constituted aiding and abetting. Participation in the bunker evacuations, however, was considered co-perpetration, because it had been undertaken with base motives—that is to say, solely to make room in the arrest cells for more prisoners to be interrogated and murdered. This activity was carried out neither in obedience to superior orders nor to aid and abet murder initiated by someone else. Boger was therefore found guilty of murder for intensified interrogations leading to death in five cases, for the bunker evacuations and executions in nine cases, and for the murder of at least one hundred people after the *Sonderkommando* uprising. Both murder and co-perpetration of murder carried sentences of life in prison. He was found guilty of aiding and abetting murder for the platform selections of at least one thousand people.

The judgments of the other excess perpetrators found guilty of murder were similar to Boger's, in that the judges ruled that defendants were sadists and common criminals; however, each individual judgment took into consideration the specific character traits of the defendant in question. The court determined, for example, that Kaduk, in contrast to Boger, was a primitive brute who was motivated less by antisemitism or hatred of Poles than by a drunken desire to kill. The verdict consistently mentioned his insobriety, as well as his indiscriminate selecting of prisoners to be tortured and murdered. He showed no mercy for the ill, and in fact proclaimed in fall of 1944 that "the 'Muslims' *(Musselmänner)* must go!" and eagerly participated in their murder. The text of the judgment also referred to Kaduk's description of these prisoners as "useless eaters," *(unnütze Esser)* and in fact used this phrase to explain why he knew that he was sending certain prisoners to their death. He was also convicted on multiple individual charges (six individual charges of murder to Boger's two) and described as "one of the cruelest, most brutal, and most vulgar SS men at Auschwitz. Almost all prisoners were afraid of him." Despite his protestations about each charge against him, the judgment quoted numerous witnesses who had seen Kaduk in action. Because he was often drunk, and clearly not very clever, he did not hide his crimes as well as other SS guards; for example, he liked to play a very public game called cap-throwing, mentioned already in the indictment. He forced prisoners to throw their hats into the restricted areas directly at the guarded fence, knowing full well that when they went to retrieve their hats (which he ordered them to do), they would be shot by the watchmen. Kaduk was convicted of murder on multiple charges of cap-throwing, even though he was not the actual shooter. The justification for this conviction lay in his having instigated the activity and acted as principal perpetrator. Most of the prisoners that he preyed upon were new to the camp and therefore had no idea of their fate if they played along; they therefore had no opportunity to resist.[60]

Kaduk was found guilty of the murder of ten people and joint murder of more than one thousand people (co-perpetration). It is interesting to note that whereas defendant Mulka was found guilty of aiding and abetting murder in selecting prisoners for the gas chambers, defendant Kaduk was found guilty of co-perpetration. The court explained his conviction as follows: "Defendant Kaduk is to be punished as a co-perpetrator. He inwardly sanctioned the killing of the victims and made it into his personal mission, and therefore demonstrated perpetrator's intent."[61] Although Kaduk was acting on orders in the case of the mass gassings, the court ruled that he had the freedom to make judgments about whom he would select. He therefore controlled the whole situation and selected many people for death when he need not have. Because Kaduk did not doubt the illegality of the gassings, because he showed zeal in selecting prisoners for death, and because in his selections he had the final say over life and death, his intent to kill was more clearly established than that of Mulka or others who participated in selections on the platform.

The court ruled that defendant Klehr was the worst offender, single-handedly responsible for the murder of at least 475 prisoners, and guilty as accomplice to the murder of at least 6,440 people in total. He was convicted of participating in murder ordered by the main camp doctor, but his life sentence was based on convictions for individually initiated selections and injections. Defendant Baretski was convicted, as an accomplice, on the same count as defendants Mulka and Höcker: "participation in the mass killing of Jewish people at Auschwitz." He was also convicted on five individual charges of murder, including the killing of a prisoner named Lischka, on April 19, 1944. Lischka was a " 'Muslim' made up only of skin and bones," whom Baretski beat with a stick until his kidneys were severely injured. He subsequently died. Baretski also drowned four prisoners in a water tank on June 21, 1944. Baretski's judgment included a section titled "Further Crimes of Defendant Baretski

That Were Not Charged and Not Included in the Indictment." Here the court determined that Baretski "loved to punish prisoners from camp section B II d (Birkenau) who illegally signaled to prisoners in the women's camp across the new selection platform"; he did so with his particular brand of sport, which consisted of exercises so strenuous and lengthy that weak prisoners could not stand up afterward. He then yelled at them, and if they did not move, pulled out his pistol and shot them. He did this to at least five prisoners. The court listed three other offenses as crimes committed by Baretski, rather than alleged acts, and determined him to be guilty. However, in the justification of all of the convictions against him, the judgment stated the following regarding the crimes for which he had not been indicted: "There can be no conviction for these crimes . . . The crimes were introduced because they point to the overall behavior of defendant Baretski at Auschwitz, and they show his inner attitude toward the prisoners and serve to help judge his character."[62] This unusual move on the court's part demonstrated the judges' desire to introduce into the judgment unsubstantiated crimes that they considered nevertheless to be representative of Baretski's brutality. This serves as a striking example of the emphasis on individual acts of cruelty, which were judged much more harshly than participation in the overall process of extermination.

Finally, defendant Bednarek was found guilty of fourteen individual instances of murder. His is an interesting case, because he was a prisoner rather than a guard at the camp. Brought to Auschwitz as a Polish political prisoner in 1941, Bednarek quickly became the senior block leader of Block 8. He was responsible for "calm, order, and cleanliness" and had to answer to the SS camp leader. Clearly, Bednarek had to follow the orders of his superiors; however, according to the judgment, Bednarek "recklessly" enforced the rules and was known among the prisoners as a "very strict boss." He was brutal, indiscriminate, and terrorizing, punishing even the most minor of "transgressions." Like defendant Kaduk, he disliked the weakest prisoners (the "Muslims"), and if they crossed his path, he brought them into Block 8 and beat them to death. Defendant Bednarek was described as a man who "loved to torment prisoners" and who had "favorite" forms of torture and cruelty; according to the judgment, "he did not limit himself to beating, abusing, and tormenting prisoners." He also played exercise games with them, suffocated them under blankets, and engaged in other crimes with eagerness and frequency.[63]

What was the legal justification given for placing Bednarek in the same category of killer as the SS men on the stand? According to the German penal code, his actions, perpetrated on his own initiative and demonstrating sadism and base motives, put him in the same category as the SS guards. The ideological motivation of the other defendants was irrelevant, as we have repeatedly seen. Just like defendant Kaduk, he took pleasure in singling out certain prisoners and killing them; just like defendants Boger and Baretski, he created his own forms of torture without orders from his superiors, demonstrating in so doing individual initiative and therefore all the elements of perpetration of murder. The judgment in fact used Bednarek's status as a prisoner as further justification for the convictions against him, to demonstrate his cruelty and malicious inner motivation: "Death came to each of the prisoners [killed by Bednarek] in a cruel manner. Defendant Bednarek inflicted extraordinary pain and physical and psychological torture upon his victims because of his unfeeling and merciless disposition . . . Defendant Bednarek knew the heavy fate of the prisoners firsthand, as he himself lived in the prisoner-unfriendly atmosphere of the camp and saw their inhuman treatment by the SS, the capos, and the senior block leaders on a daily basis."[64]

Rather than show sympathy or attempt to alleviate the pain of his fellow prisoners, Bednarek adopted the actions of the SS as his own: he demonstrated his ability to act individually and could therefore be convicted of murder. According to the judgment, "it is the opinion of the court that defendant Bednarek killed the prisoners out of lust for killing (*Mordlust*—an element of paragraph 211)." Where defendants Mulka and Höcker were given lesser sentences with the explanation that they had been "abused" by the Nazi regime and brainwashed through relentless propaganda, defendant Bednarek's murder conviction was justified by the supposition that his character had been "totally perverted at Auschwitz" to encourage his sadism and vengeful murder of innocent fellow prisoners.[65] Once again, the judges, when assessing the severity of the conviction and assigning punishment to each defendant, demonstrated a willingness to interpret the law and therefore proved that they *did* have some flexibility (which they so often denied). Whereas they had cited the ideological training in the SS to give the higher camp officials milder sentences, they cited psychological corruption at the camp to give a prisoner-functionary a stiffer sentence. Obviously, in their assessment of these matters the judges showed how far they stood from their own contentions that this was an "ordinary trial," using ordinary tools to assess guilt and assign punishment.

Another group of defendants fell somewhere between the two extremes of Mulka and Höcker, on the one hand, and the excess perpetrators on the other. These defendants—particularly Scherpe, Hantl, Dylewski, Schlage, Broad, Capesius, Lucas, and Frank—were convicted only of aiding and abetting murder, to varying degrees. They had been accused of various individual crimes that could not be proved, or had been seen committing murder with their own hands, as in the cases of defendants Scherpe and Hantl, who were charged with murdering the boys from Zamość. They still did not qualify as principal perpetrators or co-perpetrators, because of their lack of individual motivation. This is seen very clearly in Scherpe's case. Unlike defendant Bednarek, who took the SS orders and "made them his own," Scherpe demonstrated deep inner resistance. In the judgment, the second conviction against Scherpe was "the killing of at least twenty Polish boys." He was convicted of aiding and abetting joint murder. The court took pains in its legal justification to acknowledge the murderousness of the action against the boys, while convicting Scherpe of aiding and abetting murder:

> The killing of at least twenty children was murder. The children were killed treacherously. They were unsuspecting and

therefore also defenseless. They did not know what was await-
ing them . . . In addition, the killing of the children was out of
base motives . . . The fact that they were killed as members of
the Polish nation, hated at that time by the National Socialist
rulers, shows clearly not only that there was no death sentence against them, but that their right to live was in fact no
longer acknowledged, because they were members of the so-
called inferior race . . . Defendant Scherpe killed the children
under orders. Article 47 of the Military Penal Code is relevant
here. The defendant recognized that the killing of children
was a universal crime. This is clearly shown by the facts that
already before the killing action he protested to camp doctor
Rohde and that he discontinued the killing.

Despite these ostensibly damning conclusions about Scherpe, the
court determined the following: "Even though he killed the children with his own hand, it cannot be established that he acted with
the intent of a perpetrator. He followed the order only reluctantly.
He inwardly refused the killing of the children . . . It is the opinion
of the court that defendant Scherpe therefore only supported the
murder action with the intent of an accomplice."[66]

Similarly, defendant Capesius, former head pharmacist at the
camp, was accused by individual witnesses of having taken part in
selections, of dispensing phenol for the injections, and of numerous
counts of entering the woman's camp, selecting a few women, ordering them to undress, and marching them out for selections—a
charge that would carry a murder conviction if proved, because of
the individual action involved. Capesius was convicted only on the
general charge of aiding and abetting joint murder for "participation
in the mass killing of Jewish people at Auschwitz." Specifically,
Capesius was proved to have taken part in selections of incoming
transports of RSHA prisoners in spring 1944 on at least four separate
occasions. These were the Hungarian transports that took approximately four hundred thousand Hungarian Jews to their death in a
very short period of time. Because so many transports were arriving,

it was decided in a meeting in spring 1944 that camp doctors would once again have to perform platform duties. Many witnesses saw Capesius on the platform, and numerous survivors are recorded in the judgment, describing by his actions there in detail. For example, one witness, Dr. Berner, identified Capesius as the man who had taken Berner's wife and children out of the work line and into the gas chamber line. In addition, Capesius deceived Berner by telling him that they were being taken to the showers to bathe and would then rejoin him. Like the majority of the other defendants, Capesius was found to have been aware of the illegality of the selections for the gas chambers—first, because he lied to the victims about their fate and second, because he repeatedly insisted that he had never taken part in the selections. The court ruled that this refusal to admit to his participation demonstrated that "he knew very well that he was facilitating the extermination program and contributing to the death of victims through the described participation."[67] Capesius's "knowledge of the illegality of the act" (*Unrechtsbewußtsein*) was further evidenced by the following bizarre explanation:

> It has once again been mentioned that defendant Baretski, a *Volksdeutsche* (member of the German ethnic group who lived abroad) from Romania, freely admitted that he recognized the extermination of the Jews to be unjust. If even this primitive defendant recognized the injustice of the extermination of the Jews, there can be no doubt that defendant Dr. Capesius, who as an academic was essentially more intelligent and educated than defendant Baretski and is moreover married to a half-Jew, recognized that the orders regarding the mass extermination of innocent Jewish people was a universal crime—even if he was "only" a *Volksdeutsche*.[68]

Capesius had clearly attempted to use in his defense the fact that, although he was German, he had lived in Romania and therefore did not understand the full implications of the Nazi program of extermination. The court, which found this claim unconvincing, was sarcastic and impatient in its dismissal of it.

The verdicts on the other "middle-ground" defendants all contain different character assessments and therefore different explanations about why these men, although sometimes charged with individual murder and definitely involved in the extermination process, received convictions only of aiding and abetting murder, and sentences sometimes only three years in duration (as was the case with Lucas). At the core of each conviction and sentence lay the judges' perception of the inner motivation—or lack thereof—that distinguished the actions of these defendants from those of the defendants convicted of murder. The middle-ground defendants all tended to be relatively intelligent but not excessively brutal or generally "primitive." They avoided serious punishment for numerous reasons: because of the lack of specific, substantive witness testimony (this was the case with Capesius, as we will see shortly).; because they behaved decently toward prisoners and kept a low profile, as defendants Broad and Lucas did, for example; or because they demonstrated reluctance to carry out their orders, as was true of defendants Scherpe, Hantl, and Lucas. None of these defendants received a sentence of more than nine years in prison, and on average they were sentenced to approximately five years and nine months in prison. Defendant Scherpe was sentenced to only four years and six months in prison because of his reluctance to kill, despite the fact that he had led at least twenty boys, one by one, into the injection room, asked them to take off their shirts and to put their left arms above their heads, and injected phenol directly into their hearts. Defendant Hantl was sentenced to three years and six months. But both Scherpe and Hantl were immediately released at the end of the trial on time served.

Finally, it is illuminating to examine the section at the end of the judgment on the accusations that could not be proved and had not led to a verdict. Many of the charges that were dismissed appear, on first glance, to have been irrefutably criminal acts witnessed by numerous people. Many have seeped into public consciousness as just that, although they were never legally proved. Examining which charges were dismissed and why demonstrates the meticulousness of the judges in adhering, in this regard at least, to the letter of the law.

To begin with, defendants Schobert, Breitwieser, and Schatz were acquitted of all charges. Schobert was accused of having taken part in the shooting of civilians in the small crematorium. This charge was corroborated by witness Jenny Schaner, a secretary in the Political Department in charge of the "registry of crematoriums." The court determined that Schaner had been believable and reliable in her testimony that she repeatedly saw the Gestapo lead small groups of people into the crematorium, and defendant Schobert often went along with them, his gun draped over his shoulder. He returned from the crematorium with "glazed, bloodshot eyes." The problem with this testimony, and with the charges and testimony against the other two defendants who were later acquitted, was the absence of eyewitnesses to his actual participation in or perpetration of the crime. The judgment read:

> The witness did not personally see defendant Schobert partic-
> ipating in the shootings. She also heard nothing about it. The
> described circumstances surely demonstrate that defendant
> Schobert had to have been present when the civilians were
> shot. If the civilians were led into the small crematorium,
> there can be no doubt that they were killed there . . . The
> small crematorium was also—like the Black Wall—used for
> executions in many cases [that is, not just gassings] . . . The
> fact that defendant Schobert went into the crematorium, after
> the delivery of the civilians, with his gun, also clearly shows
> that the people were shot there. Because no eyewitness saw
> the shootings, it cannot be established with certainty that de-
> fendant Schobert shot the people with his own hand.[69]

The judgment went on to state that it could be assumed that defendant Schobert had played some part in the shootings and that he
definitely expedited them. But there was simply not enough proof
that Schobert had participated in any punishable way. They executions may have been the result of a "valid" death sentence, or defendant Schobert may have believed they were the result of a death sentence. Taken together, all these unknown factors led the judges
to determine that even though defendant Schobert had been seen

leading a group of civilians into the small crematorium at Auschwitz with his gun, the evidence against him was not conclusive.

The explanation for defendant Breitwieser's acquittal was based largely on the testimony given by witness Walter Petzold, mentioned in Chapter 4. The witness maintained that he had seen the defendant throw gas pellets into the cellar of Block 11, where the first gassings of Russian prisoners of war had taken place in the fall of 1941. Breitwieser insisted that he had never done such a thing, and that he did not even know at the time that people were being gassed at Auschwitz. The court admitted that there was "considerable suspicion" about Breitwieser's contention that he had been "spared a lesson about the use of Zyklon B," but there was not enough definitive proof to show that Breitwieser had actually been present at the gassings. Witness Petzold was considered unreliable because it was physically impossible for him to have witnessed the actions between Blocks 10 and 11 from Block 27, as he maintained. Because no other witness had testified to Breitwieser's participation, he had to be acquitted. The court obviously did so reluctantly, because they refused to dismiss the strong possibility that the defendant had indeed taken part in the first gassings of Russian POWs. Breitwieser's own description of the use of gas (for the disinfection of clothing, he insisted) placed him under further suspicion; however, according to the law, some form of eyewitness, some valuable testimony, and some inner motivation on the part of the defendant had to be present. These are certainly valid and important judicial qualifications that must be present for a trial under the national penal code to be fair. But these qualifications meant that many charges against volunteer SS guards at Auschwitz had to be dismissed and some could go free because of the waning memory of traumatized victims or the inaccessibility of key execution sites to the general prisoner population of the camp.

Charges were also dismissed against the defendants who were convicted. At least fourteen charges against defendant Boger, for example, were dropped, including all those made by witness Jósef Kral and the charge in the shooting death of Lilly Tofler. Defense lawyers and Ukrainian witnesses who insisted that Kral himself had been a brutal capo at the camp had called his testimony into question. In addition, the court suspected that many of what Kral described as his own experiences were actually stories told to him by others at the camp. This suspicion stemmed from his having given multiple versions of his statements, particularly to credible witness Smolen regarding the shooting of a prisoner named Wroblewski. Kral had clearly suffered immense physical and psychological torture at Auschwitz, and there was little doubt that much of what he experienced was truthfully depicted. Small details, though, ruled out his testimony.

The story of Lilly Tofler remains one of the enduring narratives of Auschwitz. Her innocence and passion inside the camp evoked sympathy from her fellow secretaries in the Political Department, and the tragedy of her death was also recounted in the famous play *The Investigation*, by Peter Weiss. Significantly, the legal insufficiencies of the case on her behalf and the decision made by the court had little impact on the public reaction to her fate. Witness Ludwig Wörl, described by Hermann Langbein as one of the kinder senior block leaders at the camp had attributed Tofler's death to Boger, in the following way,:

> When [Wörl] was imprisoned in the arrest cell of Block 11, he was once allowed [by Bunker Jacob] to go to the washroom by himself. After a short time he heard yells in Polish. Jacob told him he should disappear. The witness then left the washroom and hid in another room. He could not completely close the door to this room. Through the crack he could see the hall in Block 11. He then saw and heard Boger coming and telling Jacob: "Bring her here!" Boger then himself led Lilly Tofler into the washroom and killed her with two shots. He—the witness—heard the shots himself. Afterward he saw the body of Lilly Tofler.[70]

Boger of course denied having shot Tofler, and told a different story: One day SS officer Kirschner came with an order for execution for Tofler, after which she was shot by another officer, Gehring, in the presence of Bunker Jacob. The court determined that the witness Wörl was not necessarily reliable, as he had already misled the court regarding defendant Hantl, and it was possible that he was inventing stories "in order to convince the court." In addition, Boger's testimony on this charge was not necessarily unreliable, as it was corroborated by witness Rosenthal (as described in Chapter 2), who reported that Boger told her he would have let Tofler live had she not fallen into the hands of Grabner.[71] It was impossible to establish that Boger had committed this shooting, or that if he had, he had done it on his own initiative. He was acquitted of the charge.

Defendants met with little sympathy when they argued that they had thought the orders to kill innocent people were legal. Referring to paragraph 47 of the Military Criminal Code, this defense was discredited. However, in the case of defendant Stark, on one occasion this defense was admitted and he was acquitted of a charge against him. Specifically, Stark had participated in the killing of Russian prisoners of war under the *Kommissarbefehl* issued by the Armed Forces High Command (Oberkommando der Wehrmacht, or OKW) on June 6, 1941, described in Chapter 3. The court ruled: "Defendant Stark argues that he thought that the killing of the Russian POWs was legal because it was ordered by the OKW. This cannot be refuted. It cannot be proved with all certainty that he knew the background for the killing of the Soviet-Russian commissars . . . It is therefore possible that he believed that the shooting of the commissars followed the rule of war that allowed for the repressions of saboteurs or partisans."[72] Because the victims of these first mass executions at Auschwitz were military personnel, the court resolved that it was possible that defendant Stark truly did believe he was following a legal order. In this case, the use of the superior-orders defense paid off. It is likely that his youthfulness and impressionability were taken into account as well, as they were with the sentences imposed under the juvenile act.

Sometimes, initial testimony appeared to be damning and definitive. This was the case with Capesius, who was accused of having gone to the women's camp on more than one occasion and searched for women who had hidden during selections. Two witnesses corroborated that he had done so: Salomon and Szabo, both women who claimed to have seen Capesius in action. The judges ruled that it was unlikely that Capesius had performed this duty, which was usually reserved for SS officers of a lower rank, not the main camp pharmacist. In addition, the witnesses could not know where these women had been taken if Capesius had indeed captured them; it was possible that as a doctor, he was taking them to the HKB instead. Finally, witness Szabo had not clearly identified Capesius when she saw him and claimed that she only later learned that he had been the "officer" she was referring to.[73] Strangely, the court gave no weight to the fact that more than one witness had testified to the same action. Also, Capesius was repeatedly charged with crimes having to do with the women's camp. However, these two women were not considered reliable sources and their testimony was discounted.

The judgment of the Auschwitz Trial was an enormous, complex document that attempted to address the specific circumstances of each defendant: his personality, his actions at the camp, his inner beliefs about National Socialism and the legality of the mass murder being committed in Auschwitz, and the ways in which his actions could be judged under the West German judicial system. Although the court, and especially Judge Hofmeyer in his address at the end of the trial, insisted that he and his colleagues had had to make their decisions based solely on the law, they did so somewhat inconsistently. Depending upon the situation, they sometimes invoked the mitigating circumstances of Nazi policy, SS ideological training, or the corruption of individuals by the regime. In particular, they called up this background in the cases of defendants Mulka, Höcker, and Stark. In other circumstances, particularly when dealing with the excess perpetrators, the judges omitted references to the history of the SS and the camp, mainly because they had enough incriminating evidence anyway to convict the defendants of murder. Although in handing out milder sentences for the three defendants mentioned above, the judges relied on references to the backdrop of Nazism and the Holocaust, sometimes such references had a positive effect, as they brought the extermination of the Jews to the forefront in a conviction of "participation in the mass murder of Jewish people." The arrival of RSHA transports of Jews at the selection platform, the inclusion of a detailed description of why these particular people had been brought to the camp, and a comprehensive account of the selection, gassing, and mass execution process all demonstrated that the judges were not willing to turn their backs entirely on history and context.

The judgment thoroughly investigated and weighed all circumstances associated with every alleged murder committed by each defendant. When exact details were unavailable, as was true of the numbers of people who had arrived on transports and been taken to the gas chambers, the judges used rough calculations to determine the guilt or innocence of each defendant. With obvious reluctance, they acquitted three defendants (two—Schobert and Breitwieser—on the recommendation of the prosecution) against whom they believed there was simply not enough specific evidence. The court did not make extravagant maneuvers in an effort to exonerate any of the defendants; the judges did not have to. They had only to turn to precedent, to the general consensus at the time—that reached as high as the court of appeals—to determine that the majority of defendants were merely accomplices. And yet the judgment clearly indicates that the court did not necessarily believe these men to be innocent. Time and again, the defendants are harshly condemned for their participation in the Final Solution.

Judge Hofmeyer had indicated in his oral statement that the trial was to be conducted as an ordinary trial; it was anything but that. The prosecution did not have an ordinary goal, the defendants were not ordinary criminals, the witnesses had not experienced ordinary events at Auschwitz, and on occasion even the judges had to reach into the extraordinary history of the Auschwitz concentration camp to come to a concrete and realistic decision. The sentences, though, did not reflect the extraordinary circumstances. The sentences corresponded to the main goal of the court: to conduct a criminal trial according to the West German penal code and to determine the guilt or innocence of the defendants charged in the indictment only in accordance with the elements of each crime with which they were charged. This verdict and these sentences would be the material with which the public, the press, and cultural critics would have to contend in years to come. Open dialogue about both Auschwitz and the outcome of the trial, part of Germany's confrontation with its Nazi past, spawned a vast body of journalistic analysis and even a sensational, important play—but strangely little historical examination, until the twenty-first century. The reaction to the trial merits a closer look.

CHAPTER 6

The Response to the Verdict

I N THE HISTORY of Germany's troubled self-examinations, this trial occasioned one of the most important and most public confrontations of the 1960s. Reporters, scholars, and cultural critics all commented on the judgment quickly after its announcement. In the wide variety of responses to the trial, most newspaper reporters shared a sense of disbelief and horror at the crimes that were recounted in the judgment. Whether the response to the verdict was positive and the reporter felt that justice had been properly served, or negative and the reporter showed disappointment at the lenient sentences, this incomprehension remained. Although it is difficult to gauge public reaction to the press coverage of the trial without the benefit of an accurate survey, a glimpse into the press reports on the trial helps demonstrate how people's opinions were shaped by what they read.

In 1965 a skeptical Hannah Arendt concluded: "Exposure for twenty months to the monstrous deeds and the grotesquely unrepentant, aggressive behavior of the defendants, who more than once almost succeeded in turning the trial into a farce, had no impact on the climate of public opinion."[1] Other commentators charged that the wrong men were on trial, that the defendants were "small men" who were used as "scapegoats," for the real culprits who had created, implemented, and financed the mass murder had now been welcomed back into society; the trial therefore could not possibly have a lasting effect on German society.[2] More recently, observers have argued that such trials, especially in Germany, do bring the theme of confronting or overcoming the past *(Vergangenheitsbewältigung)* to public awareness. I would argue that all these positions are in part accurate, demonstrating the contradictory outcome of this trial. There is no doubt that the Auschwitz Trial did, at least for a short time, bring the atrocities of the Nazi regime to the fore. The daily press coverage and most especially the widely staged, important, and sensational play *The Investigation*, by Peter Weiss, provided constant reminders to the public of the crimes committed by former Nazis who were then living in freedom in Germany. Many commentators made a genuine attempt by to draw people's attention to Auschwitz, in order that they might learn lessons about the human capacity for evil. At the same time, though, most people saw the grisly crimes of the sadistic defendants as if they were part of a macabre fantasy world—"Dante's Inferno," as Martin Walser described it—and did not make a connection between the perpetrators on trial, the harmless neighbors living peacefully beside them, and their own role in the Nazi past. To them the trial seemed to have done its job, properly punishing the real monsters and leaving the rest, people who had been confused, coerced, or brainwashed into collaborating with the Nazis, to go on with their lives. These mixed results were a reflection of the trial itself, and a debate surfaced about both the legal and the historical effectiveness of the trial. Even the participants in the trial spoke extensively about its end result: the prosecution, especially Fritz Bauer, argued that it was unsatisfactory; the court insisted that the trial had fulfilled its task in the context of the West German penal code. No consensus was reached about the trial's success on the judicial, the political, or the historical level; but the dialogue was in itself a sign that the trial was having an impact on West German society.

The reaction in the major newspapers to the judgment generally mirrored the emphasis of the trial coverage itself. Greatest attention was paid to the sadistic and grotesque crimes of defendants like Kaduk, Baretski, and Bednarek. The *Frankfurter Rundschau*'s first report quoted Judge Hofmeyer's opinion that it was not the role of the court to confront the past. The article listed the sentences for each of the defendants and explained that although many of the sentences fell far short of the prosecution's requests, Hofmeyer had justified the decisions by arguing that each defendant had to be judged separately on each charge. The court had been hampered by the difficulty of determining what was valid witness testimony at this trial, which was neither a show trial nor a political trial.[3] The article did mention Hofmeyer's ruling that the dictator's order *(Führerbefehl)* to exterminate the Jews had been unlawful, and that the defendants were aware that it was. In general, though, the article did little to shed light on what the judgment meant.

The *Frankfurter Rundschau* also reported on the reaction in parliament to the Auschwitz Trial verdict. One member of parliament, who noted with gratification that the court had not accepted the superior-orders defense, saw this exclusion as a great step forward in recognizing individual responsibility. He also praised the court for imposing the most severe punishment on those defendants who had been proved to "have been directly involved in the killing operations."[4] He was slightly misguided in this interpretation of the judgment, as is clear from Chapter 5. All the defendants, even Mulka and Höcker, were directly involved in the killing operations. The speaker was referring to those who had murdered with their own hands. He argued that the federal government should not take a position on a trial by an independent court, and therefore kept his remarks to a minimum and had only positive things to say. He wished only to reiterate that this was not a trial of the entire Auschwitz complex, first of all because Auschwitz itself was not on trial, and second because Allied and Polish tribunals had already investigated and tried many other Nazi criminals. Of course, there were many thousands of camp guards who had not been tried or investigated, but his attitude was typical of those prevalent in the government and among the public at the time. People wanted to turn their attention forward, rather than back toward the past.

The most detailed newspaper analysis was in the editorials which appeared within days of the judgment. The attitude expressed toward the trial depended largely on the political orientation of the newspaper.[5] In the *Frankfurter Rundschau*, a left-leaning newspaper, writer Gerd Czechatz argued that Judge Hofmeyer's insistent refrain that this trial was not meant to overcome the past but to determine individual criminal guilt was an empty phrase when applied to crimes that "defy the imagination." Altogether, the verdict pronounced the defendants guilty in the participation of about fifty thousand murders. The author found the entire thing "difficult, no, impossible to comprehend," as did a law student with whom he spoke, who told the reporter that he had attended the trial not so much for the legal lessons but for the human ones. Czechatz too hoped that some humanitarian lessons could be learned from such a trial. Unfortunately, though, the politicians who were campaigning throughout Hesse at that time (both the chancellor and the opposition candidate) did not visit the courthouse on the day the verdict was read, because the ruling at the Auschwitz Trial was not thought to be a priority among voters. The writer addressed a public that could not understand the phenomenon of Auschwitz, could not fathom the number of people murdered, and did not question how Germany had come to support the regime that had carried out these crimes.[6] Czechatz seemed to share the general public's incomprehension of the crimes. Despite his best intentions to call attention to the trial and its lessons, the tone of his article reflected the widespread detachment from Auschwitz and the Holocaust that had characterized the press coverage throughout the trial.

Like the *Frankfurter Rundschau*, the left-leaning *Süddeutsche Zeitung* covered the verdict. In an editorial that appeared on August 20, journalist Ernst Müller-Meiningen, Jr., praised the court for refusing to acknowledge the superior-orders defense, criticized the defendants for their cowardice and the shabby pretext that they had been minor players and were being punished for the actions of their superiors, and found fault with the mild sentences given to the majority of defendants in the convictions for aiding and abetting. Müller-Meiningen emphasized the historical lessons that could be learned from the trial, despite the judge's refusal to acknowledge those as the trial's main task. "The *system* became visible" through the trial, he wrote, and although the trial had been held at an unfavorable time, twenty years after the Holocaust, when a "large, politically immature and lethargic segment of the population" wanted to close the case on the events of the past, the author argued that the public did not have the right to do so, for "the crimes cry out, if not for the blood of the guilty, then for enlightenment and the greatest requital that is humanly possible."[7] Müller-Meiningen demanded that the "horrors of Auschwitz and all the other places of death and extermination remain alive in the consciousness of our population," not only those who had lived during the Nazi period but for the next generation as well. Denial, silence, and guilty consciences about the Nazi past would lead nowhere, and the lessons of this trial, however obscured by its deficiencies, had to be learned.

Editorials that appeared in *Die Welt* and the *Frankfurter Allgemeine Zeitung*, both more conservative newspapers, took a very different tone. In *Die Welt*, editorialist Hans Schüler wrote that because the Auschwitz Trial had cast a "broad shadow" over West Germany for so long, "it could seem as though [Germany's] entire past was represented there [in the Frankfurt courtroom] in twelve dark years." A fascinating article entitled "Atonement for Auschwitz," by Johann Georg Reißmüller, appeared in the *Frankfurter Allgemeine Zeitung*. Reißmüller, who frequently contributed editorials and later became editor in chief of the newspaper, asked a larger question of the trial, while also referring to its distortion of the period of Nazi rule: "But what exactly is it that came to pass here? The civilized world's settling of accounts with Hitler's murder system? A moral and political-lesson, meant for those who lived during the era of Auschwitz who went far in the art of repression, and a signal of deterrence for the generation that followed? A historical investigation in which, in a courtroom, stroke by stroke, a narrowly circumscribed chapter of German history was recorded by living human beings? The wish itself [that the trial could serve these functions] suggests that the Auschwitz Trial could have been all this."[8]

Reißmüller recognized that the trial provided an opportunity to do all these things. Historical sources had become available that scholars rarely came across. The law, however, made it possible to address these issues only to a "narrowly restricted degree." And precisely because the legal system was that of a democratic state, it could not be altered to suit the needs of the court or of history: "The all-powerful tribunal that avenges and educates, that extorts fear . . . and that points the people toward its future path is a creation of the totalitarian state, a piece of it. [Such a trial] has to be foreign to a liberal state." The author noted that a side effect of the trial certainly was the history lessons it supplied, and that as a result of this very public proceeding, "no one can now doubt or trivialize Auschwitz." Reißmüller agreed with Judge Hofmeyer that such results, though, should be only side effects and should never be the main goal of the trial itself. In fact, according to Reißmüller, this expectation missed the point entirely: "In truth, it is exactly this that gives [the trial] value and historical and political significance: that here the liberal state atoned for boundless crimes and at no point overstepped the boundaries of the law that it had created."[9] The "superhuman strength" that all members of the court demonstrated, especially the judges and the defense, in their effort not to let this become a show trial, not to be influenced by the greater atrocity of Auschwitz itself—this was the real achievement of the trial, Reißmüller suggested, and should be seen as the great success of the proceedings against the Auschwitz perpetrators.

Gerhard Ziegler, who wrote an editorial in the *Frankfurter Rundschau* the next day, took a similar stand. He agreed with Judge Hofmeyer that there was no hope of achieving real atonement for the crimes of Auschwitz because no sufficient punishment was humanly attainable. That being established, Ziegler criticized the foreign press, and detractors in East Germany, who often expressed outrage at the mild sentences and who called the verdicts "an insult to all victims." On the contrary, argued Ziegler, "exactly these people, who suffered so unspeakably under the dictatorship of illegality, should be happy that the law is once again being upheld." He agreed that a trial like that of the Auschwitz defendants would have had a very different outcome in East Germany, but it would have been unlawful and would not have taken into account the subtleties of the issues presented in Frankfurt: for example, that these defendants were neither "born" criminals nor the "principal initiators" of the Nazi system of extermination. The defendants could therefore not all be sentenced to swift, severe punishment. That kind of punishment was typical in totalitarian states, and the Frankfurt trial represented West Germany in its "return to constitutionalism."[10] To revise or interfere with this was to shun democracy.

Leftist critics had a very different opinion of the manner in which former Nazis should be dealt with judicially. Eugen Kogon, for example, was diametrically opposed to Ziegler's position. In a commentary for the state public radio, Hessische Rundfunk, on August 21, 1965 (which appeared as an article two months later in *Neue Juristische Wochenschrift*), Kogon expressed his disappointment with the judgment. Reacting to Hofmeyer's opening statement that it was not the court's role to make a "contribution to contemporary history," Kogon agreed that it was the judge's role to uphold the law. He argued, however, that the court was missing one fundamental point: the judge could not simply close his eyes to the fact that this judgment not only was a part of history but would have an effect on history. It was the responsibility of the court to keep this in mind rather than to hide from possible repercussions behind the limitations of the law. Kogon complained, "I have never before heard such a sovereign judicial self-restriction, which does not come from ignorance or from neglect of the historical-political circumstances, but is a direct result of knowledge of them." In his criticism, Kogon stated that the judge's knowledge of the importance of the backdrop was precisely what had made him choose to ignore it, and that as such the decision had "enormous social-pedagogical implications." Kogon clearly wanted to engage the judges at the Auschwitz Trial, and the public in general, in a debate about how imperative it was that the law change and grow in response to historical developments. He agreed with Reißmüller that the trial had presented an opportunity for the judges to make an enormous leap forward and deal with crucial issues. For Kogon, however, that this was not done was the greatest shortcoming of the trial, not its greatest success. He continued: "With a few elementary initial explanations, Judge Hofmeyer cleared away current misunderstandings—misunderstandings that for many people have replaced the truth in this matter. He did it almost as if it were self-evident, obvious, reasonable, enlightening; one is supposed to simply accept . . . that the court could not question whether this trial was expedient or not, whether it fit into our politics. That could not be the concern of the court."[11]

Kogon was greatly disappointed by the arguments that Hofmeyer had used to justify the verdict. The insistence on adhering to law that had been established in 1871 and that had existed throughout the Nazi period had not, as Hofmeyer maintained, created a fair trial. Rather, it revealed a "hidden leftover National Socialist mentality." After such a judgment, the perpetrators could go back into the society unregenerate, and the only lesson from the Auschwitz Trial was that the law could deal only with "concentration camp atrocities" (*KZ-Greueln*) that were individual acts and exceptions.

The discussion of the verdict turned into a debate that engaged legal scholars, journalists, historians, and philosophers. The main questions were whether the trial had been part of a confrontation with the past, and whether that should have been the role of the trial at all. In general, those representing the legal system defended it ferociously, whereas historians called for some flexibility and willingness to adapt. The exception, as always, was Fritz Bauer. In an article entitled "In the Name of the People: The Judicial Overcoming of the Past," that appeared in a volume commemorating "twenty years after" in 1965, Bauer made his argument clear even in the title. He felt that society had to learn from the past in order to draw consequences for the present and future, and that even in trials, or perhaps especially in trials, the public is involved. The court had to take this responsibility seriously and recognize the public's involvement, just as the public had the duty to become engaged in the trial. After all, both the judges and the public were the same people who had been the judges and the public during the Nazi period. Bauer wrote: "The courts are a part of the people; that goes for the judges and the jury. True, the language of the law is not determined through the questioning of the public. But Dante's words should not be forgotten: 'The law exists, but who operates it?' "[12] Bauer felt strongly that West Germans, including the jurists, had to make connections between law and society. The law should also reflect societal and historical change. The law had to be flexible.

Bauer argued for a public and judicial awakening because of what he saw as a pervasive indifference, even resistance, to the "historical, legal, and moral lessons that these trials can provide." According to his estimate, this trial was generally not penetrating public consciousness: 40 percent of the West German population claimed never to have heard of the trial, and of the 60 percent who had, nearly 40 percent "wanted to let grass grow over the past." Even worse, on the issue of the statute of limitations, 63 percent of men and a full 76 percent of women felt that the Nazi trials should not continue and the statute of limitations should not be overturned.[13] Bauer wished to combat this public indifference and asked people to confront the Nazi past at last, recognize their own role in it, and take steps, through engagement with such trials as that of Auschwitz, toward preventing indifference from leading to oppression and persecution again.

The judgment from the trial did not make the connection between collaboration with the Nazi program—whether passive or active—and mass murder. For Bauer, this was one of the greatest disappointments of the Auschwitz Trial verdict, and the verdicts of most Nazi trials. He was especially dismayed at the judges' decision to convict most of the defendants of aiding and abetting murder. He complained:

The courts, in a large number of cases of Nazi crimes, used merely aiding and abetting rather than perpetration; this occurred not only with the "small men," but also with some of the higher functionaries in the Nazi hierarchy. Behind the much-loved adoption of the aiding and abetting conviction—by the courts all the way up to the supreme federal court—is the residual wishful fantasy that there were only a few people with responsibility in the totalitarian state of the Nazi period and the rest were merely terrorized, violated hangers-on or depersonalized, dehumanized characters who were compelled to do things that were completely contrary to their nature. Germany was not, as it were, a society obsessed by Nazism, but a country occupied by the enemy. But this had little to do with historical reality. There were virulent nationalists, imperialists, antisemites and Jew-haters. Without them, Hitler was unthinkable.[14]

Bauer went on to suggest what were, in his opinion, the real motives of the courts in letting so many Nazi criminals off with a such light sentences: "The courts made an effort to break up the entire event [the Holocaust]—for example, the mass murder of millions in the extermination camps—into episodes . . . They wished to prove in detail the individual actions of each defendant. But this desecrates the occurrence, which was not the sum of individual incidents."[15]

Bauer saw a sinister motive behind the legal flouting of the "bigger picture" of the mass murder that had gone on in the camps. He saw this phenomenon as peculiar to Nazi trials, and as a deviation from what was "usual, in fact understood, in our criminal proceedings." He was referring to the fact that under the penal code after 1954, mass murder or genocide was illegal and banned by paragraph 220 and would be prosecuted as such. The constitution banned retroactive use of laws, and many jurists argued that paragraph 220 could not be applied in trials of Nazis. But Bauer argued the opposite: consideration of the extraordinary circumstances of the Nazi Holocaust had to be incorporated into the law. Change was necessary if justice was truly to be served. For this reason, he argued, the

Auschwitz Trial, which was the longest jury trial in the history of the Federal Republic, could have been the shortest:

> There was an order to liquidate the Jews in Nazi-controlled Europe; the instruments of murder were Auschwitz, Treblinka, and so forth. Whoever operated this murder machinery is guilty of participation in murder, whatever he did, of course provided that he knew the aim of the machinery . . . If someone is a member of a band of robbers . . . or a gangster . . . then he is guilty of murder, regardless of whether he issued the murder order as the "boss" at the desk, whether he distributed the revolvers, . . . or whether he does the shooting with his own hand . . . No criminal jurist in this country would doubt this.[16]

Whereas it was usual practice for all jurists, even young ones, to recognize the justice of this representation, and to try, convict, and sentence criminals accordingly, Bauer argued that the courts had used a different standard in Nazi trials, "probably to privatize somehow and thereby blunt the collective occurrence through the atomization and parceling out of these terrible things."[17] Bauer felt that the sentences handed out at the Auschwitz Trial not only were much too mild, but constituted a mockery of the victims themselves.

Bauer was suspicious of the motivations behind the use of the regular West German penal code. He felt that this inadequate legal system contributed to lessening the magnitude of the crimes in the eyes of both the defendants and the general public and therefore was part of the Germany's failure effectively to confront its past. The "hidden motive" behind the self-justifications was the unwillingness of the "lion to look into the mirror." Bauer felt that Germans—the general public but also jurists and politicians—were reluctant to swallow the bitter pill of the Auschwitz Trial. They felt completely distanced from it by life in a thriving democratic state, where wealth was growing, where social security systems were functioning successfully, and where human rights were written into the constitution as basic and irrevocable. But Bauer wanted to bring home to them that many of the citizens of this thriving country had also been citizens of the Nazi state. Nothing precluded persecution and totalitarian domination from rising again. The seeds of perversion that had led to an event like the Holocaust lay not only in the exclusion of certain minorities, in stereotypes, or in racial hatred, but also in the "radical reduction and simplification of the facts and the proposed solutions."[18] People should not blindly accept the verdict of the court, and in the end the court itself had to look inward and find ways to promote justice that were better suited for dealing with the crimes of the Nazi period.

Kogon, Bauer, Langbein, Walser, and others, argued for a change in the legal system to ensure that the historical reality of the Holocaust could be properly addressed and criminals from that era punished through such trials. Such critics also hoped that jurists should examine their own positions on this issue and recognize that the "bigger picture" could not be wished out of existence by ignoring it. Judge Hofmeyer, who himself wrote two years after the trial's end about the trial, the judgment, and the debate that surrounded the law, argued for separating trials from history lessons. He defended the penal code and procedural code as they stood and proposed solutions that would make trials of Nazi criminals as short and swift as possible. Either way, the outcome of the Auschwitz Trial was dissatisfying to many participants and observers.

In an piece entitled "Legal Problems and the Practical Difficulties of Conducting Trials," first published in 1967, Hofmeyer directly addressed Bauer's contention that these trials of ex-Nazis could have been shorter than they were, because whoever in some way participated in the murder machinery was guilty of murder. He objected to this view as running completely contrary to the basic rights of every human being in a constitutional state. Every single defendant had the right to argue his own case, and the courts were obliged to investigate each individual count. These basic rights of each defendant had inevitably made the trials very long. In order to do justice to each case, painstaking, time-consuming work was an absolute necessity. To ignore this consideration was unjust, as "two wrongs do not make a right."[19] Hofmeyer recognized that these trials had been terribly long, and too numerous. In fact, he felt that further trials like the Auschwitz Trial should be avoided. He felt that the categorization of trials according to specific "crime complexes" (Auschwitz, *Einsatzgruppen*, death marches, for example) created all sorts of limitations, in which, for example, one group of perpetrators could exonerate itself at the cost of others. In general, trials such as this had to be curtailed if courts were to get through all the cases before them. Hofmeyer's attitude toward such trials was in exact opposition to Fritz Bauer's goal of making sure that entire "crime complexes" were judicially addressed. Whereas Bauer wanted public attention to be drawn to the big picture of the machinery of genocide, Hofmeyer felt that the West German judicial system was an inappropriate forum—and specifically, that the penal code should not be called into question. He was correct in his assessment that the law was incapable of dealing with such crimes; but he did not offer a solution to address the unavoidably present bigger picture of the extermination program. He advised instead that such trials should no longer take place. Hofmeyer, therefore, missed the point of Bauer's and Kogon's arguments. He did not entertain the possibility of updating or adapting the StGB and StPO so that they could address crimes of the magnitude of those committed at Auschwitz. Such an amendment would have been contrary to the ban in the constitution on retroactivity and therefore was not open for discussion. Hofmeyer addressed only the difficulties of witness testimony, and ignored the larger issue that especially Bauer hoped jurists would examine at length. His article was a perfect example of exactly what frustrated Bauer: the unwillingness of the public and the administrators of justice to look at the whole picture, and the tendency to simplify the problems and the solutions.

In fact, Hofmeyer questioned whether the background of the "entire event" should be addressed at all in such trials. The criminal procedural code spelled out plainly that the court could not be compelled to bring in historical documentation to broaden the case. So although such background "undoubtedly belongs to the interesting facts of history," its exclusion from trials such as the Auschwitz Trial "would certainly have limited the difficulties of such a trial." Hofmeyer substantiated his point by comparing the three Nazi trials that had taken place at the district court of Frankfurt am Main: first, the 1952 trial of a guard from Treblinka accused of cruelty and sadism, which had endeavored only to determine his individual guilt and had lasted three days; second, the 1963 Auschwitz Trial, which had lasted twenty months and had addressed the entire crime complex of Auschwitz from a historical perspective; and third, the smaller Auschwitz trial of three guards that had lasted nine months and brought to bear even more historical background. Hofmeyer felt that the trials of Nazi guards should be trials of individual defendants based upon their actions, where the nature of the criminal structure in which they had participated was almost irrelevant. Otherwise, these "gigantic trials" were taxing for everyone: the lawyers and judges, who had to learn an enormous amount of historical information that was a "psychological burden" because the "inhumanity" of the crimes was so hard to fathom; the jury, whose members had to abandon their jobs for an extremely long time; and the defendants, who were often already old men. The message in Hofmeyer's argument was that it would have been much easier for everyone not to have to confront such horrors.[20] This was especially the case because the StPO stipulated that no case could be interrupted for more than ten days, and therefore the participants in this trial were in the "grotesque" predicament of having to face the atrocities of Auschwitz relentlessly, without a break, for almost two years.

Hofmeyer wrapped up his article by pointing to what he saw as the principal problem, which encompassed all the other difficulties he had listed: "Here a political era is being investigated for its legal and illegal attributes with completely unsuitable means, namely with a criminal procedural code that never conceived of such proceedings, is not designed for them, and puts strictly constitutional principles in the foreground, principles that possibly give the defendants more protection against a misjudgment [*Fehlurteil*]."[21] Hofmeyer therefore asked that such trials be conducted as murder trials—in which the political background was borne in mind but did not become the focal point—rather than political trials. He proposed:

> Perhaps among the countless number of crimes of which each defendant is accused, the indictment can be limited to a few lesser charges that would already suffice in legal terms for the highest possible sentence. In these cases, the entire event [the Holocaust], in the sense of historical perspective, would recede into the background and possibly come up short. But it would be the only possibility to shorten these trials to lessen the responsibility of the witnesses, to shorten the length of the proceedings, and in this way to clear the way for the courts to fulfill the task that they were assigned.[22]

The most critical reaction to the Auschwitz judgment came from the East German press and from the foreign press. The East German papers expressed unanimous disapproval over the mildness of the sentences. The press wrote that the verdicts connoted a "pervasive fascism" and sympathy with the ex-Nazis in West Germany. The bulletin of the Institute for Contemporary History in East Berlin referred to the *Frankfurter Rundschau* article mentioned earlier: "The paper argues, absolutely correctly, that the Auschwitz Trial would have had a very different ending in the GDR. But that is exactly what differentiates the two states, it also adds self-assuredly. But the West German press cannot deny that the murderers from Auschwitz found benevolent judges."[23]

Neues Deutschland, a newspaper published in East Berlin, called the verdict scandalous and reported that the murderers had been handled with kid gloves, as part of a general trend in West German courtrooms where Nazi criminals were concerned. The newspaper then blasted the West German press: " 'The judgment in the Auschwitz Trial is a symbol of closure to a bloody and lost epoch,' the *Tagesspiegel* commented on Friday. Of closure? This is the impression the judgment wanted to leave. The main perpetrators, Hitler, Himmler, and Heydrich, are dead. This is true. Yet not only do the other principal perpetrators, those who thought up the murder plans right down to the last detail, live undisturbed in the Federal Republic today, but many of them hold high posts in the government and economy again."[24] The newspaper directed its chief criticism, as did most East German journalists, scholars, and lawyers (such as attorney Kaul), against big business and the focus in West Germany on capitalistic growth at all costs. In particular, *Neues Deutschland* severely condemned the role of major industrialists at IG Farben, first at Auschwitz and then in the regeneration of the West German economy.

Newspapers in London, Paris, and Zurich also expressed disappointment at the sentences. The *Neue Zürcher Zeitung* wrote that the penal code was ill equipped for such a trial; that defendants Mulka or Capesius had received such light sentences was a highly unsatisfactory outcome. *Combat*, a left-wing Parisian paper, found the sentences far too lenient but acknowledged that even death sentences would have done nothing to compensate for the crimes of the Nazis. The *Times* of London was less critical of the judgment than of the overall German public refusal to confront the crimes. The *Times* called this depressing, and suggested that the failure to do so stemmed from Germans' subconscious feeling that it was hypocritical to condemn others when they themselves felt partially responsible for and guilty of these crimes.[25] Reaction in the Polish press was similar to that of the East German newspaper coverage: *Trybuna Ludu*, the main organ of the Polish United Worker's Party, expressed disappointment that the court had refused to see the trial as a chance to indict the camp, the institution of fascism, and its most extreme consequences. According to journalist Jerzy Kowalewski, the fact that most defendants would be out of prison within a few years after the end of the trial made it much easier to forget Auschwitz.[26]

Discussion of the Auschwitz Trial tapered off in the press within a few weeks following the verdict, but for some, the trial remained of central importance. A year after the end of the trial, as part of a program for political and cultural education created by the state of Hesse, Hermann Langbein lectured in schools and at public events on the lessons to be learned from the trial. His illuminating findings after speaking with many people about the trial showed a distinct rift between the younger and older generations about the importance of these kinds of trials. One of Langbein's lectures to the community leaders in a small town in Hesse was recorded. In attendance were many young people whom Langbein had earlier visited in school. The note taker wrote of this dichotomous reaction:

> In the case of the older generation, one encounters with tiresome regularity an attempt by these people to apologize for themselves (and for most, [it was] a very superficial apology). Very often one encounters the stereotypical response, "You have to believe me: I really only discovered that Auschwitz existed in 1945." In response to these excuses the lecturer [Langbein] established that in 1934 at the latest, with the Röhm putsch, it had to be clear to every politically thoughtful person that the National Socialist regime had planned and committed crimes. There are no apologies from the younger generation. They ask about the purpose of what happened, and pose this question: "What can be done? Is there an answer that would make a recurrence impossible?"[27]

The audience became very animated during the question period, when young and old confronted one another. One older man asked why the Jews of their community had allowed themselves to be deported without a fight. Surely the rest of the town would have reacted, but as the deportation took place under "night and fog," people had known nothing. Why had the Jews not screamed out? An older woman, obviously well educated, called out, "Actually *we* should have gone out to the marketplace and screamed, 'The Jews are not to be deported!'" This remark caused a strong reaction among the young, who asked why that had not been done. When the woman responded, "Out of fear, presumably," a young man countered: "Only fear? You had no other reason than that?"[28] This public debate exemplified the growing dissonance between young and old in West Germany, dissonance that would lead to enormous protests later in the same decade, with the famous student revolutions of 1968.

But the public lecture, and other discussions with young people, also unearthed a different reaction. Many were impatient with the constant reminder of the atrocities committed against the Jews and the blaming of the German public through trials like the one in Frankfurt. Young people also argued that antisemitism was not solely a German creation, that many other countries also considered Jews the enemy and that, in fact, the Jews had brought this treatment on themselves. These sentiments closely echoed those of the older generation, leading the note taker in the article to conclude that the younger generation had learned certain attitudes in the home from parents who no longer wanted to be questioned about their activities in the past. The article further concluded: "In many parental homes and for many respectable people in general, the spirit of impatience has not been overcome." In addition, according to Langbein, the fatigue expressed by so many students when confronted with lessons on the Nazi period ("This subject *again?*") was the result of the way that students were learning: "To put it brutally, the mountain of corpses is shown too often, and the investigation into how it could have come to this is conducted too infrequently."[29] The grotesque pictures of the dead bodies had to be shown only once, argued Langbein. The constant repetition of these images led to desensitization and to resentment on the part of the young ones that the older generation, which had been much more involved in the killing, did not look at these pictures at all.

Langbein felt that young people could learn a great deal from the Auschwitz Trial. In particular, two completely different defendants —Kaduk, the sadist, and Mulka, the cold higher officer "in white gloves"—could serve to open a dialogue and create understanding about the kinds of people who made the concentration camp function. Whereas Kaduk's behavior was relatively straightforward, and his heavy punishment justified, Mulka was a more complex figure and yet the more important one for the public. He represented a more typical "everyman," who was in many ways "interchangeable" with many other Germans who by chance did or did not end up at Auschwitz as a guard. He never got his "hands dirty," in contrast with Kaduk, but must be understood as having had just as much responsibility for the mass murder as Kaduk. Why? "The Kaduks could only terrorize in that fashion because they were encouraged to do it by the Mulkas, even given special vacations and other advantages for their actions."[30] So even though quite obviously the Kaduks always got very heavy sentences and the Mulkas usually got away relatively unscathed at the German trials, the less sadistic characters should not be seen as any less guilty, despite what the verdict might instruct people to believe.

A few weeks after Langbein's public lecture, members of audience reconvened to discuss what they had learned, not only at the lecture but, in the case of the students, after talking to their parents about what their roles in Nazi Germany had been. The program organizers were especially interested in hearing from students whose parents had been in the SS, the students who had spoken about their frustration with their parents' silence at Langbein's earlier talk. In the minutes of the session, the note taker addressed two general warnings to teachers who wanted their students really to understand the nature of Nazism, antisemitism, and the Holocaust, in order to prevent its recurrence. First, German history should not be seen as having taken a "special path" that led directly to the Holocaust, which had therefore been predetermined by the events of the far-distant past. Similarly, educators should not teach their students to hide behind sweeping generalizations about the inherent nature of Germans, in which the entire nation is deemed ultranationalist and antisemitic by its very cultural and ethnic identity. These created a concept of German guilt so unwieldy and vague that it could not provide any real opening for understanding and preventive action to spring up. Rather, people had to think in terms of individual responsibility for their own actions, individual responses that had created the climate in which Hitler and antisemitic policies could flourish.

At the same time, the educators also warned against a tendency to teach about the National Socialist period as an accident of history that had simply befallen the German people, as though an enemy had suddenly occupied the country. The historical background to the advent of Nazism had to be accurately represented. Young people had to learn how that regime had come out of a climate of chaos and desperation that had led normal people to embrace a government that would oppress and persecute "outsiders." In addition, students should learn about the traditional German attitude toward authority figures, in which lawyers, bureaucrats, teachers, and government officials were not to be questioned. This attitude was attributed to the lack of a successful democratic revolution in the German history. Blind faith in authority figures caused citizens to accept the dictatorship of the Nazis more readily. Presenting this combination of factors could help students to understand how the Holocaust had come about, and although "reading the lyrical writings of Anne Frank" was important, it did not sufficiently help understand and "overcome what happened between 1933 and 1945."[31] It is important to remember that the state of Hesse organized this public forum and its probing questions, as a follow-up to the Auschwitz Trial. The fact that the state itself was concerned with how people in West Germany dealt with the past indicates an official policy, at least in the Education Department, of confrontation with the Nazi era.

The evening discussion also dealt with the topic "the Hitler in all of us," a form of *Vergangenheitsbewältigung* explored during the 1960s. People began to ask themselves whether all humans, not just Germans, and not just the demonic Hitler, were capable of actions they had never imagined possible. The legal historian Gerhard Mauz, who had written in 1968 about the Auschwitz Trial, further explored the subject. In an essay entitled "The Golgotha of the Germans," Mauz contemplated the role of the trial in German historical consciousness about Auschwitz and the Holocaust. He addressed the problem, or "puzzle," of the defendants. How do Germans understand these people? How could citizens come to grips with the existence of a Boger, who was the inventor of a torture machine, or a Klehr, who demanded that a prisoner kill his own father? In answer to this, Mauz wrote: "This is all actually not so puzzling. Not for those, in any case, who know the 'Hitler in us'; who know that everywhere and every hour people resist the memory of their own actions in the most cowardly, opportunistic, weak, and ruthless way (so that they can feel shielded). The defendants are human beings."[32]

Mauz criticized those "brief visitors," either from the press or from the public, who went to the trial for a day and came away "shaking their heads" in incomprehension at the actions of the defendants, and thus further engaging in what Martin Walser described as the distancing of normal human beings from the monsters on the stand. These characters on the stand were complex, but they were not incomprehensible if people thought long and carefully about them. The question how was on everyone's lips during the trial: the judges, the members of the press, the prosecution, and the public all asked themselves how these events had come to pass. The law made it difficult for the real answers to be found, because the prosecution was so restricted to eyewitness testimony and had to chase after minuscule details rather than find more profound answers to difficult questions. According to Mauz, the judges were both tortured and protected by the limitations of the law. They could retreat behind it when faced with criticism, but they had more difficulty explaining it to a witness whose testimony had to be excluded because he had not given enough specific evidence.[33] The lessons to be learned from the trial came not from the defendants or from the law or from the punishments allotted to the convicted. The public would not find answers about human behavior or their own actions from any of these. Mauz proposed this answer instead:

> What we can discover in Frankfurt . . . touches nearly all Germans. There was the example of witness Diamanski. Before he came to Auschwitz, he was at another camp, where one day he had to work near a lake. Suddenly he saw something bobbing in the water. He jumped into the lake and saved a woman, whose boat had capsized. When he brought the half-drowned human bundle to land, he saw—he had saved a camp guard. His friends scolded him. "I could not know who

I was saving," says the witness, stunned and confused for a moment. For an instant, there was a person in the courtroom, as a person should be; a fellow human being, a helper and a saver. This person wore a fool's clothing, because it is considered insane that someone should remain human under all circumstances. But it is to this "insanity" that the trial in Frankfurt calls all of us.[34]

Mauz hoped that everyone could learn a lesson about humanity from this trial. He also knew that people would have to search for it beyond the verdict and the law, within themselves. His attempt to dissuade people from seeing the whole event as incomprehensible was a response to the press coverage and the indifference displayed by many. The lecture series organized by the state, the Mauz book published in 1968, and the increasing discontent among young in Germany were indications that some people—not the majority, but a select group of scholars, critics, and frustrated youth—gradually turned away from the idea of the Holocaust as "incomprehensible." These people began to try to find ways to understand how it had happened.

Because the files and tapes of the Auschwitz Trial disappeared into the basement of the Frankfurt public prosecutor's office, little scholarly analysis of the trial took place until the late 1990s. In consequence, almost no research had been done into the effects of the Auschwitz Trial on the general population. However, in a book published in 1989 commemorating one hundred years of justice in Frankfurt, Heinz Haueisen, former head of the public prosecutor's office in Frankfurt, wrote about the challenge the trial posed for the legal officials involved. They had many questions about how much of the enormous mountain of evidence had to be investigated, how much could still be proved, which individual details counted, how and where suspects and witnesses were to be found, and whether a large trial of the Auschwitz complex was the best solution.[35] Once the trial had been set in motion, the prosecution did its best to prove the guilt of the defendants, but much of the judgment was disappointing to the prosecutors. In particular, Haueisen referred to the judge's determination that the SS members at the camp had been brainwashed by years of propaganda and were morally and spiritually confused by their indoctrination at Auschwitz. Haueisen, and the prosecution in Frankfurt, did not find this explanation satisfactory. He asked,

> Would the natural inhibitions that prevent people from involving themselves in this kind of extermination machinery be lessened [by propaganda and influence in such circumstances]? Was the behavior of these defendants not also influenced by the cowardice most people demonstrate, some more, some less; fear of pulling out, of explaining that one would not participate, fear of being sent to the front, with all that such a transfer could mean? It was more comfortable and less dangerous to take part in killing others at Auschwitz than to face one's own death on the Eastern Front. This was the kind of people that was needed in order to deliver the mass transports to the gas chambers in a businesslike fashion, even if one or another of these people disapproved of these actions.[36]

Even though Haueisen's article focused primarily on explaining the challenges to the prosecution, he also commented on the moral legacy of the judgment. He believed, as a representative of the state of Hesse, that the verdict had not adequately presented the crimes of the defendants and had in fact attempted to minimize their guilt. His main argument was that such men were not products merely of the National Socialist system; rather, they had existed in all different eras and were still to be found throughout the world: not only those who hid behind the superior-orders defense, but also those who took pleasure in torturing and shooting others. The judgment did not do mankind a service by whitewashing their crimes and apologizing for the defendants. The German public that witnessed this trial had to learn that everyone was capable of acting the way the defendants at Auschwitz had.

And yet Haueisen saw the trial, despite the problems with the verdict, as a positive development in Germany's confrontation with its past. It had become a part of legal history, whether Judge Hofmeyer had wanted it to or not. For Haueisen, "thanks to its [the trial's] force of law, its representation of Auschwitz cannot be called into question anymore. It assured that for all time, it is no longer possible to discuss Hitler and National Socialism without thinking of Auschwitz." Auschwitz would become a symbol, intertwined with the swastika, that could not be forgotten. And finally, this message had to be taken from the trial: "Let us not forget that in the end it was people who tortured and killed at Auschwitz, people who have always existed and will always exist. True, Auschwitz was unique. But are we certain that something similar could not somewhere, sometime, be built again? It is never too early for vigilance."[37]

One of the greatest cultural commentaries on the trial, as mentioned earlier, was the 1965 play *The Investigation*, by Peter Weiss. Based almost entirely on the oral testimony given at the trial, the play (staged only two months after the verdict) was a reaction to the trial that challenged the German public to face issues that the judgment, for all the reasons mentioned, had failed to address. Much of the dialogue in the play was taken verbatim from the testimony of both defendants and witnesses. Weiss melded their words together and put them into the mouths of a few key characters. As a staunch socialist and a harsh critic of West German capitalist society, he showed the defendants to be normal products, rather than aberrations, of a society that put industrial growth and efficiency above all other priorities. He portrayed the defendants as normal men rather than monsters; at the same time, he refused to spare the audience the most grotesque details of the trial. In this way he attempted to make connections between the crimes of the defendants at Auschwitz and the society that had created them. One character in the play, witness number 3, was Weiss's mouthpiece. Straying from the actual witness testimony given at the trial, this witness represented a fusion of historians and philosophers—Martin Broszat and Hannah Arendt, specifically—and Weiss himself. He told the audience:

> When we talk of our experience nowadays
> with people who were never in a camp
> there is always something
> inconceivable to them about it
> And yet they are the same people
> who in the camp were prisoners and guards . . .
> We must drop the lofty view
> that the camp world
> is incomprehensible to us
> We all knew the society
> that produced a government
> capable of creating such camps
> The order that prevailed there
> was an order whose basic nature
> we were familiar with.[38]

The play, which was almost four hours long, was written in the form of eleven cantos or "songs," with titles like "The Song of the Black Wall" and "The Song of the Swing"; Weiss also included, pointedly, "The Song of the Ramp" (or selection platform), to depict to the gas chamber selections as an equally criminal element of Auschwitz. Each character spoke in monotonous verse, describing in unrelenting detail the worst crimes of defendants like Boger and Baretski, while showing that all defendants, the reluctant killers included, were part of the killing machine. In turn, Weiss wanted all members of German society to question their role in making Auschwitz possible. Weiss was careful to ensure that the play "contained nothing but the facts as they were presented in the courtroom," knowing that an artistic representation of Auschwitz could not take liberties with the truth and remain historical and morally poignant.[39]

The Investigation played on fourteen stages simultaneously throughout Germany—both East and West—and in London.[40] It was widely critiqued in the press, and remains controversial among scholars, especially because Weiss does not identify the Jews as the main victims at Auschwitz, in the slave labor program, or in the Nazi extermination policy.[41] Instead, Weiss chose to emphasize the universal danger of capitalist excess, insinuating in his play that Auschwitz was the end result of a world ruled by corporations and profit. While Weiss's leftist political stance was the subject of much discussion and some suspicion in the atmosphere of the cold war, the play also put the trial, and Auschwitz, and the Holocaust—even by its absence in the play—at the center of enormous public discussion. According to an article in *Der Spiegel*, "no stage play since Hochhuth's *The Deputy* has been as widely debated, even before its staging, as *The Investigation*."[42] Through *The Investigation*, Weiss used the trial to force Germans to revisit the Nazi past, and he asked them to recognize their role in it. He did so in direct reaction to the press coverage and to what Fritz Bauer, and many others, described as public indifference to the trial. Some kind of lesson had to be learned from the trial, and since the judgment with its light sentences could not teach it, the task would be left to historians, philosophers, artists, and playwrights. Unfortunately, Weiss's message was not to be carried forward in mainstream depictions of Nazi crime.

The Auschwitz Trial had a paradoxical result. On the one hand, it illuminated the crimes of Auschwitz for a public that was almost completely—and often deliberately—ignorant of them. The extensive press coverage forced Germans to confront Auschwitz. Some did so on a very superficial level; others, as we have seen from newspaper editorials and journal articles, did so in a much deeper, more analytical way. The trial disseminated largely accurate information about the machinery of Auschwitz—its "anatomy," as historians Yisrael Gutman and Michael Berenbaum have labeled it. The historical background supplied in the indictment and the judgment, and the expert testimony by the Munich historians, were all covered by the press.

On the other hand, the public also gained a skewed understanding of Auschwitz. The sentences meted out to the defendants distorted the realities of the program of extermination at Auschwitz. The limitations of the law obscured more than they revealed, by making the prosecution dependent on the same standards of illegality the Nazis themselves had used to investigate criminal activity in the camps. This reliance on the letter of the law legitimated the criminal Nazi state and set a standard for illegal behavior in the 1960s Frankfurt courtroom that eerily echoed the laws of the Third Reich. The statements of the judges about the brutality of such defendants as Wilhelm Boger, the "Devil of Birkenau," shifted the focus in the courtroom away from Nazi genocide toward individual acts of cruelty, suggesting that, in formal legal terms at least, the Nazi orders had been acceptable: those who had herded thousands into the gas chambers were not as guilty as those who had shot prisoners without a having had a legal death sentence handed down by Nazi officials in Berlin. Defendants who had selected prisoners for death on the platform benefited from such a distortion of justice: they were convicted only of aiding and abetting murder. This was the result for the Robert Mulka and Karl Höcker, the defendants who had occupied the most senior positions of anyone on trial.

In this examination of the Frankfurt Auschwitz Trial I have attempted to tell its story. The trial, which was conducted on a grand scale, produced a vast amount of documentary and testimonial evidence. I have focused on those aspects of the proceedings—before, during, and after—that I believe capture its paradoxical essence, especially the ambitious goal of the public prosecutor's office in Frankfurt, as contrasted with the conservative objectives of the judiciary. This conflict affected the testimony as well: on the one hand that from historians and survivors who provided crucial new historical understanding and, on the other hand, that of former SS judges who lent weight and credence to the Nazi regulations, thus shielding the defendants who had acted within their confines. The press coverage brought Auschwitz into the public awareness and yet distanced most people from the reality of the camp through sensationalist presentation. The judgment reinforced this dichotomy, for in it the court acknowledged the trial's backdrop of Nazi ideology and the Holocaust yet in the end ruled that this could not overshadow the proceedings: this was to be an ordinary trial, and the defendants would be judged according to their individual actions and nothing more—and yet nobody, including the judges themselves, could realistically argue that anything about the trial had been ordinary. The law and the crimes were at odds with one another.

Why were the sentences handed down in postwar West German Nazi trials so lenient? Why did the sentences disregard the crime of systematic mass murder that had taken place during the Holocaust? Was there a tendency among the judges to view the activities of the majority of guards at the concentration camps as not ideologically motivated? Even worse, was the judges' attitude an indication of persistent and lingering Nazi beliefs? Some argue that judges in postwar West Germany found ways to reduce convictions and sentences out of fear that they too would be investigated as former members of the Nazi party. Others contend that the leniency was the result of an extreme reluctance on the part of the government, the Ministry of Justice, local courts, and the German public to try all the "murderers in their midst."[43] These arguments may hold true for certain district courts and states where ex-Nazis held positions of authority and influence; however, they are generalizations that do not present a complete picture of the complexities of trying Nazi criminals in postwar Germany under the domestic criminal justice system. In the case of the Frankfurt trial, the prosecution was determined to conduct a fair trial and expose the facts of Auschwitz criminality. Unfortunately, the prosecutors had three strikes against them: the law itself was too restrictive, legal theorists (and the federal court of appeals) had set standards that favored mild sentences for most Nazi defendants, and the judge chose not to challenge precedent.

Hence, the trial is central to German postwar reckoning with the past, and yet the lessons to be learned from it are not necessarily present in the trial proceedings and the judgment. If one were to draw conclusions and learn lessons purely from the final convictions and sentences, the majority of murderers at Auschwitz would appear to be decent men who were not ultimately responsible for committing murder by, for example, leading thousands of men, women, and children to the gas chambers. Only those whose actions exceeded the camp regulations were found guilty of perpetrating murder.

This is not the lesson that the prosecution, especially Fritz Bauer, wanted the public to learn from the Auschwitz Trial. But in many ways the misrepresentation of Nazi crime that came out of the trial is the prevalent interpretation informing people's understanding of the Holocaust to this day. Such popular films as *Schindler's List* and *The Pianist*—by far the most influential sources of public information—show either excessively cruel, drunken Nazis gleefully shooting Jews at random, or sophisticated, cultured, sympathetic middlemen who can no longer take part in the evil. Missing from these depictions are the real people who participated every day, the Scherpes and the Hantls. The mainstream image of Nazi criminality is no different from the one presented on the stand in Frankfurt. This very public trial, which was the formative moment in most of the German public's understanding of Auschwitz, certainly contributed ineradicably to the way that we understand Nazism today.

Would justice, the public, and the process of honestly confronting the past have been better served if the courts could have brought a charge of genocide or even crimes against humanity to bear? Either would have dealt with the larger crime complex—the extermination program for which the Auschwitz camp had been exclusively dreamed up and built. Surely such charges would have aided in creating a more comprehensive picture of the crime complex at Auschwitz. And yet the trials that did proceed on charges of genocide and crimes against humanity were flawed too. Justice—equity, the quality of being morally just, rectitude, the vindication of right through judgment in a court of law, and punishment—is more a pursuit than a result in trials against Holocaust perpetrators. It is a necessary one, as the Auschwitz Trial demonstrated by teaching the German public about Auschwitz for the first time and encouraging it to confront Auschwitz in a serious and concerted way that continues into the present. But the lessons learned and the punishments meted out can hardly be considered just.

Abbreviations

4 Js 444/59	Pretrial files of the First Frankfurt Auschwitz Trial
4 Ks 2/63	First Frankfurt Auschwitz Trial, December 20, 1963– August 8, 1965
BGH	*Bundesgerichtshof* (BGHSt, Federal Court of Appeals)
FBI	Fritz Bauer Institute
GG	*Grundgesetz* (Constitution)
GVG	*Gerichtsverfassungsgesetz* (court constitution)
HKB	Häftlingskrankenbau (prisoner hospital)
IAC	International Auschwitz Committee
IfZ	Institut für Zeitgeschichte (Institute for Contemporary History)
IMT	International Military Tribunal
JuNS-V	*Justiz und NS-Verbrechen: Die deutschen Strafverfahren wegen nationalsozialistischer Tötungsverbrechen* (Nazi Crimes on Trial: German Trials Concerning National Socialist Homicidal Crimes–collection of postwar German trial judgments compiled at the Institute of Criminal Law of the University of Amsterdam by Prof. Dr. C. F. Rüter and Dr. D. W. de Mildt)
LKA	Landeskriminalamt (State Criminal Department)
OKW	*Oberkommando der Wehrmacht* (Armed forces High Command)
RSHA	*Reichssicherheitshauptamt* (Central Security Department of the Reich)
SDG	*Sanitätsdienstgrad* (medical orderly)
SS	*Schutzstaffel*
StA b. LG	*Staatsanwaltschaft beim Landgericht* (public prosecutor's office at the district court)
StGB	*Strafgesetzbuch* (German penal code)
StPO	*Strafprozessordnung* (German penal procedural code)
WVHA	*Wirtschafts- und Verwaltungshauptamt* (SS Economic and Administrative Office)
ZS	Zentrale Stelle der Landesjustizverwaltung zur Aufklärung nationalsozialistischer Verbrechen (Central Office of the Land Judicial Authorities for the Investigation of National Socialist Crimes)

Pretrial Chronicle, March 1958–October 1963

1958
StA b. LG Stuttgart 16 Js 1273/58

Mar. 1, 1958	Rögner writes to StA Stuttgart regarding Wilhelm Boger.
29/05/58	Hermann Langbein, head of the IAC, gives statement re Boger.
01/10/58	Proposal for issuing arrest warrant for Boger comes from StA Stuttgart.
02/10/58	Arrest warrant against Boger is issued.
08/10/58	Boger is arrested.

1959

14/01/59	Emil Wulkan gives Thomas Gnielka documents regarding SS suspects.
15/01/59	Gnielka gives the documents to general state attorney Fritz Bauer.
06/04/59	Arrest warrants are issued against Hans Stark, Pery Broad, and Klaus Dylewski.
23/04/59	Stark is arrested.
24/04/59	Dylewski is arrested.
30/04/59	Broad is arrested.
23/05/59	Dylewski is declared exempt from arrest.
26/05/59	StA Stuttgart writes to StA Frankfurt am Main.

StA b.LG Frankfurt am Main, 4Js 444/59

15/07/59	Arrest warrants are issued against Franz Hofmann, Heinrich Bischoff, and Oswald Kaduk.
21/07/59	Kaduk and Bischoff are arrested.
03/12/59	Arrest warrants are issued against Victor Capesius, Bernhard Rakers, and Alois Staller.

1960

30/03/60	Arrest warrant is issued against Stefan Baretski.

05/04/60	Arrest warrant is issued against Helge Stiwitz.
11/04/60	Arrest warrant is issued against Johann Schoberth.
12/04/60	Baretski is arrested.
12/04/60	Arrest warrants are issued against Josef Klehr, Hans Nierzwicki, and Herbert Scherpe.
13/04/60	Staller is arrested.
16/04/60	Stiwitz is arrested.
17/04/60	Capesius is arrested.
08/06/60	Arrest warrant for Stiwitz is lifted.
20/06/60	Schobert is declared exempt from arrest.
16/09/60	Nierzwicki is arrested.
17/09/60	Klehr is arrested.
21/10/60	Arrest warrant is issued and Richard Baer is arrested.
04/11/60	Arrest warrant is issued and Robert Mulka is arrested.
04/11/60	Arrest warrants are issued against Kurt Uhlenbroock.
14/11/60	Uhlenbroock is arrested.
24/11/60	Arrest warrant is issued for Emil Bednarek.
25/11/60	Bednarek is arrested.
29/11/60	Uhlenbroock is declared exempt from arrest.
12/12/60	Arrest warrant is issued against Dylewski.
16/12/60	Dylewski is arrested.
14/12/60	Arrest warrant is issued against Arthur Breitwieser.
15/12/60	Arrest warrant is issued against Jacob Fries.
23/12/60	Broad is declared exempt from arrest.

1961

06/03/61	Mulka is released.
20/03/61	Arrest warrant is issued against Emil Hantl.
22/03/61	Dylewski is released.
23/05/61	Arrest warrant is issued against Mulka.
26/05/61	Hantl is arrested.
19/05/61	Mulka is arrested.
09/06/61	Breitwieser is arrested.
12/06/61	Fries is arrested.
22/06/61	Breitwieser is declared exempt from arrest.
06/07/61	Fries is declared exempt from arrest.
12/07/61	Proposal is made to open the preliminary judicial inquiry StA FfM 4Js 444/59 on Baer, Mulka, Capesius, Uhlenbroock, Frank, Schatz, Kaduk, Baretski, Schobert, Rakers, Bischoff, Fries, Boger, Stark, Broad, Dylweski, Klehr, Nierzwicki, Hantl, Breitwieser, Bednarek, and Staller.

09/08/61	Decision is reached on the opening of the preliminary judicial inquiry LG FfM.
15/08/61	Scherpe is arrested.
28/08/61	Addendum is filed to the proposal to open the preliminary judicial inquiry StA FfM, 4 Js 444/59 (Scherpe).
02/09/61	Addendum is filed to the decision on the opening of the preliminary judicial inquiry LG FfM (Scherpe).

1962

23/01/61	Addendum 2 is filed, StA FfM, on suspects Karl Höcker and Franz Lucas.
29/01/61	Addendum 2 is filed, LG FfM, on Höcker and Lucas.
14/02/62	Addendum 3 is filed, StA FfM, on suspect Bruno Schlage.
05/03/62	Addendum 3 is filed, LG FfM, on Schlage.
09/04/62	Addendum 4 is filed, StA FfM, on suspect Gerhard Neubert.
24/04/62	Addendum 4 is filed, LG FfM, on Neubert.
19/10/62	Decision to close the preliminary judicial inquiry LG FfM, 4 Js 444/59.

1963

16/04/63	Proposal is filed to open the main proceedings: INDICTMENT 4 Js 444/59.
24/06/63	Decision is filed to discontinue proceedings, LG FfM 3.Strafkammer, on Fries, Uhlenbroock, Rakers, and Staller.
17/10/63	Opening decree is made, LG FfM, 3. Strafkammer, 4 Js 444/59.

Source: Werner Renz, Fritz Bauer Institute, Frankfurt am Main.

SS and Concentration Camp Ranks

SS rank	Translation (U.S. Army)
Sturmscharführer	Master sergeant
Truppenführer/Hauptscharführer	Technical sergeant
Oberscharführer	Staff sergeant
Scharführer	Sergeant
Unterscharführer	Corporal
Rottenführer	Private, first-class
SS-Mann	Private
Anwärter	Recruit

SS Positions in Concentration Camps	Translation
Lagerkommandant	Camp commander
Adjutant	Deputy commander
Lagerführer	Camp leader
Rapportführer	Reporting officer
Verwaltungsführer	Administrative officer
Arbeitsdienstführer	Work recording officer
Arbeitseinsatzführer	Work detail leader
Kommandoführer	Labor group supervisor
Blockführer	Block officer
Lagerarzt	Camp doctor
Sanitätsdienstgefreiter	Medical orderly
Bewachungsmannschaft	Guard detail

Prisoner Positions in Concentration Camps	Translation
Lagerälteste	Senior camp prisoner
Blockälteste	Senior block prisoner
Blockarzt	Prisoner block doctor
Stubenälteste	Senior room prisoner
Blockschreiber	Prisoner block clerk
Oberkapo	Head capo

Kapo	Chief work overseer
Pfleger	Medical attendant
Leichenträger	Corpse bearer
Stubendienst	Room orderly

Sources: On SS ranks, see George C. Browder, *Hitler's Enforcers: The Gestapo and the SS Security Service in the Nazi Revolution* (New York: Oxford University Press, 1996), 248. On concentration camp ranks, see Abraham J. Edelheit and Hershel Edelheit, *History of the Holocaust: A Handbook and Dictionary* (Boulder, Colo.: Westview, 1994), 274.

Judges, Jury, Prosecutors, Defense Lawyers, and Defendants

Presiding judge: Hans Hofmeyer
Participating judge: Josef Perseke
Assessor: Walter Hotz
Substitute judges: Werner Hummerich, Günter Seiboldt
Jury: Gertrud Flach, Erna Grob, Else Häbich, Adolf Holzhäuser,
    Ernst Kadenbach, Emma Kotzur
Substitute jurors: Elise Knodel, Ferdinand Link, Anna Mayer
Prosecution: Dr. Hans Großmann, Joachim Kügler, Georg Friedrich Vogel,
    Gerhard Wiese
Co-plaintiffs: Henry Ormond, Christian Raabe, Prof. Dr. Karl Friedrich Kaul

Defendants: Defense attorneys
Robert Karl Mulka, Karl Höcker, Emil Bednarek: Dr. Hermann Stolting II,
    Dr. Rainer Eggert (Mulka), Dr. Herbert Ernst Müller
Wilhelm Boger: Dr. Rudolf Aschenauer, Hans Schallock
Hans Stark, Benno Erhard: Dr. Karlheinz Staiger
Klaus Dylewski, Pery Broad, Dr. Willi Frank, Dr. Willi Schatz, Dr. Victor
    Capesius: Dr. Hans Laternser, Fritz Steinacker
Johann Schobert: Engelbert Joschko, Dr. Karlheinz Staiger
Bruno Schlage: Georg Bürger, Dr. Hans Fertig
Franz Hofmann: Rudolf Heymann, Gerhard Göllner, Dr. Karlheinz Staiger
Oswald Kaduk: Dr. Friedrich Jugl, Dr. Anton Reiners
Stefan Baretski: Eugen Gerhardt, Engelbert Joschko
Arthur Breitwieser: Dr. Wolfgang Zarnack, Dr. Hans Fertig
Dr. Franz Lucas: Dr. Hans-Peter Ivens, Dr. Rudolf Aschenauer, Dr. Rainer
    Eggert
Josef Klehr: Gerhard Göllner, Dr. Hans Fertig
Hans Scherpe: Hans Knögle, Dr. Anton Reiners,
Emil Hantl: Dr. Hermann Stolting II, Dr. Rainer Eggert

The Verdict

1. Robert Mulka: for aiding and abetting the murder of 750 people on at least 4 separate occasions, 14 years in prison
2. Karl Höcker: for aiding and abetting the murder of 1,000 people on at least 3 separate occasions, 7 years in prison
3. Wilhelm Boger: for murder on at least 114 separate occasions, for adding and abetting the murder of 1,000 people, and for aiding and abetting murder of at least 10 people, life plus 5 years in prison
4. Hans Stark: for joint murder on at least 44 separate occasions, one involving the murder of at least 200 people, and another of at least 100 people, 10 years juvenile detention
5. Klaus Dylewski: for aiding and abetting murder on 32 separate occasions, 2 involving the murder of at least 750 people, 5 years in prison
6. Pery Broad: for aiding and abetting murder on at least 22 separate occasions, 2 involving the murder of at least 1,000 people each, 4 years in prison
7. Dr. Bruno Schlage: for aiding and abetting murder on at least 80 separate occasions, 6 years in prison
8. Franz Hofmann: for murder on 1 occasion, joint murder on at least 30 separate occasions, and joint murder on at least 3 other occasions of at least 750 people each, life in prison
9. Oswald Kaduk: for murder on 10 separate occasions and joint murder on at least two separate occasions, 1 involving at least 1,000 people, the other at least 2 people, life in prison
10. Stefan Baretski: for murder on at least 5 separate occasions and aiding and abetting murder on at least 11 separate occasions, one involving at least 3,000 people, 5 involving at least 1,000 people each, and 5 involving at least 50 people each, life plus 8 years in prison
11. Dr. Franz Lucas: for aiding and abetting the murder of at least 1,000 people on 4 separate occasions, $3\frac{1}{4}$ years in prison
12. Dr. Willi Frank: for aiding and abetting the murder of at least 1,000 people on 6 separate occasions, 7 years in prison

13. Dr. Viktor Capesius: for aiding and abetting the murder of at least 2,000 people on 4 separate occasions, 9 years in prison

14. Josef Klehr: for murder on at least 475 separate occasions and for aiding and abetting murder on at least 6 separate occasions, 2 involving at least 750 people each, 1 involving at least 280 people, 1 involving at least 700 people, 1 involving at least 200 people, 1 involving at least 50 people, life plus 15 years in prison

15. Herbert Scherpe: for aiding and abetting murder on at least 200 separate occasions and aiding and abetting the murder of at least 700 people, 4½ years in prison

16. Emil Hantl: for aiding and abetting murder on at least 40 separate occasions and aiding and abetting murder on 2 separate occasions, each involving at least 170 people, 3½ years in prison

17. Emil Bednarek: for murder on 14 separate occasions, life in prison

18. Johann Schobert: acquitted

19. Arthur Breitwieser: acquitted

20. Dr. Willi Schatz: acquitted.

Notes

Introduction

1. Interestingly, one of the Old French definitions of the word is "gallows," foreshadowing the fates of some major Nazi war criminals tried immediately after the war, including Rudolf Höss, former commandant of Auschwitz.

2. See Howard Ball, *Prosecuting War Crimes and Genocide: The Twentieth Century Experience* (Lawrence: University Press of Kansas, 1999); Omer Bartov, Atina Grossman, and Mary Nolan, *Crimes of War: Guilt and Denial in the Twentieth Century* (New York: New Press, 2002); Gary Bass, *Stay the Hand of Vengeance: The Politics of War Crimes Tribunals* (Princeton, N.J.: Princeton University Press, 2000); Ian Buruma, *The Wages of Guilt: Memories of War in Germany and Japan* (New York: Meridian, 1994); Lawrence Douglas, *The Memory of Judgment: Making Law and History in the Trials of the Holocaust* (New Haven, Conn.: Yale University Press, 2001); Martha Minow, *Between Vengeance and Forgiveness: Facing History after Genocide and Mass Violence* (Boston: Beacon, 1998); Aryeh Neier, *War Crimes: Brutality, Genocide, Terror, and the Struggle for Justice* (New York: Times Books, 1998); Mark Osiel, *Mass Atrocity, Collective Memory, and the Law* (New Brunswick, N.J.: Transaction, 1997).

3. Douglas, *Memory of Judgment*, 4. Similarly, Osiel examines mass atrocity trials in the role of a society's collective memory and argues that such trials can "stimulate public discussion in ways that foster the liberal virtues of toleration, moderation, and civil respect." Osiel, *Mass Atrocity*, 2.

4. Fritz Bauer, "Zu den Naziverbrecher Prozessen," in *Stimme der Gemeinde zum Kirchlichen Leben, zur Politik, Wirtschaft und Kultur* 18 (Sept. 1963): 568.

5. Two documentations written mainly during or shortly after the trial include only excerpts: Hermann Langbein, *Der Auschwitz-Prozess, Eine Dokumentation*, 2 vols. (Frankfurt am Main: Neue Kritik, 1995); and

Bernd Naumann, *Auschwitz: Bericht über die Strafsache gegen Mulka u.a. vor dem Schwurgericht Frankfurt* (Frankfurt am Main: Fischer Bücherei, 1968). Langbein was a witness who was called on the nineteenth day of testimony and could only observe in the courtroom after that, and his documentation is not in chronological but in thematic order. Naumann's account is a compilation of reports he wrote for the *Frankfurter Allgemeine Zeitung.* See also Gerhard Werle and Thomas Wanders, *Auschwitz vor Gericht—Völkermord und bundesdeutsche Strafjustiz* (Munich: Beck, 1995).

6. In April 1965 a new criminal procedure overturned this law and allowed for full transcriptions of trials; however, this was not adopted by the Frankfurt court. Langbein, *Der Auschwitz Prozess,* 13.

7. Stipulation for the recording of trial proceedings, *Strafsache gegen Mulka und andere,* First Frankfurt Auschwitz Trial, Dec. 20, 1963–Aug. 8, 1965 (hereafter 4 Ks 2/63).

8. Hermann Langbein, "Langsamer Weg zur Gerechtigkeit," *Die Welt,* Aug. 21, 1965.

9. See Werner Renz, "Der 1. Frankfurter Auschwitz Prozess: Zwei Vorgeschichten," *Zeitschrift für Geschichtswissenschaft* 50, no. 7 (July 2002): 622–641; and "Opfer und Täter: Zeugen der Schoah. Der Tonbandmitschnitt des 1. Frankfurter Auschwitz-Prozesses als Geschichtsquelle," *Tribüne: Zeitschrift zum Verständnis des Judentums* 41 no. 162 (2002): 126–136.

10. Osiel, *Mass Atrocity,* 192–193. Osiel quotes extensively from Hannah Arendt and Ian Buruma on the importance of the Auschwitz Trials.

11. Norbert Frei, paper presented at the conference "Vom Prozess zur Geschichte," Jan. 1998.

12. Robert Moeller, in his book on postwar "selective memory" of German suffering at the end of the war, argues convincingly that the West German government and public consciously avoided confronting the Nazi past by emphasizing German victimization at the hands of the Soviets. Robert Moeller, *War Stories: The Search for a Usable Past in the Federal Republic of Germany* (Berkeley: University of California Press, 2001). In contrast, W. G. Sebald argues that after the war, German writers were peculiarly silent about German wartime suffering; W. G. Sebald, *On the Natural History of Destruction,* trans. Anthea Bell (New York: Random House, 2003).

13. Buruma, *Wages of Guilt,* 149.

14. "An Act can only be punished if the punishability of said act was already legally established before it was committed." *Grundgesetz für die Bundesrepublik Deutschland* (Bonn: Bundeszentrale für die Politische Bildung, 1996), paragraph 103, section 2.

15. The Sonderkommandos, described most movingly by Primo Levi, were prisoners selected to perform the grisliest task at the camp: they had to herd people into the gas chambers and unload their bodies from the gas chambers into the crematoriums. They were generally killed every few months and a new group of men (most often) were selected to perform this duty. Primo Levi, *The Drowned and the Saved*, trans. Raymond Rosenthal (New York: Summit, 1986), 36–61.

16. 4 Js 444/59, 63: 11714–11722 and 4 Ks 2/63, Mar. 9, 1964, tapes 4–5.

17. The "Canada" bunker was the building in which all the valuable goods were stored—gold, money, clothing, jewelry—and therefore was given the name of a stereotypically bountiful country.

18. In 1965 Martin Walser wrote a searing indictment of the press coverage of the trial (published several years later), from which I borrow the discussion of Auschwitz as hell: Martin Walser, "Unser Auschwitz," *Heimatkunde: Aufsätze und Reden* (Frankfurt am Main: Suhrkamp, 1968).

19. See Christopher Browning, *Ordinary Men: Reserve Police Battalion 101 and the Final Solution in Poland* (New York: HarperCollins, 1992); George C. Browder, *Hitler's Enforcers: The Gestapo and the SS Security Service in the Nazi Revolution* (New York: Oxford University Press, 1996); Daniel Jonah Goldhagen, *Hitler's Willing Executioners: Ordinary Germans and the Holocaust* (New York: Knopf, 1996); Robert R. Shandley, *Unwilling Germans? The Goldhagen Debate* (Minneapolis: University of Minnesota Press, 1998); Edward Westermann, " 'Ordinary Men' or 'Ideological Soldiers'? Police Battalion 310 in Russia, 1942," *German Studies Review* 21 (1998): 41–68; Stanley Milgram, *Obedience to Authority: An Experimental View* (New York: Harper and Row, 1974); Zygmunt Bauman, *Modernity and the Holocaust* (Ithaca: Cornell University Press, 1989); Eric A. Zillmer, Molly Harrower, Barry A. Ritzler, and Robert P. Archer, *The Quest for the Nazi Personality: A Psychological Investigation of Nazi War Criminals* (Hillsdale, N.J.: Lawrence Erlbaum, 1995); and Robert Jay Lifton, *The Nazi Doctors: Medical Killing and the Psychology of Genocide* (New York: Basic Books, 1986).

20. The word "Holocaust" was not yet being applied to the systematic annihilation of Europe's Jews. This term refers to a sacrificial burnt offering—giving the event theological significance—and came to be widely used only in the 1960s. Michael Marrus, *The Holocaust in History* (New York: Meridian, 1987), 3. According to the *Oxford English Dictionary*, the term was used in 1942 by a newspaper to describe the mass murder of the Jews but was not picked up by historians until the 1950s.

21. Norbert Frei, "Der Frankfurter Auschwitz Prozess und die Deutsche Zeitgeschichtsforschung," in *Auschwitz: Geschichte, Rezeption und Wirkung*, ed. Fritz Bauer Institute (Frankfurt am Main: Campus, 1996)

124. See Lucie Adelsberger, *Auschwitz: a Doctor's Story*, trans. Susan Ray (Boston: Northeastern University Press, 1995); H. G. Adler, Hermann Langbein, and Ella Lingens-Reiner, eds., *Auschwitz: Zeugnisse und Berichte* (Frankfurt am Main: Europäische Verlagsanstalt, 1962); Hannah Arendt, *Eichmann in Jerusalem: A Report on the Banality of Evil* (New York: Viking, 1964); Karl Dietrich Bracher, *The German Dictatorship*, trans. Jean Steinberg (New York: Praeger, 1970); Karl Jaspers, *The Question of German Guilt*, trans. E. B. Ashton (New York: Capricorn, 1961); Eugen Kogon, *The Theory and Practice of Hell*, trans. Heinz Norden (New York: Berkeley, 1985); Ota Kraus and Erich Kulka, *Die Todesfabrik* (Berlin: Kongress, 1957); Alexander and Margaret Mitcherlich, *The Inability to Mourn: Principles of Collective Behavior* (New York: Grove, 1984); Wolfgang Scheffler, *Judenverfolgung im Dritten Reich, 1933–1945* (Berlin: Colloquium, 1960); and Jan Sehn, *Konzentrationslager Oswiecim-Brzezinka: Auf Grund von Dokumentation und Beweisquellen* (Warsaw: Wydawnictwo Prawnicze, 1957). On the response to Arendt's book, see Gary Smith, ed., *Hannah Arendt Revisited: "Eichmann in Jerusalem" und die Folgen* (Frankfurt am Main: Suhrkamp, 2000).

1. Pretrial History

1. Fritz Bauer, "Im Namen des Volkes: Die strafrechtliche Bewältigung der Vergangenheit," in Helmut Hammerschmidt, ed., *Zwanzig Jahre danach: Eine Deutsche Bilanz, 1945–1965* (Munich: Desch, 1965): 303–304. For similar statistical reports, see Dick de Mildt, *In the Name of the People: Perpetrators of Genocide in the Reflection of Their Post-War Prosecution in West Germany—The "Euthanasia" and "Aktion Reinhard" Trial Cases* (The Hague: Martinus Nijhoff, 1996), 20–21; and Adalbert Rückerl, *The Investigation of Nazi Crimes, 1945–1978: A Documentation*, trans. Derek Rütter (Heidelberg: C. F. Müller, 1979).

2. Bauer, "Im Namen des Volkes," 304.

3. Ibid.

4. Annette Weinke, *Die Verfolgung von NS-Tätern im Geteilten Deutschland: Vergangenheitsbewältigung, 1949–1969, oder: Eine Deutsch-Deutsche Beziehungsgeschichte im Kalten Krieg* (Paderborn, Germany: Ferdinand Schöningh, 2002); Volker Zimmerman, *NS-Täter vor Gericht: Düsseldorf und die Strafprozesse wegen nationalsozialistischer Gewaltverbrechen* (Düsseldorf: Achim Freudenstein, 2002). See also Ulrich Battis, Gunther Jakobs, and Eckhard Jesse, *Vergangenheitsbewältigung durch Recht: Drei Abhandlungen zu einem deutschen Problem* (Berlin: Duncker & Humblot, 1992); de Mildt, *In the Name of the People*; Ralf

Dreier, *Juristische Vergangenheitsbewältigung* (Baden-Baden: Nomos, 1995); Norbert Frei, Dirk van Laak, and Michael Stolleis, eds., *Geschichte vor Gericht: Historiker, Richter und die Suche nach Gerechtigkeit* (Munich: Beck, 2000); Kerstin Freudiger, *Die juristische Aufarbeitung von NS-Verbrechen* (Tübingen: Mohr, 2002); Henry Friedlander, "The Judiciary and Nazi Crimes in Postwar Germany," in *Simon Wiesenthal Center Annual 1* (New York: Rossel Books, 1984), 27–44; Michael Greve, *Der justitielle und rechtspolitische Umgang mit den NS-Gewaltverbrechen in den sechziger Jahren* (Frankfurt am Main: Lang, 2001); Christa Hoffmann, "Die justitielle 'Vergangenheitsbewältigung' in der Bundesrepublik Deutschland: Tatsachen und Legenden," in Rainer Zitelmann, ed., *Die Schatten der Vergangenheit: Impulse zur Historisierung des Nationalsozialismus* (Berlin: Propyläen, 1990), 497–521; Barbara Just-Dahlmann and Helmut Just, *Die Gehilfen: NS-Verbrechen und die Justiz nach 1945* (Frankfurt am Main: Athenäum, 1988); Ingo Müller, *Hitler's Justice: The Courts of the Third Reich*, trans. Deborah Lucas Schneider (Cambridge, Mass.: Harvard University Press, 1991); Michael Ratz, *Die Justiz und die Nazis: Zur Strafverfolgung von Nazismus und Neonazismus seit 1945* (Frankfurt am Main: Röderberg, 1979); Alan S. Rosenbaum, *Prosecuting Nazi War Criminals* (Boulder, Colo.: Westview, 1993); Rückerl, *Investigation of Nazi Crimes*; Uwe Schulz, ed., *Grosse Prozesse: Recht und Gerechtigkeit in der Geschichte* (Munich: Beck, 1996); Jürgen Weber and Peter Steinbach, eds., *Vergangenheitsbewältigung durch Strafverfahren? NS-Prozesse in der Bundesrepublik Deutschland* (Munich: Olzog, 1984).

5. Michael Marrus, *The Nuremberg War Crimes Trial, 1945–1946, A Documentary History* (Boston: Bedford Books, 1997), 3, 10.

6. Gary Jonathan Bass, *Stay the Hand of Vengeance: The Politics of War Crimes Tribunals* (Princeton, N.J.: Princeton University Press, 2000), 58–105.

7. Telford Taylor, *The Anatomy of the Nuremberg Trials: A Personal Memoir* (New York: Knopf, 1992), 21.

8. *American Draft of Definitive Proposal, Presented to Foreign Ministers at San Francisco, April 1945*, in Marrus, *Nuremberg War Crimes Trial*, 34–35.

9. Ibid., 46.

10. *Charter of the International Military Tribunal, August 8, 1945*, ibid., 52–53.

11. For example, Telford Taylor explained about Major William Walsh, an American prosecutor: "Walsh began his presentation with documents dealing with Nazi persecution of Jews during the prewar years on the

stated basis that prewar crimes against German Jews were part of the preparation for waging aggressive wars. No objection was raised at the time, but ultimately the Tribunal held that the evidence did not support such a conclusion and declined to treat prewar persecutions as crimes under the Charter." Taylor, *Anatomy of the Nuremberg Trials*, 210.

12. Marrus, *Nuremberg War Crimes Trial*, 56.

13. International Military Tribunal (IMT), *Trial of the Major War Criminals before the International Military Tribunal, Nuremberg, 14 November 1945–1 October 1946*, 42 vols. (Nuremberg: International Military Tribunal, 1947), 1: 27–95; Rückerl, *Investigation of Nazi Crimes*, 26–27.

14. Ibid., 66.

15. On German resentment toward the Allied and Soviet involvement in "victor's justice," see Jörg Friedrich, "Nuremberg and the Germans," in *War Crimes: The Legacy of Nuremberg*, ed. Belinda Cooper (New York: TV Books, 1998), 87–106.

16. Rückerl, *Investigation of Nazi Crimes*, 36.

17. Ibid., 26. Control Council Law No. 10 ratified the charter of the IMT in an official Allied code that would apply to all subsequent trials. Paragraph 6 of the IMT charter, which became paragraph 2, listed the four major crimes to be tried. In addition, it stipulated the appropriate punishment for these crimes.

18. Ohlendorf was sentenced to death, and executed in June 1951, a few years prior to another Einsatzgruppen trial (the West German Ulm trial of 1959).

19. Rückerl, *Investigation of Nazi Crimes*, 28. Jeffrey Herf, *Divided Memory: The Nazi Past in the Two Germanys* (Cambridge: Harvard University Press, 1997), 204. On the Dachau trials, see Harold Marcuse, *Legacies of Dachau: The Uses and Abuses of a Concentration Camp, 1933–2001* (Cambridge: Cambridge University Press, 2001).

20. Rückerl, *Investigation of Nazi Crimes*, 30, 34. Despite the fact that Law No. 10 was designed to provide a "uniform legal basis in Germany for the prosecution of war criminals and other similar offenders," the Allies allowed exceptions in some cases. Specifically, German courts could try Nazi criminals on the charge of crimes against humanity if those crimes were unrelated to the war of aggression, but not for "crimes against peace" or war crimes as these directly affected the Allies. According to Henry Friedlander, the Germans were rarely allowed to try Nazis for crimes, however, because in almost all cases the Allies considered crimes against humanity to be linked to war crimes and therefore subject to Allied jurisdiction. IMT, *Trials of War Criminals before the Nuremberg Trials, Military Tribunals under Control Council Law No. 10. Nuremberg,*

October 1946–April 1949 (Washington, D.C.: U.S. GPO, 1949–1953), xvi–
xix.

21. Friedlander, "Judiciary and Nazi Crimes," 31, 32.

22. Rückerl, *Investigation of Nazi Crimes,* 35–36. For more on denazificat-
ion, see Herf, *Divided Memory;* Rebecca L. Boehling, *A Question of Pri-
orities: Democratic Reforms and Economic Recovery in Postwar Germany:
Frankfurt, Munich, and Stuttgart under U.S. Occupation* (Providence,
R.I.: Berghahn, 1996); Norbert Frei, *Vergangenheitspolitik: Die Anfänge
der Bundesrepublik und die NS-Vergangenheit* (Munich: Beck, 1996);
Klaus Dietmar Henke and Hans Woller, eds., *Politische Säuberung in
Europa: Die Abrechnung mit Faschismus und Kollaboration nach dem
Zweiten Weltkrieg* (Munich: DTV, 1991); Ernst Klee, *Persilscheine und
falsche Pässe: Wie die Kirchen den Nazis halfen* (Frankfurt am Main:
Fischer, 1991); and Clemens Vollnhals, *Entnazifizierung: Politische
Säuberung und Rehabilitierung in den vier Besatzungszonen, 1945–1949*
(Munich: DTV, 1991).

23. Gordon Craig, *The Germans* (New York: Meridian, 1982), 36. This argument has been thoroughly debated, and many historians argue that this
outlook is far too simplistic, for many important political figures from the
Nazi era—and before—remained powerful and regained key political
posts. Recent analysis has generally contended that the hasty denazification and release of many investigated former Nazis led to the continuation of conservative political trends and the preservation of powerful
elites in both government and the economy. The most glaring example
was Hans Globke, appointed as Adenauer's personal secretary, who had
been a civil servant in the Ministry of Justice in the Nazi period and
wrote commentary on the Nuremberg Laws. Dennis L. Bark and David
R. Grees, eds., *A History of West Germany: From Shadow to Substance,
1945–1963,* 2d ed. (Oxford: Blackwell, 1993), 85. See also Geoffrey J.
Giles, ed., *Stunde Null: The End and the Beginning Fifty Years Ago*
(Washington, D.C.: German Historical Institute, 1997); Christa Hoffmann, *Stunden Null? Vergangenheitsbewältigung in Deutschland, 1945–
1989* (Bonn: Bouvier, 1992); and Stefan Krimm and Wieland Zirbs, eds.,
*Nachkriegszeit: Die Stunde Null als Realität und Mythos in der deutschen
Geschichte* (Munich: Bayerischer Schulbuch-Verlag, 1996).

24. Herf, *Divided Memory,* 226.

25. According to the historian Michael Kater, eight million Germans were
members of the Nazi party at the end of the war. Michael Kater, *The
Nazi Party: A Social Profile of Members and Leaders, 1919–1945* (Cambridge, Mass.: Harvard University Press, 1983), 262.

26. Herf, *Divided Memory,* 203, 209.

27. Craig, *The Germans*, 44. Herf, *Divided Memory*, 209, 224.
28. Herf, *Divided Memory*, 224, 225. For more on Adenauer's legacy and the early postwar attitudes toward confrontation with the Nazi past, see Ulrich Brochhagen, *Nach Nürnberg: Vergangenheitsbewältigung und Westintegration in der Ära Adenauer* (Hamburg: Junius, 1994); Gotthardt Jasper, "Wiedergutmachung und Westintegration: Die halbherzige justizielle Aufarbeitung der NS-Vergangenheit in der frühen Bundesrepublik," in Ludolf Herbst, ed., *Westdeutschland, 1945–1955: Unterwerfung, Kontrolle, Integration* (Munich: Oldenbourg, 1986): 183–202; Hoffmann, "Die justitielle 'Vergangenheitsbewältigung'"; Manfred Kittel, *Die Legende von der "Zweiten Schuld": Vergangenheitsbewältigung in der Ära Adenauer* (Berlin: Ullstein, 1993); and Robert G. Moeller, ed., *West Germany under Construction: Politics, Society, and Culture in the Adenauer Era* (Ann Arbor: University of Michigan Press, 1997).
29. Herf, *Divided Memory*, 226.
30. Konrad Adenauer, quoted ibid., 271.
31. Bauer, "Im Namen des Volkes," 301–302.
32. Ibid.
33. Rückerl, *Investigation of Nazi Crimes*, 44, 46.
34. Ibid., 47.
35. Ibid., 53. The ZS still exists today, not only for purposes of official investigation but as an important archival and historical source for a broad array of information on Nazi crimes.
36. Adalbert Rückerl, "Nazi Crime Trials," in *The Nazi Holocaust*, ed. Michael Marrus (Westport: Meckler, 1989), 9:627.
37. De Mildt, *In the Name of the People*, 20–21, 403. De Mildt states that many crimes prosecuted were "final phase crimes"—for example, the execution of German soldiers who had deserted, or "political denunciation," that is to say informing on fellow German citizens to the Gestapo. Few trials actually had to do with the Final Solution, the killing of Jews in the death camps and gas chambers.
38. Friedlander, "Judiciary and Nazi Crimes," 36–37, 32.
39. See Nicolas Berg, *Der Holocaust und die westdeutschen Historiker: Erforschung und Errinnerung* (Göttingen: Wallstein, 2003); Jean-Paul Bier, "The Holocaust, West Germany, and Strategies of Oblivion, 1947–1979," in Anson Rabinbach and Jack Zipes, eds., *Germans and Jews since the Holocaust: The Changing Situation in West Germany* (New York: Holmes and Meier, 1986): 185–207; Michael Burleigh, ed., *Confronting the Nazi Past: New Debates on Modern German History* (London: Collins and Brown, 1996); Frei, *Vergangenheitspolitik*; in English *Adenauer's Germany and the Nazi Past*, trans. Joel Golb (New York: Columbia Uni-

versity Press, 2002); Ulrich Herbert and Olaf Groehler, *Zweierlei Bewältigung: Vier Beiträge uber den Umgang mit der NS-Vergangenheit in den beiden deutschen Staaten* (Hamburg: Ergebnisse, 1992); Herf, *Divided Memory*; Jeffrey Herf, "The 'Holocaust' Reception in Germany: Right, Center, and Left," in Rabinbach and Zipes, *Germans and Jews since the Holocaust*, 208–233; Eckhard Jesse and Konrad Low, eds., *Vergangenheitsbewältigung* (Berlin: Duncker & Humbolt, 1997); Ian Kershaw, "Beware the Moral High Ground," *Times Literary Supplement*, Oct. 10, 2003; Peter Graf Kielmansegg, *Lange Schatten: Vom Umgang der Deutschen mit der nationalsozialistischen Vergangenheit* (Berlin: Siedler, 1989); Erich Kuby, *Deutschland: Von verschuldeter Teilung zur unverdienten Einheit* (Rastatt, Germany: Arthur Moewig, 1990); Alf Lüdtke, " 'Coming to Terms with the Past': Illusions of Remembering, Ways of Forgetting Nazism in West Germany," *Journal of Modern History* 65 (1993): 542–572; Charles Maier, *The Unmasterable Past: History, Holocaust, and German National Identity* (Cambridge, Mass.: Harvard University Press, 1988); Hans Mommsen, *Auf der Suche nach historischer Normalität: Beiträge zum Geschichtsbildstreit in der Bundesrepublik* (Berlin: Argon, 1987); Moeller, *West Germany under Construction*; Peter Reichel, *Vergangenheitsbewältigung in Deutschland: Die Auseinandersetzung mit der NS-Diktatur von 1945 bis heute* (Munich: Beck, 2001); and Rolf Steininger, ed., *Der Umgang mit dem Holocaust: Europa-USA-Israel* (Vienna: Bohlau, 1994).

40. Nigel G. Foster, *German Law and Legal System* (London: Blackstone, 1993), 1–2. John H. Langbein, *Comparative Criminal Procedure: Germany* (St. Paul, Minn.: West Publishing, 1977), 1, 68–71.

41. StGB, 90. The law defines genocide as "whoever, with the intention of wholly or partially destroying a national, racial, religious or ethnically distinct group as such, 1) kills members of a group; 2) inflicts serious physical or mental injury . . . 3) subjects the group to living conditions likely to cause death to all or some of the members; 4) imposes measures designed to prevent births within the group; 5) forcible transfers children from one group to another." *The Penal Code of the Federal Republic of Germany*, trans. Joseph Darby (Littleton, Colo.: Fred B. Rothman, 1987), 182.

42. Ibid., 36–37.

43. The *Schwurgericht* has now been abolished; although the term still exists to describe large criminal cases, the court now has only two lay and three professional judges. Langbein, *Comparative Criminal Procedure*, 62.

44. Gerhard Dannecker and Julian Roberts, "The Law of Criminal Procedure," in *Introduction to German Law*, ed. Werner F. Ebke and Matthew W. Finkin (The Hague: Kluwer, 1996), 420.

45. Foster, *German Law and Legal System*, 81.

46. Heribert Schumann, "Criminal Law," in *Introduction to German Law*, ed. Ebke and Finkin, 384.

47. *Penal Code*, 47.

48. Foster, *German Law and Legal System*, 170. Schumann, "Criminal Law," 388.

49. Schumann, "Criminal Law," 394. Foster, *German Law and Legal System*, 170. Paragraph 46 falls into title II of the StGB, "The Assessment of Punishment."

50. *Penal Code*, 57.

51. Rückerl, *Investigation of Nazi Crimes*, 65.

52. RGSt, 74:84, in Friedlander, "Judiciary and Nazi Crimes," 36.

53. Devin O. Pendas, "Displaying Justice: Nazis on Trial in Postwar Germany," Ph.D. diss., University of Chicago, 2000, 82.

54. Jürgen Baumann, *Alternative Draft of a Penal Code for the Federal Republic of Germany*, trans. Joseph Darby (South Hackensack, N.J.: F. B. Rothman, 1977); *Beschränkung des Lebensstandards anstatt kurzfristiger Freiheitsstrafe* (Neuwied, Germany: Luchterhand, 1968); *Kleine Streitschriften zur Strafrechtsreform: 10 Beitrage* (Bielefeld, Germany: Gieseking, 1965); Werner Hardwig, "Über den Begriff der Täterschaft: Zugleiche eine Beschprechung der Habilitationsschrift von Claus Roxin 'Täterschaft und Tatherrschaft' " *Juristenzeitung* 20, no. 21 (1965): 667–671; Richard Henkys, *Die nationalsozialistischen Gewaltverbrechen: Geschichte und Gericht* (Stuttgart: Kreuz, 1964); Claus Roxin, *Kriminalpolitik und Strafrechtssystem* (Berlin: de Gruyter, 1970); Roxin, *Täterschaft und Tatherrschaft*, 6th ed. (Berlin: de Gruyter, 1994).

55. Pendas, "Displaying Justice," 87–88.

56. Baumann, "Die strafrechtliche Problematik der nationalsozialistischen Gewaltverbrechen" in Henkys, *Die nationalsozialistischen Gewaltverbrechen*, 308.

57. Friedlander, "Judiciary and Nazi Crimes," 37, 44n63,, 36.

58. Dannecker and Roberts, "Law of Criminal Procedure," 426.

59. Foster, *German Law and Legal Procedure*, 182, 178. See also Langbein, *Comparative Criminal Procedure*, 101.

60. Generally, the prosecutor's office is in the court building itself; for example, the state attorney's office in Frankfurt is right in the regional court. The files of the pretrial investigation therefore remain within the prosecutor's office before, during, and after the trial.

61. Foster, *German Law and Legal Procedure*, 179, 185. Langbein states that lay judges rarely disagree with the judgment of the professional judges; when they do, they usually (in almost 80 percent of cases) concede to the majority opinion, and the "traceable overall effect of the lay judges on

the verdicts of German courts is indeed small." Langbein, *Comparative Criminal Procedure*, 135, 137.

62. Foster, *German Law and Legal Procedure*, 186.

63. For a list of defendants, lawyers, judges, and jurors, see p. 284.

64. StGB, 88. Friedlander, "Judiciary and Nazi Crimes," 34. Why the Nazi judicial system chose to adopt language utilized by other European countries at this juncture is perplexing, to say the least.

65. Rückerl, *Investigation of Nazi Crimes*, 42.

66. Alfred Bongard, "Der Unterschied zwischen Mord und Totschlag," in *Die Justiz und die Nazis: Zur Strafverfolgung von Nazismus und Neonazismus seit 1945*," ed. Michael Ratz (Frankfurt am Main: Röderberg, 1979), 81. This comes from the BGH decision in Criminal Matters (BGHSt) 18, 37, 39.

67. Rückerl, *Investigation of Nazi Crimes*, 64. Rückerl maintains that the use of "base motives" to determine accomplice status became even more widespread after May 1969, when new laws were passed stating that "an accessory merely acting under orders could be punished only if it was demonstrated that his contribution to the crime sprang from base motives or that he was aware of the cruel or malicious nature of the crime at the time of its commission."

68. Bongard, "Der Unterschied zwischen Mord und Totschlag," 82. These are precedent decisions announced in the *Neue Juristische Wochenschrift*, a Frankfurt law journal, in 1968–1969.

69. Ibid.

70. Ibid., 83.

71. BGHSt 8, ibid., 85.

72. For examples of such rulings, see the collection of judgments compiled by the Institut für Strafrecht der Universität von Amsterdam, C. F. Rüter and Dick de Mildt, at http://www1.jur.uva.nl/junsv/.

73. Rückerl, *Investigation of Nazi Crimes*, 43.

74. Ibid., 52. Fritz Bauer, "Die Verjährung der nazistischen Massenverbrechen," *Tribüne* 12 (1964): 1251. This is another example of a change made by the Nazis that was not repealed in the postwar period.

75. Rückerl, *Investigation of Nazi Crimes*, 54.

76. Peter Steinbach, *Nationalsozialistische Gewaltverbrechen: Die Diskussion in der deutschen Öffentlichkeit nach 1945* (Berlin: Colloquium, 1981), 55.

77. Rückerl, *Investigation of Nazi Crimes*, 57.

78. Bauer, "Die Verjährung," 1253.

79. Steinbach, *Nationalsozialistische Gewaltverbrechen*, 60.

80. Bauer, "Die Verjährung," 1254.

81. Rückerl, *Investigation of Nazi Crimes*, 65.

2. Pretrial Investigations

1. Adolf Rögner, letter of March 1, 1958, in 4 Js 444/59, 1:1, 1R, 2.
2. The IAC, based in Vienna and Warsaw, was made up of survivors of Auschwitz. It was dedicated to finding survivors and gathering information on crimes committed there and perpetrators who might still be alive.
3. Judicial Officer Wasserlos, Report on the Interrogation of Prisoner Adolf Rögner, 16 Js 1273/58, Hohenasperg, May 6, 1958, in 4 Js 444/59, 8.
4. Dr. Rudolph, Senior Executive Officer, State Penitentiary Bruchsal: official letter to the senior prosecutor at Munich, Re: Request of penitentiary inmate Adolf Rögner, Apr. 9, 1958, ibid., 25.
5. Public Prosecutor Weber, Memo, Stuttgart, May 15, 1958, ibid., 7.
6. Hermann Langbein, *Der Auschwitz-Prozess, Eine Dokumentation*, 2 vols. (Frankfurt am Main: Neue Kritik, 1995), 22–23.
7. The warrant charges Boger under the StGB (criminal code) with murder, (paragraph 211) stating that he "is accused of killing a person at Auschwitz in April 1943, out of bloodthirstiness, in that as SS Oberscharrführer at the concentration camp, in an unauthorized execution that he knew to be illegal, he shot a prisoner with his pistol out of pleasure in killing. The accused is urgently suspected in this act and therefore a flight risk." 16 Js 1273/58, Staatsanwaltschaft bei dem Landgericht Stuttgart, Oct. 1, 1958, in 4 Js 444/59, 1:128–129.
8. Langbein, *Der Auschwitz-Prozess*, 25. On November 14, 1958, Langbein sent to the public prosecutor's office in Stuttgart a list of eighteen other members of the Political Department at Auschwitz who were suspected of having committed murder between 1940 and 1945. Among those named were men who later appeared as defendants at the trial in Frankfurt, including Hans Stark, Klaus Dylewski, and Pery Broad. Ibid., 26.
9. *Urteil und Urteilsbegründung im Verfahren gegen Liebehenschel und andere* (Judgment and Explanation in the Proceedings against Liebehenschel and Others), Polish People's Tribunal 5/47, Dec. 22, 1947, in 4 Js 444/59, 49:8291–8513.
10. 9352 E–791/61, Sentence of the Soviet Military Courts in the state of Saxony, August 25, 1947, ibid., 74:13829–13840. The late appearance of this document in the pretrial files—in August 1962—was a result of the difficulties the West German courts faced in communicating with the Soviet court systems, which reluctantly and after much silence and procrastination finally handed over the trial documents.
11. Fritz Bauer, "Zu den Naziverbrecher Prozessen," in *Stimme der Gemeinde zum Kirchlichen Leben, zur Politik, Wirtschaft und Kultur* 18 (Sept. 1963): 564.

12. On July 13, 1959, the prosecution in Frankfurt released its first interoffice memorandum regarding various arrest warrants. This memo includes documentation of the request for transfer of Dr. Kremer from Münster and of Pery Broad from Ludwisgburg, among others.

13. 16 Js 1273/58, StA Stuttgart, "Antrag auf Haftbefehle," Apr. 3, 1959, in 4 Js 444/59, 5:770.

14. Thomas Gnielka, letter of Jan. 15, 1959, in AR-Z 13/59, Zentrale Stelle der Landesjustizverwaltungen, 72. Letter also appears on files of 4 Js 444/59.

15. In actuality, the federal courts ruled on April 14, 1959, to move the investigation to Frankfurt; two months passed before all documents concerning the proceedings arrived in Frankfurt.

16. 4 Js 444/59, 10:1490–1496.

17. Bauer, "Zu den Naziverbrecher Prozessen," 574.

18. Ibid., 568.

19. Ibid.

20. Fritz Bauer, "Nach den Wurzeln des Bösen Fragen," *Die Tat*, Mar. 7, 1964.

21. Fritz Bauer, Barbara Just-Dahlmann, and Golo Mann, "NS-Verbrechen vor Deutschen Gerichten—Versuch einer Zwischenbilanz," *Diskussion—Zeitschrift für Fragen der Gesellschaft und der Deutsch-Israelischen Bezeihungen* 14 (1964): 4.

22. For more on Bauer see his collected works in Joachim Perels and Irmtud Wojak, eds., *Die Humanität der Rechtsordnung: Ausgewählte Schriften von Fritz Bauer* (Frankfurt am Main: Campus, 1998).

23. 4 Js 444/59, 14:2272–2273.

24. Ibid., 17:2670–2671.

25. Nov. 30, 1959, ibid., 19:2967–2969.

26. Tadeusz Paczuła, letter to 4 Js 444/59, 1959, ibid., 4:623.

27. Tadeusz Paczuła, official interrogation of witness for the head prosecutor in Frankfurt, Oct. 22, 1959, ibid., 16:2549.

28. Ibid., 2555.

29. Tadeusz Paczuła, official interrogation of witness for the head prosecutor in Frankfurt, Nov. 23, 1960, ibid., 40:7064–7065.

30. Ibid., 7065.

31. Ibid., 7066.

32. Paczuła, ibid., 16:2551.

33. Ibid., 2552.

34. Scheerer describes these events in extraordinary detail on pages 2199–2220 of his testimony, stating that in mid-March 1944 at 2:00 PM, forty prisoners from the Corpse Commando at Birkenau were brought into the corpse cellar of Block 28, accompanied by Klehr, Boger, and Hofmann

among others; Hofmann closed the cellar doors, and a ten-minute shooting spree ensued. Scheerer states that he was then called into the cellar to undress and spray the blood from the bodies. Scheerer, prosecutor's interrogation, Sept. 23, 1959, ibid., 14:2199–2220. Paczuła states that this is impossible, for as an SDG Klehr never participated in shootings, only injections.

35. Paczuła, 16:2573.

36. Stanisław Głowa, Nov. 21, 1960, ibid., 40:7057. Such questions of guilt or complicity cannot be addressed here at length but fall very much into the domain of Primo Levi's "Gray Zone" and demonstrate another layer of criminality in the system at Auschwitz, which the prosecution could not very well ignore in its search for the "perfect" witness. Determining the motivation of people at Auschwitz who committed murder or at least somehow aided in its execution was crucial to the prosecution. A survivor such as Głowa, who had clearly been forced into such activities (although one could argue that his complicity in the injections was what allowed him to survive) was therefore not suspected of criminal behavior in the same way as Scherpe or the prisoner Bednarek, for example, who was prosecuted because of his extraordinary cruelty and display of individual initiative.

37. Dr. Stanisław Kłodziński, pretrial interrogation conducted by the prosecution, Oct. 26, 1959, ibid., 16:2589. Kłodziński's report on the incident shows some lapses in memory, as he stated that only twenty to thirty boys were to be executed and that the event had taken place in 1942 (rather than 1943). Further investigation by the prosecution would show that the accounts of Głowa and Paczuła were more accurate.

38. Langbein, ibid., 68:12711.

39. Dr. Hans-Günther Seraphim, expert testimony in the jury trial at the Ulm District Court, from 22AR 75/60, ibid., 30:5047, 5049, 5050.

40. Christopher Browning, *Ordinary Men: Reserve Police Battalion 101 and the Final Solution in Poland* (New York: HarperCollins, 1992). Browning deals with this subject particularly in chapter 18.

41. 4 Js 444/59, 5055.

42. Ibid., 5065.

43. Ibid., 5066. Seraphim used as his proof speeches by Himmler in Posen to his SS leaders. On the subject of refusal to obey orders, Himmler had this to say: "He who carries out an order does so as a "loyal Walter," as a faithful representative of the power of an order. If one first thinks, this is right and this is not right, in fact wrong, there are two possibilities. When someone thinks he cannot go through with an order, then he has to report it truthfully: I can't be responsible for this, I would like to excuse my-

self. Then, in most cases, the order will come, You must carry this out. Or one would think, his nerves are finished, he is weak. Then one can say: Good, go and withdraw." 75–75, Himmler's "Posener Rede," PS-1919, ibid.

44. Official interrogation of Maryla Rosenthal by the LKA Baden-Württemberg for the Sonderkommission der Zentrale Stelle der Landes-justizverwaltungen, Mar. 2, 1959, ibid., 4:506–507.

45. Ibid., 510.

46. In her memoirs, Raja Kagan corroborates Rosenthal's depiction of Boger as a kind boss: "Marilla [sic] was an excellent worker, and the horrible Boger, whose secretary she was, acknowledged her, took care of her, nourished her with food from his own plate, and gave her clothing and shoes." Kagan's descriptions of Boger, however, are far more negative than Rosenthal's, as I shall discuss later in this chapter. Raja Kagan, "Frauen und der Kanzlei der Hölle," 171, ibid., 8:1260a.

47. Ibid., 4:512.

48. Ibid., 513.

49. Ibid., 512.

50. Letter from Siegfried Rosenthal to the StA, Stuttgart, Mar. 2, 1959, ibid., 516–517.

51. Interestingly, Rosenthal did indeed appear at the trial and testify about Boger some four years later. Her reasons for her change of heart are not documented in the trial files, and her testimony in the trial itself was also quite vague. Ibid., 20:3183–3186.

52. Interrogation from the Embassy of the Federal Republic of Germany, Mar. 31, 1959, ibid, 5:762.

53. Langbein, Apr. 4, 1959, ibid., 812.

54. Dounia Wasserstrom, testimony from the Auschwitz Trial, Apr. 23, 1964, in Langbein, *Der Auschwitz-Prozess*, 421. Unfortunately, Wasserstrom declined to have her testimony recorded, and her statements at the trial itself are therefore available only through secondary sources.

55. Ibid.

56. *Frankfurter Rundschau*, Apr. 24, 1964.

57. Raja Kagan in 4 Ks 2/63, tape 31A, July 31, 1964.

58. It is not surprising that after the difficult task of appearing at the trial in 1964, Kagan disappeared from public view and wished to be left in peace by anyone seeking information on her experiences at Auschwitz. Lore Shelley, *Secretaries of Death: Accounts by Former Prisoners Who Worked in the Gestapo of Auschwitz* (New York: Shengold, 1986), 265.

59. Zimetbaum is an important symbol of spiritual resistance at Auschwitz, in that, by cutting her wrists before being hanged, she deprived the SS of

the chance to make an example of her and yelled out, "You will all die like dogs, but I shall die as a heroine!" Kagan, acknowledging the courage and higher meaning of Mala's attempted escape, wrote that her flight had become a legend because it had not been mere freedom, but rather the determination to tell the world of the atrocities at Auschwitz and Birkenau that had driven Mala to escape. Kagan, 208, in 4 Js 444/59, 8:1262.

60. Raja Kagan, "Frauen in der Kanzlei der Hölle," 144, ibid., 1256–1257.

61. Raja Kagan, official prosecution interrogation, Dec. 8, 1959, ibid., 19:3155.

62. Ibid., 3156.

63. 4 Ks 2/63, tape 4A, Mar. 6, 1964.

64. Hannah Arendt, *Eichmann in Jerusalem: A Report on the Banality of Evil* (New York: The Viking Press, 1964, 14–15.

3. The Indictment

1. For a record of the changes, see p. 279. Although three subsequent Frankfurt Auschwitz trials took place between 1964 and 1976, in which seven defendants were tried and two of these acquitted, the files of the Auschwitz Trial sat in a closed office for thirty-three years. A couple of years ago, the prosecution reopened them, in the hope of finding some of the suspects still alive and eligible to stand trial.

2. *Antrag auf Eröffnung der gerichtlichen Voruntersuchung: Anklageschrift,* in 4 Js 444/59, 52:9442.

3. 4 Js 444/59, 9383.

4. For example, the reporting officer (*Rapportführer*—represented on the stand by defendant Kaduk), was actually the most important link between the camp itself and its commander. There were only two at Auschwitz. Ibid., 9411.

5. Ibid., 9441.

6. Ibid.

7. Arendt, *Eichmann in Jerusalem: A Report on the Banality of Evil* (New York: Viking Press, 1964), 16.

8. 4 Js 444/59, 52:9486.

9. Raul Hilberg first coined this phrase in his seminal work *The Destruction of the European Jews*. It remains one of the best discussions of the subject. It was first published in 1961 and appeared in Germany in 1964. Raul Hilberg, *The Destruction of the European Jews*, rev. ed., 3 vols. (New York: Holmes & Meier, 1985).

10. Auschwitz in particular fell under the jurisdiction of both offices (which

often had conflicting aims), as it was both a deportation camp for the Jews (controlled by the RSHA) and an enormous slave labor camp (controlled by the WVHA). Helmut Krausnick, Hans Buchheim, Martin Broszat, and Hans-Adolf Jacobsen, *The Anatomy of the SS State*, trans. Richard Barry, Marian Jackson, Dorothy Long (New York: Walker and Company, 1968), 483–484.

11. 4 Js 444/59, 52:9525. Notice the adoption of Nazi terminology for extermination or murder in the use of the word "liquidate" *(liquidieren)*, which in the indictment appeared as "exterminate" *(vernichten)*. Such influences were often evident in the trial and pretrial investigations, an uncanny aspect of the regression into Nazi standards that was sometimes inevitable.

12. Krausnick, Broszat, Buchheim, and Jacobsen, *Anatomy of the SS State*, 399.

13. Adelheid L. Rüter-Ehlermann, and C. F. Rüter, eds., *Justiz und NS-Verbrechen: Sammlung deutscher Strafurteile wegen nationalsozialistischer Tötungsverbrechen* (hereafter *JuNS-V*) 22 vols. (Amsterdam: Amsterdam University Press, 1968), 15:2–9.

14. Ibid., 17:88–115.

15. These sections within the indictment provided only the skeleton of what would be later be published as *The Anatomy of the SS State*; the book included new chapters with much more in-depth analysis of the SS mentality (see chap. 3, "Command and Compliance") and the Final Solution as a whole (see chap. 1, "The Persecution of the Jews"). This important historical documentation was touched upon in the indictment of the trial but fleshed out more fully in the book. Krausnick, Broszat, Buchheim, and Jacobsen, *Anatomy of the SS State*.

16. *Anklageschrift*, 78:14721.

17. Nuremberg Document 2533-PS, ibid., 14740.

18. Nuremberg Document 778-PS, ibid., 14741.

19. Ibid.

20. Ibid., 14744. This passage also appears verbatim in *Anatomy of the SS State*, with new accompanying explanations.

21. Krausnick, Broszat, Buchheim, and Jacobsen, *Anatomy of the SS State*, 432.

22. Nuremberg Document 1063 (a-b)—PS, in 4 Js 444/59, 78:14749.

23. Nuremberg Document 645-PS, 4 Js 444/59, 78:14751.

24. *Anklageschrift*, 14751.

25. Ibid., 14751, 14757.

26. The term *Abspritzen* was camp jargon for the phenol injections. Ibid., 14714–14715, 14797.

27. The term *Lagerältester* is defined as a "prisoner functionary appointed by the SS to be a camp representative—but answering to the SS. . . Within the hierarchy of the camp, this was the highest rank that could be attained by a prisoner." "Concentration Camp Slang and Idioms: A Lexicon" (unpublished, compiled by the United States Holocaust Memorial Museum Library, Washington, D.C.), 14.

28. 4 Js 444/59, 78:14793. *Muselmänner*, or "Muslims," was slang for starved, skeletal prisoners. This term was given to them because "these inmates seemed to resemble stereotyped pictures of Arabs: brown skin, huge eyes, always wrapped in blankets." "Concentration Camp Slang and Idioms: A Lexicon" (compiled by the United States Holocaust Memorial Museum Library, Washington, D.C.), 16.

29. See Primo Levi, *The Drowned and the Saved*, trans. Raymond Rosenthal (New York: Summit Books, 1986), particularly the chapter "The Gray Zone." See also Filip Müller, *Auschwitz Inferno: The Testimony of a Sonderkommando*, trans. Susanne Flatauer (London: Routledge and Kegan Paul, 1979), and Tadeusz Borowski, *This Way for the Gas, Ladies and Gentlemen, and Other Stories*, trans. Barbara Vedder (London: Cape, 1967). See also Richard Glazar, *Trap with a Green Fence: Survival in Treblinka*, trans. Roslyn Theobald (Evanston, Ill.: Northwestern University Press, 1992). These are among the most famous accounts, but many other survivor memoirs include details of prisoners who tortured others in order to survive.

30. 4 Js 444/59, 78:14799.

31. Ibid., 14801; Nuremberg Document 2199-PS, 14802.

32. *Anklageschrift*, 14814.

33. The swing was made famous in the trial and witness testimony about the effects of such an interrogation on the victim has appeared in Chapter 2. The Boger swing figured prominently in Peter Weiss's play *The Investigation*. See Figure 2.

34. Nuremberg Document 1531-PS, in 4 Js 444/59, 14815–14816.

35. *Anklageschrift*, 14815.

36. Ibid., 14819. Grabner's description in his notes is intentionally vague.

37. Krausnick, Broszat, Buchheim, and Jacobsen, *Anatomy of the SS State*, 525.

38. Nuremberg Document 52-PS, 4 Js 444/59, 78:14821.

39. Nuremberg Document 338 EC, ibid., 14824.

40. *Anklageschrift*, 14827. Pilecki uses the word *abtransportiert* to describe the taking away of prisoners on the trucks. The prefix *ab-*, like the *ab-* in *abspritzen*, was a euphemism for murder.

41. Ibid., 79:14838.
42. Ibid., 14854. In fact, at this time both the historians and the prosecution overestimated the number of victims at Auschwitz. They quote a figure estimated by survivor and witness Kazimierz Smolen, director of the Auschwitz museum, who thought at least three million people had been murdered there. More recent estimations stand at between 1 and 1.5 million people.
43. Ingo Müller, *Hitler's Justice: The Courts of the Third Reich*, trans. Deborah Lucas Schneider (Cambridge, Mass.: Harvard University Press, 1991), 255.
44. 4 Js 444/59, 79:14889–14890.
45. Ibid., 14892–14893.
46. Court order, July 8, 1963, ibid., 85:16136–16155. This final attachment to the indictment appeared as an addendum, part of the ongoing process of refining the charges.
47. Memo of Feb. 1963, ibid., 77:14595.
48. Nov. 14, 1960, ibid., 40:7007r.
49. Report of public prosecutor Kügler, Hamburg, Nov. 14, 1960, ibid., 7003.
50. Memo ibid., 77:14596.
51. Court order of the District Court in Frankfurt am Main, 3. Strafkammer, June 24, 1963, ibid., 85:16138.
52. Ibid., 16137.
53. Monowitz, also known as Auschwitz III or Buna, was a massive work camp where prisoners worked either in the Buna synthetic rubber works or for IG Farben.
54. JuNSV, 14:734–738.
55. Interrogation of Jacob Fries by the Zentrale Stelle: Landeskriminalamt Baden-Württemberg Sonderkommission, Feb. 9, 1959, in 4 Js 444/59, 3:437.
56. 4 Ks 2/63, July 16, 1964, tape 26B.
57. *Anklageschrift*, 78:14619–14662. The titles given to the various guards at Auschwitz are often difficult to translate, as the job descriptions are overlapping and vague, created specifically for the camp context. The translations here are in part from "Concentration Camp Slang and Idioms" and Abraham J. Edelheit and Hershel Edelheit, *History of the Holocaust: A Handbook and* Dictionary (Boulder, Colo.: Westview, 1994). For a complete list of ranks, both within the SS and within the camp, see p. 282.
58. *Anklageschrift*, 78:14620.
59. Testimony of Ludwig Wörl, ibid., 79:14925.
60. Pretrial interrogation of Hermann Langbein, ibid., 68:12704.

61. Ibid., 79:14934.
62. Ibid.
63. *Anklageschrift*, 78:14634.
64. Ibid., 14647.
65. Ibid., 15005–15006.
66. Ibid., 15006–15007.
67. Ibid., 15007.
68. Ibid., 15020, 15035–15036.
69. Ibid., 80:15150.

4. The Trial

1. In my examination of the audiotapes I selected a cross section of witnesses, and from this research I construct here a picture of the courtroom.

2. Unfortunately, the trial proceedings were not always recorded, as anyone on the stand could decline to be taped "for securing of the memory of the court." Documentation of testimony by those who refused to be taped does appear, however, in Bernd Naumann, *Auschwitz: A Report on the Proceedings against Robert Karl Ludwig Mulka and Others before the Court at Frankfurt*, trans. Jean Steinberg (New York: Praeger, 1966).

3. Peter Novick, *The Holocaust in American Life* (Boston: Houghton Mifflin, 1999), 275.

4. Yisrael Gutman, "Auschwitz—An Overview" in *Anatomy of the Auschwitz Death Camp*, eds. Yisrael Gutman and Michael Berenbaum (Bloomington: Indiana University Press, 1994), 11.

5. Otto Wolken, *Chronik des Lagers Auschwitz II (B II s)*, 1945, in 4 Js 444/59, 33:5648a-5659.

6. Prosecutor's Interrogation of Otto Wolken, ibid., November 14,1960, 40: 6948.

7. 4 Ks 2/63, Feb. 27, 1964, tape 2B. Laternser, in an attempt to defame Wolken, went so far as to ask him about a case in which he had been tried and sentenced, during the war. Wolken responded: "But I was a Jew."

8. 4 Ks 2/63, Mar. 5, 1964, tape 3A.

9. Ibid.

10. Ibid.

11. Ibid.

12. 4 Ks 2/63, March 2, 1962, tape 2B.

13. Ibid.

14. 4 Ks 2/63, Mar. 5, 1964, tape 3A.

15. 4 Ks 2/63, Mar. 26, 1964, tape 6A, and Naumann, *Auschwitz: A Report on the Proceedings*, 329.

16. 4 Ks 2/63, May 8, 1964, tape #7A.

17. At this point in the trial tapes, the clear sound of children playing outside the courthouse can be heard, creating an eerie dichotomy between the dialogue in the courtroom and the sound of children's laughter outside.

18. 4 Ks 2/63, May 29, 1964, tape 15B.

19. 4 Ks 2/63, May 8, 1964, tape 7A.

20. 4 Ks 2/63, May 8, 1964, tape 8B.

21. Ks 2/63, May 15, 1964, tape 11A.

22. 4 Ks 2/63, May 15, 1964, tapes 11A-B.

23. 4 Ks 2/63, May 25, 1964, tapes 14B-15A.

24. Lawrence Langer, *Admitting the Holocaust* (New York: Oxford University Press, 1995), 89.

25. Ibid., 89, 97. Langer uses this phrase twice to encapsulate his understanding of the trial.

26. Martin Walser, "Unser Auschwitz," in *Heimatkunde: Aufsätze und Reden* (Frankfurt am Main: Suhrkamp, 1968), 10.

27. One former SS member, Georg Engelschall, was not sworn in but was arrested instead. 4 Ks 2/63, July 16, 1964, tape 27A. Others, like Friedrich Ontl, who had worked for the main camp doctor, were offered the possibility of remaining silent, in order not to implicate themselves, but did not. 4 Ks 2/63, June 4, 1964, tape 17A.

28. The confiscation of Jews' belongings and the relation this practice at Auschwitz bore to "Aktion Reinhard" is dealt with in Bertrand Perz and Thomas Sandkühler, "Auschwitz und die 'Aktion Reinhard,' 1942–45: Judenmord und Raubpraxis in neuer Sicht," *Zeitgeschichte* (Innsbruck: Studienverlag, September–October 1999), 5:283–316. The authors briefly discuss the appearance of Dr. Morgen to investigate individual guards suspected of stealing goods.

29. At Nuremberg, Morgen gave a bizarre version of events in which the extermination camps were not run by the SS but by a criminal commissioner named Wirth, an officer of Hitler's chancellery. Morgan, who was not taken seriously, was not cross-examined by the prosecution. Gerhard Reitlinger, *The Final Solution: The Attempt to Exterminate the Jews of Europe 1939–1945* (Northvale, N.J.: Jason Aronson, 1987), 123–124.

30. Jan. 26, 1961, 30 UR 9/58 LG Köln, in 4 Js 444/59, 48:8515–8516.

31. Ibid., 8517–8518.

32. Konrad Morgen, Mar. 8, 1962, ibid., 63:11716.

33. Ibid., 11718.

34. 4 Ks 2/63, Mar. 9, 1964, tape 4A.

35. Ibid.
36. Ibid.
37. Ibid.
38. Gerhard Reitlinger corroborates in his book on the Final Solution this representation of Morgen's. Reitlinger recalls Morgen's appearance at the Nuremberg trial and says, "He seems to have been a boastful man of some integrity, though not enough. Although he knew how to keep his mouth shut when the clues became dangerous, he got the reputation of a Nosey Parker in SS circles . . . In the end Morgen's fellow-captives overcame their repugnance, recognizing in him a man whom the Allies might consider respectable." Reitlinger, *Final Solution*, 123–124.
39. 4 Ks 2/63.
40. Reitlinger, *Final Solution*, 453.
41. 4 Js 444/59, 63: 11721.
42. Reitlinger, *Final Solution*, 453. This characterization contradicts his earlier comments about Morgen's mendacity.
43. Alfred-Maurice de Zayas, "The Wehrmacht Bureau on War Crimes," *Historical Journal* (Cambridge: Cambridge University Press), 35 (2): 397.
44. 4 Ks 2/63. It is quite telling that Morgen was not punished for his direct disobedience to one of the highest officials of the SS. We already know that no one was ever punished for refusing to follow his or her orders; presumably, Morgen was reprimanded for doing his duty with too much zeal and without any proper order from Berlin. This was also the standard Morgen himself applied in investigating the guards at Auschwitz.
45. After the war, Grabner was tried in 1947 at the big Polish tribunal against Auschwitz perpetrators, where he was sentenced to death and executed.
46. 4 Ks 2/63.
47. Ibid.
48. Ibid.
49. Ibid.
50. Ibid.
51. Ibid.
52. Ibid.
53. Mar. 23, 1960, in 4 Js 444/59, 28:4752. He repeated this statement on the stand in his trial testimony.
54. Wilhelm Reimers, June 6, 1961, ibid., 51:9132.
55. Ibid., 9133.
56. Langbein, *Der Auschwitz-Prozess*, 337.
57. Dr. Werner Hansen ibid., 338.
58. Heinrich Hannover, "Vom Nürnberger Prozeß zum Auschwitz-Prozeß," *Auschwitz—Ein Prozeß*, ed. Ulrich Schneider (Cologne: Papy-Rossa, 1994), 73.

59. Devin O. Pendas, " 'I Didn't Know What Auschwitz Was': The Frankfurt Auschwitz Trial and the German Press, 1963–1965," *Yale Journal of Law and Humanities* 12, (2000), 2:397, 421–422.

60. Walser, "Unser Auschwitz," 8.

61. Hannover, "Vom Nürnberger Prozeß zum Auschwitz-Prozeß," 72.

62. "Auschwitz Zeuge: Menschenfleisch im Versuchslabor: Jede Woche zwei große Töpfe . . . 'Kleinkinder fast immer in die Gaskammern geschickt,' " *Frankfurter Rundschau,* June 9, 1964.

63. Ibid.

64. Ibid.

65. Walser, "Unser Auschwitz," 8–9. In discussing the tendency of the reporters to present the SS officers as beasts and devils, Walser largely attributes this to the inability of the press to view Auschwitz as a reality. He does not address the law itself and its emphasis on the excessive cruelty of these defendants.

66. Ibid., 11.

67. Heinz Abosch, Ursula Rütt, and Arthur Miller, "Auschwitz," *Blätter für deutsche und internationale Politik* 4 (1964): 300–301.

68. "SED sichert Auschwitz-Angeklagten Integrität zu," *Frankfurter Rundschau,* June 12, 1964. In this paragraph, the reporter changed his language from "alleged," to present the crime as fact. Klehr was not convicted on this charge.

69. Ibid.

70. Sybille Bedford, " 'The Auschwitz Business': Horror and Courtesy in a German Court," *Observer,* Jan. 5, 1964. Bedford is most famous for her book *The Faces of Justice: A Traveller's Report* (New York: Simon & Schuster, 1961), which documents the novelist's journey throughout the European courts in the late 1950s; in it she demonstrates the differences in French, German, and English, Austrian and Swiss courts.

71. Otmar Kauck, "Die Mordmaschinerie von Auschwitz: 22 Männer auf der Anklagebank im Frankfurter Römer," *Frankfurter Neue Presse,* Dec. 13, 1963.

72. H. G. Adler, Hermann Langbein, and Ella Lingens-Reiner, comp., *Auschwitz: Zeugnisse und Berichte* (Frankfurt am Main: Europäische Verlagsanstalt, 1962). The book includes documents from Auschwitz, excerpts of the Höss diary (which is banned from publication in Germany), and witness testimony—including that of Tadeusz Paczuła, Dr. Stanisław Kłodziński, and others who also testified at the trial.

73. Kauck, "Die Mordmaschinerie von Auschwitz."

74. While a prisoner of the Poles in postwar Kraków, Rudolf Höss wrote his account of being the commandant at Auschwitz; the book is a startling inside look not only at the grisly duties of the commandant but also at the

psyche of the man who seemed quite capable of ordering and overseeing mass executions during the day and tending his beautiful garden in the evening. Rudolf Höss, *Kommandant in Auschwitz: Autobiographische Aufzeichnungen* (Stuttgart: Deutsche Verlagsanstalt, 1958). Höss was tried and sentenced to death in 1947; he was hanged on the gallows in Auschwitz I, beside Crematorium 1, very near his former office.

75. Kurt Ernenputsch, "Die Angeklagten von Auschwitz: Als Mitläufer eingestuft, lange Jahre unerkannt—Am 20. Dezember in Frankfurt vor Gericht," *Frankfurter Allgemeine Zeitung*, Dec. 17, 1963.

76. Many journal articles that dealt with the trial in a more thoughtful manner criticized the public's deliberate ignorance about the "murderers in their midst": see Horst Krüger, "Im Labyrinth der Schuld: Ein Tag im Frankfurter Auschwitz-Prozeß," *Der Monat* 188 (1964): 19–29; Hermann Langbein, "Probleme des Auschwitz-Prozesses," *Hessische Blätter für Volksbildung* 1 (1964): 25–36. In the opening speech for an Auschwitz exhibition in the Paulskirche (St. Paul's church) in Frankfurt, Eugen Kogon expressed sentiments similar to Walser's and bemoaned the idea that the "audience" at the trial heard only about the incomprehensible, the disgusting, and remained removed from the world of Auschwitz, created as it was by a highly civilized, recognizable society. Eugen Kogon, "Auschwitz und eine menschliche Zukunft," *Frankfurter Hefte* 12 (1964): 830–838.

77. A large body of literature exists on the psychological reaction (or lack thereof) in postwar Germany. The most famous studies are Karl Jaspers, *The Question of German Guilt*, trans. E. B. Ashton (New York: Capricorn Books, 1961); Alexander and Margaret Mitscherlich, *The Inability to Mourn: Principles of Collective Behavior* (New York: Grove Press, 1984); Theodor Adorno (and others), *The Authoritarian Personality*, 2 vols. (New York: Wiley, 1964); and more recently, Jeffrey Herf, *Divided Memory: The Nazi Past in the Two Germanys* (Cambridge, Mass.: Harvard University Press, 1997). See also Erich Kuby, *Deutschland: Von verschuldeter Teilung zur unverdienten Einheit* (Rastatt, Germany: Arthur Moewig, 1990).

78. Letter to the editor, *Frankfurter Rundschau*, Dec. 21, 1963.

79. Letter to the editor, ibid.

80. Lothar Vetter, "Es bleiben die Angst und die Schuld: Beobachtungen und Gespräche am Rande des Auschwitz-Prozesses," *Frankfurter Rundschau*, Feb. 15, 1964.

81. Walser, "Unser Auschwitz," 12.

82. Ibid.

83. Werner Wiechmann, "20.000 mal den Tod gebracht . . . Ungeheuerliche

Vorwürfe gegen Auschwitz-Sanitäter Josef Klehr," *Frankfurter Rundschau*, Apr. 25, 1964.

84. Bastian, "Die Sache mit dem Apfel," *Frankfurter Rundschau*, Apr. 24, 1964.

85. "Die Phantasie Versagt," *Frankfurter Rundschau*, May 30, 1964. The title of this article refers to the public's (and the reporter's) incomprehension of the perpetrators on the stand and perception of them as inhuman beasts.

5. The Summations and the Judgment

1. "Anklage Plädoyer" (Prosecution closing argument), May 7, 1965, 4 Js 444/59, 2.

2. Ibid., 4–5.

3. 4 Js 444/59, 9.

4. Ibid., 10.

5. Ibid., 16.

6. Ibid., 16–17.

7. This was the constant refrain of defendant Mulka, for instance, who insisted that he had never been inside the actual camp, let alone on the platform.

8. Großmann describes all these events in detail in his summation, 4 Js 444/59, 22–28. Intentionalism is the argument that Hitler had a plan for the extermination of the European Jews before he took power, and that he carried out his plan through war. On the opposite side of the debate, functionalists argue that Hitler had not created a blueprint for the Holocaust and only sometime in 1941 or 1942 did he initiate the Final Solution and the concerted effort to exterminate the Jews. See Christopher Browning, *The Path to Genocide: Essays on the Launching of the Final Solution* (Cambridge: Cambridge University Press, 1992); Lucy Davidowicz, *The War against the Jews* (New York: Holt, Rinehart and Winston, 1975); Gerald Fleming, *Hitler and the Final Solution* (Berkeley: University of California Press, 1984); Christian Gerlach, "The Wannsee Conference, the Fate of German Jews, and Hitler's Decision in Principle to Exterminate All European Jews," *Journal of Modern History* 70 (1998): 759–812; Eberhard Jäckel, *Hitler's World View: A Blueprint for Power* (Cambridge, Mass.: Harvard University Press, 1981); Ian Kershaw, "Improvised Genocide? The Emergence of the 'Final Solution' in the 'Warthegau,'" *Transactions of the Royal Historical Society*, sixth series, no. 2 (1992): 51–78; Hans Mommsen, "Anti-Jewish Politics and the Implementation of the Holocaust," in Konrad Kwiet, ed., *From the Emancipa-*

tion to the Holocaust: Essays on Jewish Literature and History in Central Europe (Sydney: UNSW Press, 1987), 63–78; Karl Schleunes, *The Twisted Road to Auschwitz: Nazi Policy towards German Jews, 1933–1939* (Chicago: University of Illinois Press, 1990).

9. 4 Js 444/59, 34. This Posen speech is not to be confused with Himmler's much more famous speech two days earlier to the leaders of the SS, also in Posen.

10. Ibid., 35.

11. Georg Friedrich Vogel, "Anklage Plädoyer," May 10, 1965, 4 Js 444/59, 3, 10.

12. According to Hermann Langbein in the commentary accompanying his documentation of the trial, this was actually a high number of petitions for life sentences. Langbein, *Der Auschwitz-Prozess*, 867. A life sentence was the maximum punishment, for West Germany did not have the death penalty.

13. In his initial interrogation during the trial proceedings Breitwieser gave the court a graphic description of the gassing process and his role in it. He explained the way the gas pellets were thrown into the chamber and how quickly the pellets turned into gas. He insisted that he had gleaned this information only by disinfecting clothing, and the evidence was not sufficient to prove otherwise. Breitwieser reported, "The gas disagreed with me; I developed stomach problems and asked to be transferred." Dec., 30, 1963, ibid., 786.

14. Henry Ormond and Christian Raabe were responsible for the proposal that the court conduct an on-site investigation at the Auschwitz concentration camp, which occurred in December 1964.

15. Bernd Naumann, *Auschwitz: A Report on the Proceedings against Robert Karl Ludwig Mulka and Others before the Court at Frankfurt*, trans. Jean Steinberg (New York: Praeger, 1966), 386.

16. Henry Ormond, "Plädoyer im Auschwitz-Prozess," *Sonderreihe aus gestern und heute* 7 (1965): 1. The table of contents for Ormond's summation includes such topics as "The Fairy Tale of the Collective Innocence of the Waffen SS," "The Myth of the Iron Discipline of the SS in Auschwitz," and "The Legend of Helpfulness to Camp Prisoners."

17. Ibid., 26.

18. Ormond, "Plädoyer im Auschwitz-Prozess," 49, 50.

19. Ibid., 61.

20. Naumann, *Auschwitz: A Report on the Proceedings*, 388.

21. Dr. Hermann Stolting II, "Plädoyer im Auschwitz-Prozess," gift from Werner Hummerich, substitute judge in the Auschwitz Trial, courtesy of the Fritz Bauer Institute, 6.

22. Naumann, *Auschwitz: A Report on the Proceedings*, 389.
23. Ibid., 2, 5.
24. Ibid., 391–393. Naumann, who is critical of Aschenauer's summation, states that his defense of Boger consisted of a "several hours-long speech about the background against which the actions of the defendant must be seen."
25. Ibid., 394, 395. Laternser wrote a book about his experience as a defense lawyer at the Auschwitz Trialwhich includes his closing statement. Hans Laternser, *Die Andere Seite im Auschwitz-Prozess, 1963–1965* (The Other Side in the Auschwitz Trial, 1963–1965) (Stuttgart: Seewald, 1966).
26. Naumann, *Auschwitz: A Report on the Proceedings*, 395.
27. Ibid., 399.
28. Ibid., 403.
29. "*Auschwitz-Urteil*," in Naumann, *Auschwitz: A Report on the Proceedings*, 270–271, and *Auschwitz Urteil*, 4 Ks 2/63, Landgericht Frankfurt am Main. See Appendix 4.
30. Naumann, *Auschwitz: A Report on the Proceedings*, 414.
31. Ibid., 415.
32. Ibid.
33. Fritz Bauer, "Zu den Naziverbrecher Prozessen," *Stimme der Gemeinde zum Kirchlichen Leben, zur Politik, Wirtschaft und Kultur* 18. (1963): 563–574. Quotation on 568.
34. Naumann, *Auschwitz: A Report on the Proceedings*, 416.
35. This part of Hofmeyer's public address came directly from the written judgment. Specifically, it came from the section on evidence pertaining to the case of defendant Mulka. Before dealing with the specific evidence against Mulka, the judgment had a section called "Overall Preliminary Remarks to the Evaluation of Evidence." 4 Ks 2/63, 107–110.
36. Naumann, *Auschwitz: A Report on the Proceedings*, 416.
37. Ibid., 417–418.
38. 4 Ks 2/63, 95. It is clear from the verdict that the judge chose to use the term "mass murder" in order to recognize the existence of a crime complex; however, he did not let this terminology affect the convictions, for it was not legally acceptable at the time the crimes were committed.
39. Ibid., 103–105.
40. Ibid., 126.
41. Ibid., 130.
42. Ibid., 131–135.
43. Ibid., 136. The court reinforced this knowledge of the illegality of the act by pointing to the testimony of SS witnesses and other defendants, such

as Baretski, who spoke of their understanding that the extermination of the Jews was a horrible crime. The justification in the judgment stated that "if even Baretski, who is a simpleton and is less intelligent than all the other defendants, could clearly recognize the illegality of the extermination actions, then the decision is final, that the rest of the defendants also knew that the ordered mass murder of Jewish people was criminal." This is another good example of the innovative ways that the court had to determine innocence or guilt.

44. Ibid., 137.

45. In the judgment on Mulka, the court referred to the distinction between paragraphs 47 and 49: "The co-perpetrator is the one who intends the crime principally; the accomplice is the one who supports the crime of another." Mulka was determined to have been the perpetrator in the murder of a prisoner whose death he ordered. The prisoner was on the selection platform and spoke with others, which was strictly forbidden (by Mulka). Because Mulka instigated the order to kill, he was the murderer. No conviction could be reached, however, because Mulka was never officially charged with this incident (it came to light during the trial) and it did not appear in the indictment. 4 Ks 2/63, 138, 144, 147.

46. Ibid., 173.

47. Ibid., 150.

48. Ibid.

49. Ibid., 151.

50. Ibid., 152.

51. Ibid., 152–153.

52. Ibid., 175.

53. Ibid., 176. This seems like a weak argument for reducing a sentence, as virtually every former SS officer who had participated in the extermination of the Jews—even persons such as Boger and Kaduk—went back to a normal, law-abiding life. As Hannah Arendt has observed, this was one of the main reasons that the public was indifferent toward these defendants and did not feel a pressing need to put them on trial. Hannah Arendt, *Eichmann in Jerusalem: A Report on the Banality of Evil* (New York: Viking, 1964), 16.

54. Many of the charges against Boger emphasized the zeal with which he made certain that no prisoners selected for the gas chambers returned to the line for prisoners who would be admitted into the camp. Because of this, at least ten prisoners were always taken directly to the gas chambers.

55. 4 Ks 2/63, 182.

56. Ibid., 185–186.

57. Ibid., 188.

58. Ibid., 189–190.
59. Ibid., 201, 230.
60. The judgment for Kaduk reads: "There is no doubt that Kaduk knew precisely that the prisoners he picked out would be killed, because as useless eaters they no longer served a purpose." A hint of sarcasm crept into the tone of the judgment at this point. Ibid., 393, 399, 390, 405–406.
61. Ibid., 410.
62. Ibid., 423, 427–428, 450.
63. Ibid., 713–714.
64. Ibid., 739.
65. Ibid., 740
66. Both quotations ibid., 868–869.
67. Ibid., 519, 551.
68. Ibid., 552–553.
69. Ibid., 746, 747.
70. Ibid., 816.
71. In his first interrogation by the prosecution, Wörl testified to having seen defendant Hantl inject more than one prisoner, but in his second interrogation, by the court's investigating judge, he said that he had seen Hantl in the injection room and had witnessed naked prisoners being led into the room, but he did not state that he had seen the actual injections. In the courtroom, Wörl insisted that he had seen defendant Hantl inject at least one person. The defense lawyers questioned him on his inconsistency, and finally Wörl could only retreat to the explanation that "he wanted to meet him [the defense lawyer] halfway." Ibid., 698, 817; 4 Js 444/59, 4:513.
72. 4 Ks 2/63, 838.
73. Ibid., 884–885.

6. The Response to the Verdict

1. Hannah Arendt, foreword, in Bernd Naumann, *Auschwitz: A Report on the Proceedings against Robert Karl Ludwig Mulka and Others Before the Court at Frankfurt* trans. Jean Steinberg (New York: Praeger, 1966), xi.
2. See Heinrich Hannover, "Vom Nürnberger Prozeß zum Auschwitz-Prozeß," In Ulrich Schneider, ed. *Auschwitz—Ein Prozeß*, (Cologne: Papy-Rossa Verlag, 1994), 71–72. Hannover is extremely critical of the choice of defendants on the stand and the fact that Germany's postwar "capitalist reflorescence" has made German industrialists who worked at IG Farben were important players in the new economy and therefore valued members of society. He deplores the fact that most of these former

Nazis (including former SS judges like Konrad Morgen) openly led public lives, came to testify at the trial, and ran no danger of being prosecuted themselves.

3. "Urteil im Auschwitz-Prozeß gefällt: Sechs Angeklagte erhielten lebenslang Zuchthaus/Dreimal Freispruch," *Frankfurter Rundschau*, Aug. 20, 1965.

4. "Vielsichtiges Echo auf das Auschwitz-Urteil: Die Bundesregierung hebt Nichterkennung des Befehlsnotstandes hervor/ Ablehnung im Ostblock," *Frankfurter Rundschau*, Aug. 21, 1965.

5. This phenomenon is carefully examined in Devin O. Pendas' article, " 'I Didn't Know What Auschwitz Was': The Frankfurt Auschwitz Trial and the German Press, 1963–1965," *Yale Journal of Law and Humanities* 12 (2000): 397–446.

6. Gerd Czechatz, "Die Ersten kamen schon kurz nach sechs Uhr: Nach 182 Verhandlungstagen wurden im Frankfurter Auschwitz-Prozeß die Urteile gesprochen," *Frankfurter Rundschau*, Aug. 20, 1965.

7. Ernst Müller-Meiningen, Jr., "Nach dem Auschwitz-Urteil," *Süddeutsche Zeitung*, Aug. 20, 1965.

8. Hans Schüler, "Auschwitz: Die Schuld der Zwanzig; Ein Stück deutscher Geschichte; Der Sinn des Prozesses," *Die Welt*, Aug. 20, 1965; Johann Georg Reißmüller, "Sühne für Auschwitz," *Frankfurter Allegemeine Zeitung*, Aug. 20, 1965.

9. Reißmüller, "Sühne für Auschwitz." The reference in the second quotation to a tribunal evoked memories of the Nuremberg trials as well. This evocation was surely intentional on the author's part.

10. Gerhard Ziegler, "Gegen Mulka und andere," *Frankfurter Rundschau*, Aug. 21, 1965. Although Ziegler's commentary struck a tone similar to that of the more conservative Reißmüller, he also pointed out that the jurists and judges involved in the trial had to recognize their involvement in the Nazi past and had to acknowledge the need for an ongoing confrontation with the past that should not at any time simply be declared complete.

11. Eugen Kogon, "Umwelt und Recht: Rechtsgrundsätze des Auschwitz Urteils," *Neue Juristische Wochenschrift* 41 (1965): 1901.

12. Fritz Bauer, "Im Namen des Volkes: Die strafrechtliche Bewältigung der Vergangenheit," In Helmut Hammerschmidt, ed. *Zwanzig Jahre danach: Eine Deutsche Bilanz, 1945–1965* (Munich, Vienna, Basel: Desch, 1965), 301–302.

13. Ibid. Bauer did not cite any references for these statistics.

14. Ibid., 307.

15. Ibid.

16. Ibid., 308.
17. Ibid.
18. Ibid., 312.
19. Hans Hofmeyer, "Prozessrechtliche Probleme und Praktische Schwierigkeiten bei der Durchführung der Prozesse," in *Probleme der Verfolgung und Ahndung von nationalsozialistischen Gewaltverbrechen* (Munich: Beck'sche Verlag, 1967), C39.
20. Ibid., C42, C43.
21. Ibid., C43.
22. Ibid.
23. "Zum Urteil im Auschwitz-Prozeß," *Dokumentation der Zeit* 342 (1965): 3.
24. "Skandalösen Urteil," *Neues Deutschland*, Aug. 21, 1965.
25. All quotations in this paragraph come from *Die Welt*, Aug. 21, 1965.
26. Jerzy Kowalewski "Polen kritisiert Urteile im Auschwitz-Prozeß," in *Begegnung mit Polen* 10 (1965): 579.
27. Hermann Langbein, "Stimmen der Bevölkerung zum Auschwitzprozeß: Protokoll eines Referates," *Hessische Blätter für Volksbildung* 4 (1966): 323–324. This publication was the mouthpiece for the Hesse State Central Office for Political Education (*Hessische Landeszentrale für politische Bildung*). The harshly critical voice of the note taker throughout the article provides an illuminating glimpse into the earnest attempt this state agency made to educate the young and the old about the Nazi past.
28. Ibid., 324.
29. Ibid., 324–325.
30. Ibid., 325.
31. Ibid., 332. This historical discussion regarding the path of German history became the *Sonderweg* debate, in which historians like Hans Ulrich Wehler and Fritz Fischer on one hand argued for a German "special path" that had led to the rise of Nazism, whereas others, like Geoff Eley and David Blackbourn, argued for a more complex constellation of events leading to Nazism. For an introduction to this debate, see David Blackbourn, and Geoff Eley, *The Peculiarities of German History: Bourgeois Society and Politics in Nineteenth-Century Germany* (Oxford: Oxford University Press, 1984); Geoff Eley, *From Unification to Nazism: Reinterpreting the German Past* (Boston: Allen & Unwin, 1986); Fritz Fischer, *From Kaiserreich to Third Reich: Elements of Continuity in German History, 1871–1945*, trans. Roger Fletcher (Boston: Allen & Unwin, 1986); Thomas Nipperdey, *Deutsche Geschichte, 1866–1918* (Munich: Beck, 1992); and Hans-Ulrich Wehler, *The German Empire, 1871–1918*, trans. Kim Traynor (Dover, N.H.: Berg Publishers, 1985);

32. Gerhard Mauz, "Die Schädelstätte der Deutschen: Der erste Auschwitz-Prozeß," in *Die Gerechten und die Gerichteten* (Frankfurt am Main: Verlag Ullstein, 1968), 227.

33. Ibid., 230–231.

34. Ibid., 233.

35. Heinz Haueisen, "Auschwitz—eine Herausforderung an die Frankfurter Justizbehörden," in Horst Henrichs and Karl Stephan, eds., *Studien zur Frankfurter Geschichte 27: Ein Jahrhundert Frankfurter Justiz* (Frankfurt am Main: Verlag Waldemar Kramer, 1989), 190–191.

36. Ibid., 194.

37. Ibid., 200.

38. Peter Weiss, *The Investigation*, trans. Jon Swan and Ulu Grosbard (New York: Atheneum, 1984), 107–108.

39. "Weiss: Gesang von der Schaukel," *Der Spiegel* 43 (1965), 162.

40. Ibid., 152.

41. Both Lawrence Langer and James Young have criticized the play as distorting the events of the Holocaust in order to promote Weiss's radical socialist ideological view of West German society. Langer later revised his opinion and, in *Admitting the Holocaust*, argued that it filled the gaps that had been so glaring in the trial itself. Says Langer, "Weiss created from a futile courtroom dispute a fresh vision of the clash in Auschwitz between moral space and destructive place." Lawrence L. Langer, *Admitting the Holocaust* (New York: Oxford University Press, 1995), 97–98. See also Lawrence L. Langer, *The Holocaust and the Literary Imagination* (New Haven, Conn.: Yale University Press, 1975); Alvin H. Rosenfeld, *A Double Dying: Reflections on Holocaust Literature* (Bloomington: Indiana University Press, 1980); Sidra DeKoven Ezrahi, *By Words Alone: The Holocaust in Literature* (Chicago: University of Chicago Press, 1980); James E. Young, *Writing and Rewriting the Holocaust: Narrative and the Consequences of Interpretation* (Bloomington: Indiana University Press, 1988). An excellent essay that carefully examines the debate surrounding Weiss's omission of the word "Jew" is Robert Cohen, "The Political Aesthetics of Holocaust Literature: Peter Weiss's *The Investigation* and Its Critics," *History and Memory* 10, no. 2 (1998), 43–67.

42. "Weiss: Gesang von der Schaukel," 155.

43. Hannah Arendt, *Eichmann in Jerusalem: A Report on the Banality of Evil* (New York: Viking, 1964), 16. Historian Dick de Mildt voices similar sentiments, by pointing to a 1952 survey by the U.S. High Commission for Germany which showed that only one in ten Germans wanted further Nazi war crimes trials. The survey stated that "the main reason for this much debated popular aversion was undoubtedly formed by the deeply

rooted unwillingness among the German population at large to face up to the vilest aspects of a political system they had so enthusiastically supported." De Mildt, *In the Name of the People: Perpetrators of Genocide in the Reflection of Their Post-war Prosecution in Germany—The "Euthanasia" and "Aktion Reihard" Trial Cases* (The Hague: Martinus Nijhoff, 1996), 23.

Primary Sources

Judicial Records

4 Js 444/59. Ermittlungsakten des 1. Frankfurter Auschwitz-Prozess (Pretrial Files of the First Frankfurt Auschwitz Trial). Public prosecutor's office at the district court of Frankfurt am Main, 128 vols. Frankfurt am Main: Mar. 1958–Dec. 1965.

4 Ks 2/63. "Strafsache gegen Mulka und andere" (Criminal Proceedings against Mulka and Others). Jury trial at the district court of Frankfurt am Main. Tapes 01–101. Wiesbaden, Germany: Hessisches Staatsarchiv, Dec. 20, 1963–Aug. 8, 1965.

4 Ks 2/63. "Das Urteil im Frankfurter Auschwitz-Prozess" (Auschwitz Trial Judgment). Landgericht Frankfurt am Main: Aug. 1965.

Dr. Hermann Stolting II. "Plädoyer im Auschwitz-Prozess." Gift from Werner Hummerich, substitute judge at the Auschwitz Trial, Fritz Bauer Institute.

Grundgesetz für die Bundesrepublik Deutschland (Basic Law for the Federal Republic of Germany). Bonn: Bundeszentrale für die Politische Bildung, 1996.

International Military Tribunal. *Trial of the Major War Criminals before the International Military Tribunal, Nuremberg, 14 November 1945–1 October 1946.* 42 vols. Nuremberg: International Military Tribunal, 1947.

Strafgesetzbuch mit 77 Nebengesetzen (StGB), 34th. ed. Munich: Beck'sche Verlagsbuchhandlung, 1963.

The Penal Code of the Federal Republic of Germany. Trans. Joseph Darby. Littleton, Colo.: Fred B. Rothman, 1987.

Trials of War Criminals before the Nuremberg Military Tribunals under Control Council Law No. 10. Nuremberg, October 1946–April 1949. 15 vols. Washington: U.S. Government Printing Office, 1949–1953.

Newspapers

Frankfurter Allgemeine Zeitung, October 1963–December 1965.
Frankfurter Neue Presse, October 1963–December 1965.
Frankfurter Rundschau, October 1963–December 1965.
Observer, January 1964.

Acknowledgments

There are many people without whom I could not have begun or finished this book. I am grateful to the DAAD and the University of Toronto for supporting my research trip to Frankfurt Germany. Thanks go also to Hanno Loewy and Werner Renz at the Fritz Bauer Institute, and to chief public prosecutor Ursula Solf at the public prosecutor's office in Frankfurt am Main, as well as to the staff at the state archive in Wiesbaden. On a personal level, Jenny Farrell, Devin Pendas, Nina Reich, Jannis Skalieris, and Svenja Stolze were wonderful friends to me in Germany. Herr and Frau Hoffmann took me into their home on many occasions and nourished me physically and intellectually.

This book would not have been possible without the guidance and generosity of the Holocaust Educational Foundation and most especially Theodore (Zev) Weiss, its committed and extraordinary president. I owe inexpressible thanks to Zev, who has always been my champion and who helped me along through every stage of my work.

Many scholars of Holocaust studies and German history were open and giving of their time and advice. Christopher Browning was a careful reader and helpful mentor; I thank him for his advice and guidance. I also wish to thank the many others who assisted me, including Michael Allen, Omer Bartov, Peter Black, Rebecca Boehling, Jeffry Diefendorf, Lawrence Douglas, Geoffrey Giles, Peter Hayes, Jeffrey Herf, Dagmar Herzog, Konrad Kwiet, Allan Mitchell, and Michael Phayer. The Center for Advanced Holocaust Studies at the United States Holocaust Memorial Museum provided a much-needed fellowship, thereby affording me the time to finish the project. Robert Ehrenreich, Wendy Lower, Jürgen Matthäus, and Paul Shapiro were enormously helpful and accommodating. I am also grateful to Michael Marrus, Jacques Kornberg, and James Retallack, who offered me the best possible advice. Jacques Kornberg's fine scholarship and nuanced approach were the inspiration that sealed my determination to delve into the topic. I could not have asked for a more engaged reader of the first draft than Michael Marrus; his scrupulous attention to my writing infinitely improved this book, and his dependability and promptness on all fronts were reassuring to an anxious mind.

My former colleagues at Marquette University as well as my current colleagues at the University of Toronto at Mississauga and the University of Toronto history department offered me valuable support. Thanks also to Linda Mastalir for her help.

Portions of *Beyond Justice* have appeared, though in a different form, in the other publications. A section of Chapter 2 appeared as "The Wheels of Justice Turn Slowly: The Pre-Trial Investigations of the Frankfurt Auschwitz Trial, 1963–1965," *Central European History* 35, no. 3 (2002), 345–378; and "Indicting Auschwitz? The Paradox of the Auschwitz Trial," *German History* 21, no. 4 (2003), 505–532. Two separate sections of Chapter 4 appeared as "Telling the Story: Survivor Testimony and the Narration of the Holocaust," *GHI Bulletin*, no. 32 (Spring 2003), 93–101; and "Legitimating the Criminal State: Former Nazi Judges on the Stand at the Frankfurt Auschwitz Trial," in *Lessons and Legacies VI: New Currents in Holocaust Research*, ed. Jeffry Diefendorf (Chicago: Northwestern University Press, 2004).

My friends near and far have been an integral support system for me. Thank you to Angela Andersen, Paige Arthur, Suzanne Brown-Fleming, Weronika Cwir, Andrew Donson, Anne Fenn, Adam Gilders, Robin Green, Jennifer Jordan, Claire Moorsom, Minna Niva, Wynter Rosen, and Anna Bauer-Ross and Craig Ross, and Fran Sterling, whose friendship helped me maintain perspective on the wonderful things in life. I also wish to thank the Stewart family, George and Barbara Hylands, and Eva Schiffer. Thanks go to my brothers Jeffery and Patrick and their families, who have made me a very lucky, happy sister and aunt. They have all encouraged me along the way, and I feel eternally grateful to be related to them all.

John Zilcosky has been my partner and colleague throughout the greater part of the writing process. I have learned from him in so many ways: as a writer, a scholar, and as a person. I am deeply grateful to have such a loving and generous supporter, as well as a rigorous and challenging reader. His input and engagement have shaped this book immeasurably.

Finally, my parents, Horst and Evelyn Wittmann, pointed out to me when I was struggling in Germany that the reason they left is the reason I went back. They are the reason for everything.

Index